NEW VOICES IN CATHOLIC THEOLOGY

ANNA BONTA MORELAND AND
JOSEPH CURRAN,
EDITORS

A Herder & Herder Book
The Crossroad Publishing Company
New York

The Crossroad Publishing Company
www.CrossroadPublishing.com
© 2012 by the Trustees of Boston College, acting by and through The Church in the 21st Century Center

In continuation of our 200-year tradition of independent publishing, The Crossroad Publishing Company proudly offers a variety of books with strong, original voices and diverse perspectives. The viewpoints expressed in our books are not necessarily those of The Crossroad Publishing Company, any of its imprints or of its employees. No claims are made or responsibility assumed for any health or other benefit.

Printed in the United States of America

The text of this book is set in Sabon

Project Management by
The Crossroad Publishing Company
John Jones
For this edition numerous people have shared their talents and ideas, and we gratefully acknowledge Anna Bonta Moreland and Joseph Curran, who have been most gracious during the course of our cooperation.

We thank especially:
Cover design: Piper Wallis   Text design: WebFusion
Proofreading: Sylke Jackson   Printing: Sterling Pierce

Package, and market positioning by The Crossroad Publishing Company

Library of Congress Cataloging-in-Publication Data available from the Library of Congress Books published by The Crossroad Publishing Company may be purchased at special quantity discount rates for classes and institutional use. For information, please e-mail info@CrossroadPublishing.com

"A Herder & Herder book."
Includes bibliographical references and index.
ISBN 978-0-8245-4950-3

In Memoriam

On behalf of all the authors who have worked with
John Jones (1964–2012) over the years,
we thank him for his generosity of spirit,
editorial insight, and spiritual depth.
He will be greatly missed.

Contents

Part Four: New Directions in Systematic Theology

Introduction:
Theology as Prayer and Reflection in Lifelong Conversation

THIS COLLECTION OF ESSAYS GROWS out of a weekend symposium held in honor of Michael J. Buckley, S.J. at Boston College in October of 2009. The symposium drew together many of Michael Buckley's former students in order to honor his teaching and mentorship. Simone Weil writes that "nothing among human things has such power to keep our gaze fixed ever more intensely upon God, than friendship for the friends of God."[1] As a mentor, Buckley created a community of scholarship, prayer and charity that was based upon intellectual friendship. Drawing upon years of experience with the formation of members of the Society of Jesus, Buckley paid careful attention to the intellectual, spiritual and social development of his students, many of whom were lay people. As a result of Buckley's attentive efforts, his graduate students built a community based on the integrity of faith and reason. These friendships enriched our graduate experience and made us better theologians. This collection represents some of the fruits of this community of prayer and scholarship. It is offered in a spirit of deep gratitude for Buckley's life and work as a teacher of theology and a mentor to many theologians.

The essays collected here represent the broad scope and wide influence of Buckley's work. The authors have in each case engaged an insight, problem or theme indicated by Buckley's work. In some cases we have brought these insights to bear on the new questions of the 21st century. In other cases we have challenged Buckley's conclusions in light of the different cultural conditions that have emerged since the publication of his work. In each case we have tried to extend and continue the rigorous and charitable theological conversation into which Buckley initiated us.

What Michael Buckley embodied throughout his life as a theologian, Nicholas Lash explicates in his essay for this volume. In "Oracles, Dissent and Conversation: Reflections on Catholic Teaching," Lash reminds us that human community is sustained by conversation, and conversation is marked at least at times by disagreement and discussion. Lash argues that the movement to a more oracular model for church teaching, a model that emphasizes obedient and passive reception over conversation and conversion, rejects the very essence of teaching as a dynamic exchange that fosters true learning.

Lash defines teaching in terms that a student of Michael Buckley would immediately recognize. The next group of essays takes Buckley's now-classic works on modern atheism and transposes them into the arena of religious pluralism. Grant Kaplan builds on Buckley's analysis of the rise of modern atheism by offering a critical appraisal of two of the most perceptive genealogists of modernity and its twin, secularism—Charles Taylor and René Girard. In *Denying and Disclosing God,* Buckley describes the risks and inherent contradictions of any defense of belief that would bracket the personal nature of the experience of God. Anna Bonta Moreland argues that the opposite approach—a defense of belief that depends exclusively upon the personal and subjective without reference to the rational and speculative—is also problematic. This question is posed in the context of contemporary theology of religious pluralism. Dominic Doyle takes Richard McKeon's description of interpretation as a coordinate of philosophical pluralism and transposes it into a theological key, suggesting four approaches to interpretation that allow one to sort the array of theological positions. Christian Krokus then analyzes St. John of the Cross in light of contemporary interreligious dialogue.

In the next group of essays, each author builds upon Buckley's work in *The Catholic University as Promise and Project: Reflections in a Jesuit Idiom.* Joseph Curran considers Buckley's suggestion of the use of justice as a "new humanism" in Catholic education. Curran argues from the tradition of the Religious Sisters of Mercy that the humanistic foundation that Catholic higher education requires should be based not only on justice but on hospitality, mercy and service as well. Examining Buckley's argument that theology should be utilized by the Catholic university as an architectonic discipline, Brian Hughes suggests that this settlement can overcome the fragmented nature of theological discourse, thereby serving theology as a discipline as well as the university as a whole. John Montag, S.J. examines the establishment of the Jesuit school at Salamanca in the 16th century, arguing that the Jesuit challenge to Dominican hegemony set a new course for Jesuit higher education and theological instruction.

The final set of essays in this volume addresses pressing theological questions in a manner inspired by Buckley's methodology in teaching theology and forming professional theologians. Richard W. Miller draws upon the work of John H. Wright, S.J. in order to construct a theology of providence that preserves the dialogical character of God's activity with respect to free creatures as revealed in scripture. Cara Anthony takes Buckley's argument that religious belief finds its most compelling evidence in religious experience, and proposes that an experience of ecclesial community that integrates ecology, community and worship will enhance and strengthen belief in the triune God. Using Buckley's argument that human religious experience brings together the categorical experience of God and the transcendental orientation to God, Randall Rosenberg explores the theological foundations of sainthood. Thomas Kelly situates Buckley's intentional effort to engage in the formation of lay people as theologians within the context of the wider movement in the post-Vatican II church to emphasize the role and vocation of the laity, particularly with regard to a commitment to justice for the poor.

The years since the publication of Alasdair MacIntyre's *After Virtue* and James Burtchaell's *The Dying of the Light* have seen much hand-wringing over the fragmented nature and seemingly difficult future of Catholic higher education. We hope that this collection of essays shows how a small community of prayer and scholarship in the fleeting years of graduate school can lead to substantive contributions to theological reflection at a variety of Catholic academic institutions. It is offered, then, in a spirit of hope for the promise and project of the Catholic university in the 21st century.

Part One:

TEACHING AND AUTHORITY

Oracles, Dissent, and Conversation:
Reflections on Catholic Teaching

NICHOLAS LASH, CAMBRIDGE UNIVERSITY

MICHAEL BUCKLEY AND I FIRST met in the summer of 1976, when he was teaching in the summer session at the Graduate Theological Union in Berkeley, and I was doing the same, across the bay, in the University of San Francisco. I was therefore well-placed to attend the great parade, in Golden Gate Park, celebrating the Fourth of July. My favorite float carried the message, spelled out in flowers: "200 years of having fun." This struck me as an optimistic reading of American history—even by California standards!

The final chapter of Eamon Duffy's history of the popes is entitled "The Oracles of God."[1] I shall suggest that oracularity should have no place in the relations between bishops and their flocks.

"If," said a leading article in *The Tablet* in 2009, "the Catholic Church is to look like the People of God it has to be an inclusive family, able to contain dissent and embrace dissenters on left and right, not an ever-shrinking sect reserved for the pure."[2] I have no wish whatsoever to belong to some sect reserved for the pure. Nevertheless, I propose to argue that there are good reasons for strenuously resisting the language of "dissent."

"Human community," says Timothy Radcliffe, "is sustained by conversation."[3] That he regards this as an ecclesiological, and not merely an anthropological principle, is clear from his later remark that "sharing our faith is always more than stating our convictions: it is finding our place in that conversation which has continued ever since Jesus began to talk with anyone whom he met in Galilee, and which is the life of the Church."[4] Disagreement, I shall suggest, is an unavoidable feature of serious conversation about the things that matter most. David Woodard, the brilliantly effective but somewhat eccentric parish priest whose curate I had the privilege of being in the early 1960s, came back one day after visiting a neighboring parish, and exclaimed: "Those people are completely lacking in Christian charity: they can't even disagree with one another!"

The School of Christianity

The theme of the Teape Lectures I gave in India in 1994 was that "the modern dissociation of memory from argument, of narrative from reason, made us forget how deeply all understanding and imagination are shaped by memory, coloured by circumstance, constituted by tradition. With this forgetfulness we lost sight of the extent to which the ancient traditions of devotion and reflection, of worship and enquiry" which we now think of as "religions" have seen themselves as *schools*: schools "whose pedagogy has the twofold purpose—however differently conceived and executed in the different traditions—of weaning us from our idolatry and purifying our desire."[5]

This suggestion would, I think, reconnect our sense of what is meant by Christian "teaching" with the account given in the single most influential study of the subject ever written: namely, Augustine's *De Doctrina Christiana*. For Augustine, Christian doctrine is far more fundamentally a matter of the *process* through which, by God's grace, we learn, and learn to share what we have learned with others, than it is about the *contents* of that process. As he puts it at the beginning of Book One: "There are two things on which all interpretation of Scripture depends: the process of discovering what we need to learn, and the process of presenting what we have learnt."[6] Accordingly, his first three Books deal with "discovery" and the fourth with "presentation."

It follows that the most fundamental truth about the *structure* of Christian teaching cannot lie in distinctions between teachers and pupils—although such distinctions may be drawn and are not unimportant—but in the recognition that *all* of us are called to lifelong learning in the Spirit, and *all* of us are called to embody, to communicate, and to protect what we have learned.

As Vatican II ended, several of the bishops who took part told me that the most important lesson they had learned through the conciliar process had been a renewed recognition that the Church exists to be, for all its members, a lifelong school of holiness and wisdom, a lifelong school of friendship (a better rendering of *caritas* than "charity" would be.)[7]

Aspects of Instruction

The concept of "instruction" is ambiguous. If I am "instructing" someone, I may be teaching them, or I may be issuing a command. Someone who is "under instruction" is being educated, but to say "I instructed him to stop" reports a command. "Instructions for use," however, provide information, and hence would seem to be educational. There may be cases in which it is not easy to decide the sense. It is, however, important not to confuse the two senses, and even more important not to *subordinate* instruction as education to instruction as command. As Ring Lardner memorably put it: "Shut up! He explained."[8]

I have long maintained that the heart of the crisis of contemporary Catholicism lies in just such subordination of education to governance, the effect of which has too often been to substitute, for *teaching*, proclamation construed as command.[9] It is, said Yves Congar, impossible to make the function of teaching an integral element of jurisdiction because it is one thing to accept a teaching, quite another to obey an order: *"Autre chose est agréer une doctrine, autre chose obéir à un ordre."*[10]

A few years ago, the Dominican canon lawyer, Robert Ombres, "paid tribute to the pioneering work of Congar, the second part of whose 1954 study, *Jalons pour un théologie du laïcat*, was divided into chapters considering 'the laity in terms of the Church's priestly, kingly and prophetical functions'. Ombres pointed out that, through Congar, this tripartite distinction between sanctifying, governing and teaching offices had entered Vatican II and become 'fundamental to the new canon law', inasmuch as the 1983 Code 'has a separate Book on the teaching office of the Church (Book III on the *munus docendi*) and a separate Book on the sanctifying office of the Church (Book IV on the *munus sanctificandi)*'. It does not, however, have a 'separate Book on the governing office of the Church (the *munus regendi).*'"[11]

Ombres said that he did not know—and nor do I—why the new Code has no separate Book on governance. It is, however, difficult to avoid the suspicion that this may be because the powers that be imagine no such extra book to be needed, presuming that, at the end of the day, teaching and sanctifying are but aspects of governance.

The Threefold Office

Reflection on Christ's threefold office—as Prophet, Priest, and King; as teacher, sanctifier, and ruler—goes back at least as far as the fourth century, to Eusebius of Caesarea.[12] It was only in the sixteenth century, however—and then, originally, in Protestant theology—that the topic came to be treated as not only Christological but also ecclesiological.

I still believe that the finest ecclesiological treatment of the topic is John Henry Newman's 1877 Preface to the third edition of the *Via Media*.[13] And here we have a puzzle. Congar (who was a great admirer of Newman) took close interest in the threefold office from as early as 1932[14] and, as I have already mentioned, used it to structure the second part of *Lay People in the Church*. Some years ago, I rather rashly said that, in doing so, he was "drawing upon a text which he regarded (as I do) as one of the richest and most profound reflections on the doctrine of the Church in modern times": namely, the 1877 Preface.[15]

I am no longer sure that Congar was even familiar with the text. He certainly knew of its existence, having taken a very active part in a Colloquium in Strasbourg in 1960, at which Msgr. Henry Francis Davis (who first taught me to read Newman) discussed and quoted from the Preface in his paper on *"Le rôle et l'apostolat de la hiérarchie et du laïcat dans la théologie de l'Eglise chez Newman."*[16] Nevertheless, the Preface is nowhere mentioned either in *Lay People in the Church*, or in Congar's lengthy and detailed review of Schick's exhaustive study of the threefold office (which, in turn, makes no mention of it).[17]

Avery Dulles, who seems to have misread the Preface,[18] deplored Newman's apparent lack of familiarity with nineteenth-century European Catholic studies of the threefold office, and said that the Preface "does not seem to have significantly influenced the developments that led from Vatican I to Vatican II."[19] When we add that the Preface is nowhere mentioned in the five volumes of the *History of Vatican II* edited by Alberigo, it seems clear that it played no significant part in the drafting of articles 10 to 13 of *Lumen gentium*.

I would now like to list some of the salient features of the Preface, from the point of view of the topics which I am trying to consider in this essay.

"The institutional element in Christianity," said Robert Murray over forty years ago, "by which I mean especially social structure and law, *is not part of the Gospel*."[20] Perhaps as a result, it is only too easy to treat of institutional questions—questions of "authority" and "dissent," for example—as if we were discussing entirely secular phenomena. One of the strengths of Newman's Preface is that it provides consideration of such questions with a properly theological context.

A second feature is Newman's insistence that he is writing about *offices*, about tasks and duties, rather than about "officers."

In the third place, he is writing about offices in which, in some measure, *all* Christians share. It is, says Congar, the people, the Church, that is prophetic, priestly, and royal.[21] This, it seems to me, is something that is often overlooked in discussion about "magisterium."

In the fourth place, Newman speaks of "three offices, which are indivisible, but diverse."[22] Aquinas spoke of the Apostles' *authority* of governance, *faculty* of teaching, and *power* of confirming doctrine through working miracles.[23]

Perhaps the most important feature of the Preface is Newman's insistence that the three offices operate, as it were, like forces in tension, each one correcting and moderating the direction of the others. An extended quotation can give the sense of his argument.

> *Christianity, then, is at once a philosophy, a political power, and a religious rite: as a religion, it is Holy; as a philosophy, it is Apostolic; as a political power, it is imperial, that is, One and Catholic. As a religion, its special centre of action is pastor and flock; as a philosophy, the Schools; as a rule, the Papacy and its Curia.*[24]

Had he lived after Vatican II, he might, optimistically, have said "the episcopal college"!

> *Truth is the guiding principle of theology and theological inquiries; devotion and edification, of worship; and of government, expedience. The instrument of theology is reasoning; of worship, our emotional nature; of rule, command and coercion. Further, in man as he is, reasoning tends to rationalism; devotion to superstition and enthusiasm; and power to ambition and tyranny....*

> *Arduous as are the duties involved in these three offices, to discharge one by one, much more arduous are they to administer, when taken in combination. Each of the three has its separate scope and direction; each has its own interests to promote and further; each has to find room for the claims of the other two; and each will find its own line of action influenced and modified by the other, nay, sometimes in a particular case the necessity of the others converted into a rule of duty for itself.*[25]

"Concepts have dates" was the first thing said by Bernard Lonergan to my uncle, Sebastian Moore, on the occasion of their first meeting. Always fearful of "relativism," and usually resistant to change, the thought patterns of what we might call "official Catholicism" tend to operate as if this were not the case: as if what words mean now is (more or less) what they have always meant. Gary Macy is surely correct when he says, in the opening sentence of his erudite study of female clergy in the medieval West: "The fact that women were ordained for the first twelve hundred years of Christianity will surprise many people."[26] It will surprise them, I suggest, because they will take for granted that "ordination" meant, during the first millennium, what it has come to mean since Trent. But, as a matter of fact, it did not. In quest of a deepened sensitivity to the *historicality* of Christian doctrine, even a model as sophisticated as that of Newman's Preface is of little help. The problem is exacerbated by the considerable difficulty "Rome" experiences in admitting that a Pope has got something important badly wrong. Here are three illustrations of this difficulty.

Parables from the Past

Urban VIII and Mary Ward

Galileo was not the only person to meet with disapproval from Pope Urban VIII. Mary Ward had, for a number of years, been seeking papal approval for the institute which she had founded, and which, in contrast to the enclosure of most orders of nuns, modeled its lifestyle on that of the Jesuits. Urban received her kindly in audience in 1630, but the following year he issued a Bull, *Pastorali romani pontificis*, suppressing her order. He made the finality of his decision rather clear:

> *After mature consideration with our Venerable Brothers, Cardinals of the Holy Roman Church, specially deputed by the same See as general Inquisitors against heretical depravity... we decree and declare with Apostolic authority and by the contents of this present document, that the pretended Congregation of women or virgins called Jesuitesses and their Sect and state was and is from its very beginning null and void and of no authority and importance. And because indeed they have made progress, with the same authority we totally and completely suppress*

and extinguish them, subject them to perpetual abolition and remove them entirely from the Holy Church of God; we destroy and annul them, and we wish and command all the Christian faithful to regard and repute them as suppressed, extinct, rooted out, destroyed and abolished.[27]

In case he had not made his meaning clear, he then had Mary Ward imprisoned for heresy.

Mary Ward and her colleagues were not given to "dissent," but neither were they put off by bullying. It took some time to sort things out. A fresh petition by the general superior, in 1693, was refused by Innocent XII. In 1749, Benedict XIV approved the "Institute of Mary," on condition that Mary Ward was not claimed to be its foundress. Only in 1909 was she acknowledged as foundress, and it was not until 2004 that the Roman branch of the order adopted the full Ignatian Constitutions, the Ignatian fourth vow and the name "Congregation of Jesus."[28]

Anglican Orders

My second example of the temporary nature of "perpetual" papal decisions has, so far, a more confusing outcome. On September 13, 1896, Pope Leo XIII issued the Bull *Apostolicae curae*, which declared Anglican orders to be "absolutely null and utterly void." Just over a century later, on June 29, 1998, Cardinal Ratzinger, in a "doctrinal commentary" on John Paul II's Apostolic Letter *Ad tuendam fidem*, listed *Apostolicae curae* among the definitive and irreversible teachings, failure to give assent to which excludes someone from "full communion with the Catholic Church."[29] Meanwhile, in 2006, in another part of the forest, Cardinal Kasper, addressing the House of Bishops of the Church of England on the work undertaken by the Anglican Roman Catholic International Commission, referred to the Commission's "thorough historical and theological discussion" of *Apostolicae curae*. Although these discussions "have not," he said, "led to a conclusive resolution or to a full consensus... they achieved a pleasing rapprochement which justifiably aroused promising expectations."[30]

Actions, they say, speak louder than words. Archbishop Michael Ramsey was deeply moved when, in 1966, Pope Paul VI gave him his own episcopal ring. Many years later, John Paul II gave Professor Henry Chadwick a priestly stole and, in November 2006, Archbishop Rowan Williams was invited to celebrate the Eucharist at the high altar of Santa Sabina in Rome, a celebration at which the Gospel was read by a senior official of the Roman Curia.[31] If I were asked what "the Church's teaching" is on Anglican orders, I would have to say that I have absolutely no idea.

Humanae vitae

My third example, perhaps predictably, is the tragedy of *Humanae vitae*. The Pontifical Commission on Problems of Marriage and the Family, established by John XXIII in 1963, consisted of six people. By the beginning of 1965, the membership had expanded to 55 and, apart from a wider range of academic and technical expertise, it now included three married couples. In February 1966, two months before it began its fifth and final session, 16 cardinals and bishops were added. Cardinal Ottaviani was now president, with Cardinals Doepfner and Heenan as vice-presidents. (These heavy pastoral guns were added, it seems, because everyone now assumed that the commission was going to propose a significant change in Catholic teaching on birth regulation.)

On June 28, 1966, the commission's report was presented to Paul VI by Cardinal Doepfner and Fr. Henri de Riedmatten, the secretary-general of the Commission. Two years later, after much agonized thought, Paul VI set aside the Commission's report and issued the encyclical *Humanae vitae*.

Now let's go back a bit. In April 1966, Cardinal Ottaviani, asked in an interview whether he foresaw an end to the Commission's work, said: "I do not know if the Holy Father in every respect will wish to or can accept the conclusions of our studies," but there could be no question of departing from "the teachings given by Popes Pius XI and Pius XII because they are founded on natural law."[32]

Article 13 of *Humanae vitae* includes the assertion that "The Church, calling men back to the observance of the norms of the natural law, as interpreted by her constant doctrine, teaches that each and every marriage act must remain open to the transmission of life."

A key moment in the Commission's work, according to John Marshall (who had been one of the original six members) came in April 1964, when the four theologians who eventually found themselves unable to sign the report "acknowledged that they could not demonstrate the intrinsic evil of contraception on the basis of natural law and so rested their case on

Authority and the fear of possible consequences of change both to Authority and to sexual morality."[33]

In other words, the Commission was *unanimous* that the intrinsic evil of contraception cannot be demonstrated on the basis of natural law. In the encyclical, the sentence in Article 13 which I quoted refers, in a note, to Pius XI's 1930 Encyclical, *Casti connubii*, and to an address by Pius XII. As John Marshall noted, "although it is asserted" in the Encyclical "that contraception is contrary to the natural law, no theological argument is proposed to support this view. The reason for its absence is that none has been forthcoming."[34]

In other words, Paul VI's decision to reject the Commission's report was not grounded on better arguments in the ethics of reproduction, but on considerations of church authority: he could not bring himself to disagree with his predecessors. And yet, from slavery to usury, the list of not unimportant issues in the moral order on which the Church has changed its teaching over time is rather long. I speak of the "tragedy" of *Humanae vitae* because it seems, in the event, to have been his refusal to countenance change which undermined the confidence of so many Catholics in the very authority which he sought to uphold.[35]

Magisteria?

On, then, to "magisterium." The Oxford English Dictionary knows no theological use of the term in English earlier than 1866, when *The Dublin Review* announced that "Roman Catholics, throughout the world, are instructed in certain *doctrines*; are exhorted to certain *practices*; are encouraged and trained in certain *tempers* and *dispositions*. The Church's office in providing for this is called her 'Magisterium'." Robert Murray notes that "it is important for ecclesiology that *magisterium* till about the mid-nineteenth century referred to the *activity* of authorized teaching in the Church. The use with a capital 'M', to denote episcopal and especially papal *authority*, was developed mainly in the anti-Modernist documents."[36]

A little over twenty-five years ago, Frank Sullivan sketched the history of theological uses of the term with characteristic lucidity. Noting Aquinas's distinction between the "'magisterium cathedrae pastoralis' of the bishop, and [the] 'magisterium cathedrae magistralis' of the theologian," he agreed with those "who feel that the effort to reclaim the term *magisterium* for the role of theologians is ill-advised."[37] A few years later, that other master of magistracy in Boston, Ladislas Örsy, said: "I am inclined to agree with Sullivan, given the evolution of the concept of magisterium and its meaning *today*. To speak of two magisteria could lead to endless confusion."[38]

I have no wish to stir up "endless confusion," and I am sure that neither Michael Buckley nor I will lose sleep if our magisterial dignity is not terminologically acknowledged. Nevertheless, it seems to me that simply accepting the use of some concept "today" may, for a number of reasons, be very dangerous.

In the first place, it is an implication of the "perichoresis" which obtains between the elements of Christ's threefold office that it is never possible, in fact, sharply to *separate* the tasks of education, edification, and governance—all the more reason, however, to keep a sharp eye on the necessary *distinctions* between them.

In the second place, we must never forget that it is the *Church*, the *whole* Church, which shares in the threefold office, and not merely, or even primarily, the Church's officers. (The sequence of chapters in *Lumen gentium* is exemplary in this respect.)

In the third place, the nineteenth-century shift from the name of a *function*—that of teaching—to the name of a group of "functionaries," was, for two reasons, most unfortunate. It was unfortunate because it created the impression that, in the Church, *only* bishops bear responsibility for witnessing to the Gospel (we should never forget that most bishops were first catechised by their mothers). It was unfortunate, secondly, because bishops seldom do much teaching in the ordinary sense, being preoccupied with the cares of middle management. As a result, the contraction of the range of reference of "magisterium" to the episcopate alone serves only to deepen that subordination of education to governance that I earlier deplored.

There are, of course, exceptions to the claim that most bishops seldom do much teaching in the ordinary sense. Cardinal Martini, when he was archbishop of Milan, could fill his cathedral with people who came to hear him interpret the Scriptures. And an encyclical such as *Caritas in veritate* is surely a quite straightforward exercise in teaching. (I once knew a priest who served as secretary to the Bishop of Clifton. Four or five times a week, for ten years, he would accompany the bishop into some space—a church, a school, a parish hall—filled with people who had come to listen to their bishop. On each occasion, as they entered the room, the bishop would turn to his secretary and say: "Oh, father! It makes you wish you had something to say!")

I have referred to the contraction of the range of "official teachers" to the episcopate. In fact, of course, during the twentieth century, "magisterium" contracted even further. John Paul II's encyclical *Veritatis splendor* is addressed "to all the bishops of the Catholic Church." Near the end, the pope says: "This is the first time, in fact, that the Magisterium of the Church has set forth in detail the fundamental elements of this teaching,"[39] thereby contracting the range of reference still further—to himself.

Shifts in sense and reference often mark shifts in power: they occur in the interests of some people and not of others. I agree with Sullivan and Örsy that there is little to be gained by speaking, today, of the "magisterium" of theologians. But it does not follow from this that there are not good reasons for vigorously contesting many of the ways in which the concept of magisterium is used "today."

"Pastoral" Magisterium

The description of episcopal office as "pastoral" has a very ancient history and yet, in the preparation of Vatican II, and since that Council, it has often been a difficult concept to pin down, usually being defined, it seems, by indirection, in *contrast* to something else. Thus, for example, *Gaudium et spes* was entitled a "*Pastoral* Constitution," in contrast to the "*Dogmatic* Constitutions," *Dei verbum* and *Lumen gentium*.

When Gregory Baum says that "the teaching of the Holy See has an obligatory character, not because it is necessarily a definitive statement of Christian truth, but, rather, because it is a *pastoral* measure in proposing the safest solution for grave and urgent problems, overcoming dangerous controversy in the Church and steering the energy of theologians along a more unified path,"[40] his description not only brings out the *practical* character of pastoral leadership, but gives a sense of shepherds guiding their flock to safer pastures, of the helmsman of the barque of Peter guiding the ship through choppy water.

Eamon Duffy, who always uses the notion positively in his history of the popes, speaks of John XXIII's "determination that this should be a pastoral Council devoted to opening up the Church, not barricading it in"; he says that Cardinals Montini and Suenens saw that the Council "must present a pastoral not a bureaucratic vision," and that John Paul I "established himself at once as a pastoral figure, opposed to all pomp, refusing, for example, to be crowned."[41]

We may be tempted to take for granted that to describe something as "pastoral" is warmly to praise it for its humanity, its lack of defensiveness, its simplicity. There is, however, another side to the story.

"'Pastoral'," said Giuseppe Alberigo, "is a key word that expresses the central aspect of Roncalli's ecclesiology." John XXIII used it to indicate that he saw no place in his Council for dogmatic definitions or for condemnations, and to emphasize "the urgency of a commitment to a renewal of the Church's spirit and forms of witness and of its evangelical presence in history."[42]

During the preparatory period, however, although it was generally understood that "the Pope wished the… Council to be primarily 'pastoral' in nature," not everyone understood this in the same sense. Doctrinal questions were assigned to the Theological Commission (under Cardinal Ottaviani), and "all the practical 'pastoral' questions" were assigned to the other Preparatory Commissions. This enabled the view, propagated by the Theological Commission, to prevail, according to which "doctrinal clarification, over which it had a monopoly, was the primary role of the Council, with 'pastoral' considerations something that bishops could see to when they returned to their sees."[43] Only the Liturgical Commission "consistently refused this fatal disjunction" between the doctrinal and the "merely" pastoral.[44]

According to Alberigo, "it was only on the very eve of the Council that a stronger meaning of the term 'pastoral' began to gain ground: the subordination of every other aspect of the church's life to the image of Christ as 'Good Shepherd.'"[45] As well, of course, in the years since the Council ended, we have only too often seen the significance of the Council's teaching downplayed again, on the grounds that it was, after all, merely a "pastoral" Council.

Oracles of God

According to Duffy, John Paul II, like Pius XII before him, "saw the pope as first and foremost a teacher, an oracle."[46] Where Pius XII is concerned, I am reminded of Jean Leclercq's description of him (in conversation with Sebastian Moore): "*il assiste à sa propre vie comme à une drame historique*" ("he attends his own life as if it were an historical drama"). Nevertheless, however accurate, in descriptive *fact*, the image of Pius XII (or John Paul II, for that matter) as an "oracle," I am not persuaded of the appropriateness, in principle, of the description. In other words, any pope who behaves, within the Church, as an oracle misunderstands his office.

Chambers Dictionary defines an oracle as "a person with the reputation, or an air, of infallibility or great wisdom." So far, no harm done: someone like Michael Buckley, perhaps! But the *Dictionary* offers another definition: "a medium or agency of divine revelation": a definition matched by one in the *Oxford English Dictionary*, for which an oracle is "the mouthpiece of the deity."

If "teaching" in the Church occurs in all *three* aspects of the threefold office, then we need, perhaps, to differentiate between the "doxological," "declaratory" and "critical" or "exploratory" dimensions of the Christian quest for and expression of God's truth.[47] "Declaratory" teaching, that which most resembles governance, includes, for example, dogmatic definitions (which also pertain, of course, to the doxological, because they are acts of *faith*) and the resolution of doctrinal disputes. (Where this last category is concerned, I wish modern popes more often followed the example of Clement VIII and Paul V who, in the *"de auxiliis"* controversy, exercised their office by refusing to condemn either side in the dispute. *Quaestiones disputatae* are rarely well resolved by fiat!)[48]

Where the proclamation of the Gospel to those who have not heard it is concerned, it may well be appropriate to speak of the "oracular" because, in such proclamation, the Church does indeed serve as a "medium or agency of divine revelation." But the case is entirely different *within* the Church.

The image of the oracle is of one who brings fresh messages from God. This, no pope can do, for the Church he serves as its chief bishop has *already* heard the Word, and lives by that faith which is its God-given response. It is the duty of those who hold teaching office in the Church to articulate, to express, to clarify, the faith by which we live.

Hence the importance of the doctrine of "reception." There is, somewhere, a sermon of Augustine's in which he says: "When I hold up the host before communion, I say 'Corpus Christi,' and you reply 'Amen,' which means: 'Yes, we are.'" The response of the faithful to sound teaching in the Church is to say "Yes, that's it." Where this response is lacking, the teaching is called in question.

Securus judicat orbis terrarum. In the months leading up to the first Vatican Council, Newman insisted that he "put the validity of the Council upon its reception by the orbis terrarum."[49] And when, after the Council, he hesitated before accepting the definition of papal infallibility, Lord Acton remarked: "He was waiting for the echo."[50]

Dissent and Disagreement

I have said that Catholic Christianity is a lifelong school of friendship, holiness, and wisdom. And yet, the tasks of those exercising "pastoral magisterium" seem not, in fact, primarily to be "teaching," at least as this activity is understood in most schools.

In 1975, a plenary session of The International Theological Commission issued a series of theses on "the relationship between the magisterium and theology." In 1966, Paul VI had addressed an international congress on "The Theology of Vatican II" on the same topic, and the Commission introduced its theses with two "brief quotations" from that address. The Commission defined ecclesiastical magisterium as: "the office of teaching which, by Christ's institution, is proper to the college of bishops or to individual bishops joined in hierarchical communion with the Supreme Pontiff." According to Paul VI, the function of this magisterium is to "safeguard" revelation.[51]

Notions such as "safeguarding" and "protecting" may carry defensive, even negative overtones. Perhaps for that reason, Örsy prefers to describe the specific "charism" of the episcopate as being that of bearing "*witness* [to] God's mighty deeds."[52]

What terminology might be appropriate to describe what someone was doing when, for whatever reason, they sought to take issue with some particular instance of magisterial "teaching"? "Disagreeing" is the term that comes to mind. But because (I maintain) "teaching" is, in this context, usually in *fact* construed as governance, as *command*, such taking issue is described, in the recent literature, not as "disagreement" but as "dissent."

Frank Sullivan, reminding his readers that Pius XII, in *Humanae generis*, announced that "when a pope, in an encyclical, expresses his judgement on an issue that was previously controverted, this can no longer be seen as a question for free discussion by theologians," points out that "there is no such statement in any of the documents that were approved by the Council."[53] Nevertheless, in 1987, four years after the publication of Sullivan's *Magisterium* (from which I have just quoted), John Paul II, addressing the American bishops in Los Angeles, said, without qualification: "It is sometimes claimed that dissent from the Magisterium is totally compatible with being a 'good Catholic' and poses no obstacle to the reception of the sacraments. This is a grave error that challenges the teaching office of the bishops in the United States and elsewhere."[54]

Sullivan's study, *Magisterium*, seemed nevertheless content to work with the terminology of "dissent." Örsy, on the other hand, is more troubled by the notion. "Dissent has," he says, "become one of the dominant themes in Catholic theology in the United States," but "is mentioned less in European writings." It is, he says, "an imperfect term under several aspects": it is purely negative; it implies "deep-lying internal antagonism"; it is historically loaded; and so on. "It follows that if we abandoned the word 'dissent' altogether, we would lose little and gain much." I agree. And yet, "all these arguments notwithstanding," he concludes, "it appears that for the time being at least," we must "live with an unsuitable word."[55] For goodness' sake, why?

Here is a very simple model. "Yes" or "No"? The teacher looks for understanding, the commander for obedience. Where teaching in most ordinary senses of the term is concerned, if a pupil's response to a piece of teaching is "Yes," they are saying something like either "I see" or "I agree." If the response is "No," the pupil is saying either "I don't see" or "I don't agree." When subordinates say "Yes" to a command, they obey; when they say "No," they disobey. Dissent is disobedience. The entire discussion about the circumstances in which it may be permissible or appropriate to "dissent" from magisterial utterances makes clear that what is at issue is when, and in what circumstances, it may be virtuous, and not sinful, to disobey. There could, in my opinion, be no clearer evidence that what we call "official *teaching*" in the Church is, in fact, for the most part not teaching but governance.[56]

I am not in the least denying that governance, the issuing of instructions and commands, has its place in the life of the Church, as of any other society. That is not at what is at issue. The point at issue is, once again, that commands direct, they do not educate. "It is one thing to accept a teaching, quite another to obey an order."[57]

The Mandatum Docendi *of Episcopal Conferences*

A striking illustration of the confusion of *teaching* and *governance* is provided by the way in which, during the 1980s, the question of the teaching authority of episcopal conferences was handled. While the National Conference of Catholic Bishops in the United States "was preparing its pastoral letter 'The Challenge of Peace,' several of its members were invited to Rome in 1983 to discuss this project with representatives of some European episcopal conferences. Cardinal Joseph Ratzinger, who chaired the meeting, proposed five points for discussion, the first of which... [stated that]: 'A bishops' conference as such does not have a *mandatum docendi*. This belongs only to the individual bishops or to the College of bishops with the pope.'"[58] The manner of the proposal left little doubt that it expressed the Cardinal's own view of the matter.[59]

Two years later, in November 1985, the presidents of all the conferences gathered in Rome for the Synod that "Pope John Paul II called 'to celebrate and reflect on the Second Vatican Council twenty years after its conclusion.' It seemed inevitable that this synod would have something to say about episcopal conferences."[60] Accordingly, the International Theological Commission, meeting under Ratzinger's chairmanship a few months before the Synod assembled, issued a document entitled "Select Themes of Ecclesiology," which endorsed the Cardinal's position on the issue—not, however, without some difficulty. According to a former member of the Commission, it "was deeply divided... but in a narrow vote (with a large number of abstentions) the CDF claimed the support of the ITC that no episcopal synod had magisterial authority. They then sacked all who had voted against the proposal or abstained!"[61]

Conclusion: Educators in Christian Conversation

Commenting on *Veritatis splendor*, Herbert McCabe contrasted manuals and rule books. The manual helps you to acquire some skill: as a football player, maybe, or a piano-tuner or, if we extend the range of skills to those habits which we call the virtues, as a just or generous person. The manual is an instrument of education. As well as manuals there are rule books, which tell you what, in some particular context, you are and are not allowed to do. "The rule book does not tell you anything about acquiring skills in football; it simply tells you the rules and the kinds of action that would break them."[62] The rule book is an instrument of governance. What worried McCabe about *Veritatis splendor* was that it is, he said, "in great part, an attack on those who want to read the rule book as a manual by those who want to read the manual as though it were a rule book."[63]

Nowhere in *Veritatis splendor* does John Paul II discuss disagreement in the Church, or the duty of episcopal authority to monitor and guide it. Indeed, near the end of the encyclical, in a passage denouncing "dissent" and "opposition to the teaching of the Church's pastors," he comes close to claiming that there is simply no place for disagreement, on moral questions, in the Church: "While exchanges and conflicts of opinion may constitute normal expressions of public life in a representative democracy, moral teaching certainly cannot depend simply upon respect for such a process."[64] "Cannot depend *simply*" upon "exchanges and conflicts of opinion"—fair enough. But might we not have expected him to say something about the part which such "exchanges" should play?

If, as I have argued, "dissent" is disobedience, its counterpart is, presumably, obedience.[65] The term preferred, it seems, by the Holy See, is *riconoscimento* or "recognition." On February 4, 2009, the Secretariat of State issued a "Note... Concerning the Four Prelates of the Society of Saint Pius X," the second article of which began: "A full recognition [*il pieno riconoscimento*] of the Second Vatican Council and the Magisterium of Popes John XXIII, Paul VI, John Paul I, John Paul II and Benedict XVI himself is an indispensable condition for any future recognition [*riconoscimento*] of the Society of Saint Pius X."[66]

Where the second occurrence of the term is concerned, the "recognition" of the Society would presumably be a matter of canonically regularising its place within the Catholic Church. But what about the first occurrence? What would count as "full recognition" of the "Magisterium" of those five Popes? Hit the button for the "Magisterium" of Benedict XVI on the website of the Holy See, and up pops a list, not only of encyclicals and motu proprios, but letters, addresses, messages, speeches, the daily Angelus, his appreciation of a concert in honour of the fourth year of his election—just about everything the good man has said in public. Perhaps it's just as well that most bishops seem more restrained in requiring "full recognition" of their magisterium! For the first time in my life, I feel some sympathy for the Lefebvrists!

"Human community is sustained by conversation."[67] And disagreement, as I said at the beginning, plays an integral part in any serious conversation about the things that matter most. In his study of the Catholic University, Michael Buckley sketched the gravity of the situation in which he believes American Catholic universities find themselves.[68] On a much broader front, I am troubled by the quality of public disagreement between Catholics, in this country—I think—especially, but also elsewhere.

In necessariis unitas, in dubiis libertas, in omnibus caritas.[69] It seems to me that, where the relationships between governance and education, and between the episcopate and teachers of theology, are concerned, there are few more important tasks for the bishops to undertake than to act as moderators of disagreement, educators in Christian conversation. And so long as the Church in this country is served by teachers as erudite and ecclesially committed as Michael Buckley, the prospects for the effective resolution of our difficulties cannot be that bad!

Part Two

NEW DIRECTIONS
IN RELIGIOUS PLURALISM

Widening the Dialectic:
Secularity and Christianity
in Conversation

GRANT KAPLAN, SAINT LOUIS UNIVERSITY

PART OF THE LORE AROUND Fr. Buckley involves an anecdote with a pope. When Buckley presented John Paul II a copy of his first book on atheism, the Pope asked, "And what was it that lay at the origins of modern atheism?" Without skipping a beat, Buckley responded, "Theologians, Your Holiness." This anecdote captures the provocative nature of Buckley's argument: Modern, Western atheism arose, at least in part, due to a contradiction in early modern theism itself. As Buckley puts it in *At the Origins of Modern Atheism*: "Atheism must be seen not as a collation of ideas which happened to arise in Western thought but as a transition whose meaning is spelled out by the process and whose existence is accounted for in terms of the ideas which preceded it."[1] In tribute to Buckley's important work, in this essay I ask a more expansive question: can one understand modernity and the development of Western secularism according to this same pattern suggested by Buckley? Here I argue that Charles Taylor and René Girard offer a parallel account of modernity and its Christian roots that widens Buckley's dialectical thesis on atheism.

Of course, to enter a discussion of modernity opens the door to previous analyses of the genesis and nature of modernity. *Modernity* normally signifies an anti- or post-Christian worldview that has made an explicit attempt to dispose some central, pre-modern religious and philosophical tenets in order to manifest itself. These discussions of modernity, held by some of the greatest lights of the intellectual scene, go beyond the scope of this essay. Those familiar with such discussions, one would hope, will find the accounts of Taylor and Girard compelling and provoking. For with these two, the discussion of the relationship between Christianity and modernity does not ultimately aim towards a moral or intellectual judgment as to its legitimacy. Instead, the two offer a genetic account similar to Buckley's treatment of the origins of modern atheism. It is posited here, without bringing Taylor and Girard into direct discussion with other genealogists of modernity, that this genetic account provides a much more helpful and illustrative picture of modernity. The brunt of this analysis aims to bring Taylor and Girard into conversation with one another, but also with Buckley.

To execute this argument, this essay aims to cover the following ground: first, it examines the nature of Buckley's dialectical method. Next, it briefly mentions two dominant trends concerning secularity and modernity. Then it turns to Charles Taylor and René Girard and compares their accounts of modernity's relationship with Christianity under the following categories: 1) the relationship of Christianity to religion; 2) the nature of Christianity; 3) the nature and cause of modernity; 4) the impact of these theses on 21st-century Christian apologetics.

1. Buckley's Dialectic of Atheism

Buckley's research into modern atheism and early modern history of ideas has substantially affected the academic assessment of the history of atheism and has also deepened our understanding of modernity's emergence.[2] At the heart of his investigative method lies an assessment about our capacity to understand the emergence, power, and dissolution of ideas. A review and assessment of this method is central in order to bring Buckley into conversation with Charles Taylor and René Girard.

In the "Introduction" to At the Origins of Modern Atheism Buckley asks:

> *Does atheism also depend upon theism for its very existence? ... Does theism not only shape, but generate its corresponding atheism? Does theism not only set the meaning, but also generate the existence of the atheism which emerges in the middle of the eighteenth century? Is the content of god, the idea of the divine, so internally incoherent that it moves dialectically into its denial? (16)*

After five chapters covering the religious apologetics of Leonard Lessius and Marin Mersenne, the philosophical system of René Descartes and the mechanics of Isaac Newton, their applications by Nicolas Malebranche and Samuel Clarke, and the atheistic mutations of these systems by Denis Diderot and Baron Paul Henri d'Holbach, his conclusion revisits the questions raised in his Introduction. Upon observing that the meaning of atheism has always been parasitic on the meaning of theism, Buckley pushes further: "If the meaning of atheism is shaped by the going theism, is this also true of its *existence*? ... If theism is responsible for the patterns of atheism, did it also generate its actual birth" (338)? In his concluding chapter, Buckley affirms that an internal contradiction in Christian theology generated atheism: "There was a contradiction between this content [of the theists] and the form in which it was advanced.... In this process of self-alienation, religion denied itself both a proper form to reflect upon this issue and commensurate evidence by which it could be resolved—and all of this before the question had even been raised by the intellectual culture in which the theologians wrote" (346). For Buckley, the *nature* of theological argument helped generate modern atheism. Its contradiction consisted in arguing through impersonal means—natural theology—for a personal God.

To describe this process of generation through contradiction, Buckley uses the language of *dialectic*. On the last page of his conclusion he writes: "The dialectical contradiction is pervasively present; it effects a dynamic continuity in the paradoxical developments toward and into atheism and it gives existence and shape to what emerged" (363). The language and import of this "dialectic" emerge as central to Buckley's aim and method in *At the Origins of Modern Atheism*. Several scholarly reviews of *At the Origins* noticed the centrality of this dialectical method and centered their critique on it. After praising Buckley for writing a "highly readable book" that "has set the terms for subsequent discussions," James Force, for example, criticizes the book's "narrowly epistemological focus."[3] He later complains about Buckley's appropriation of theists in accounting for the "dialectical" origin of modern atheism. Force writes that this appropriation makes him "uneasy" and argues for a more historical and contextual reading than Buckley's "litany of logical begats."[4] Another reviewer, David Wilson, calls the work "a big book with bold claims." Unlike Force's assessment, Wilson focuses specifically on the dialectical method employed. Even if the historical claims of Buckley are true, asks Wilson, is the Hegelian account necessary? Wilson's judgment is in the negative: "Buckley ... may well be right in his broad causal claim: Christian theologians probably did play some causal role in the rise of atheism. But this role can be expressed in non-Hegelian terms that anyone can understand."[5] Paul Casner's review resonates with the assessments of Force and Wilson. Although complimentary about the research and orientation of *At the Origins*, Casner bristles at the method: "Ironically, Buckley weakens his position by excessive dependence upon a Hegelian philosophical perspective."[6] For these scholars, the heuristic of dialectical method does more harm than good because it imports a Hegelian superstructure upon the data under consideration.

These concerns also entered into more explicitly theological assessments of Buckley's thesis. Buckley's concern with highlighting "internal contradiction," fears John Milbank, tends to understate the importance of social and economic factors. Although Milbank admits the "general validity" of Buckley's claims, his judgment echoes the complaints above: "One should be suspicious both of his methodological agenda and the over-neat fit of this agenda with a subject-matter which is itself all too-precisely defined."[7] This *agenda* is the dialectical approach. As an alternative, Milbank proposes a more radically historicist approach that would meet the concerns of French postmodern theorists, in particular Deleuze and Foucault. Of the dialectical method, Milbank avers, "One notices that [Buckley] insinuates all sorts of *intellectual* (not historical) necessities where none exist." Like Force, Casner and Wilson, Milbank criticizes what he considers Buckley's arbitrary use of evidence, and an etiology that produces a narrative and a conclusion that is "over-tidy and over-achieved."[8]

Almost two decades after the appearance of *At the Origins*, Buckley published *Denying and Disclosing God*, which both encompasses his earlier argument and advances it into the nineteenth and twentieth centuries. Buckley does not modify his method; rather, he doubles down on dialectic. In the preface he alludes to Milbank's review and responds: "Nevertheless, additional research has not weakened the evidence that such a dialectical negation was vitally present. On the contrary, it has strengthened the conviction that this dialectical pattern did in fact obtain and was to be found in the genesis of atheism elsewhere."[9] Buckley uses the studies of atheism by Alan Kors and James Turner to support his claim, which he takes up most directly in the second chapter, "A Dialectical Pattern in the Emergence of Atheism."[10] Here Buckley addresses Milbank's criticisms and reflects on the conclusions of his previous work. He remarks that *At the Origins* proposed the thesis "that the remarkable development of atheism in modernity exhibits a dialectical structure."[11]

Clearly, then, the dialectical method remained central to Buckley's approach over a span of nearly two decades. In order to understand this method with greater precision, and to address the accusation of Buckley's alleged crypto-Hegelianism, a brief historical overview in conversation with Buckley's own understanding of dialectics follows below.

Buckley's work makes both an empirical claim and a more theoretical point about dialectics. The empirical claim is "that atheism as an argument and theorem was generated by the very intellectual forces enlisted to counter it."[12] His assertions about the development of atheism ultimately rely on historical evidence that either supports or undermines his thesis. It lies outside the scope of this essay to revisit these empirical claims, but it is worth reminding readers of Buckley's own modesty about the breadth of his conclusions:

> *Does so faulty a strategy comprehensively account for the origins of modern atheism? Obviously not! Many other critically important influences, social as well as ideological, obtained during these two centuries.... These factors and many more...would have to be charted if one were to write a comprehensive study of "the origins of modern atheism." The dialectical contradiction...is not all. It is still only "at" the origins of modern atheism.*[13]

The concern in this essay is with the theoretical claim about the ability of dialectics to narrate and distinguish patterns in intellectual history. A cursory look at the history of dialectics, with an emphasis on Hegel's application, is in order.

Dialectic originated among the Greeks and already had multiple meanings by the time of Aristotle.[14] It could refer to the art of conversation, an element of formal logic, or a method of argumentation. For Plato and Aristotle, dialectic is a positive term, although both imply a pluriform understanding of dialectic. In the *Republic*, the dialectical man "grasps the reason for the being of each thing," and in the *Cratylus* the dialectical man "knows how to ask and answer questions."[15] In the *Topics* Aristotle places dialectic between the apodictic conclusions of philosophy and the eristic of the Sophists.[16] The Stoics identify dialectic as the art of asking and answering questions correctly. Cicero gives a more precise definition than that of the Stoics when he calls dialectic "the entire science of discerning the essence of things, of judging their qualities, and of conducting a systematic and logical argument."[17] In the context of his definition, Cicero chides Epicurus for not doing what dialectic demands: offering a clear and precise definition—in this case, of happiness. If he had done so, he suggests, he would have not run into such great confusion.

Buckley locates the model for his method of inquiry in Plato's *Seventh Epistle*. According to Plato, since words do not define themselves, and individual cases do not explain themselves, some method is necessary. As Buckley puts it, "The need for the dialectical method lies precisely in the discontinuity among these three, and the movement of the dialectical conversation is toward their resolution, toward a coincidence of word, thought, and thing."[18] Similar to the references above, Buckley associates dialectic with good reasoning so as to get to the heart of the realities in question. In his conclusion he returns to Plato's text. After distancing himself slightly from Plato's method, he states, "This *Epistle* and the dialectical tradition suggested the devices with which the indeterminacy of the situation of modern atheism could be given some determination and its inner consistencies discovered."[19] Yet the reviewers cited above explicitly criticized his Hegelianism, *not* Buckley's reverence for classical dialectic. What has changed in modern dialectic, and does Buckley incorporate this modern transition into his method of enquiry?

The meaning and application of dialectic takes many important turns between Cicero and modernity. It is worth noting, however, that whereas some medievals began to equate dialectic with philosophy itself, Descartes criticized it as a lamentable, unscientific discipline ruinous to reason. It came to mean for Descartes what eristics had meant for Plato and Aristotle, a shoddy way of thinking that dialectic had served to correct. For Descartes, dialectic became the problem. This criticism and transformation continued with Kant, who addressed the problem of *"Dialektik"* in his *Critique of Pure Reason*. In the beginning of both the "Transcendental Logic" and the "Transcendental Dialectic," he refers to dialectic as the "logic of illusion" (B 86; B 349-55) because it fails to take into account the warnings proscribed in his critical method about our inability to know realities beyond the grip of empirical confirmation. Despite evincing familiarity in his references to how the ancients used dialectic, Kant equates it with the bad metaphysics and "school philosophy." He does, however, try to transform the practice of dialectic with what he calls a "transcendental dialectic." This dialectic does not transgress the limits of metaphysical speculation.

Kant's transcendental dialectic raised the stakes among the German Idealists, especially Hegel, who has done the most to give the term its current connotation. For Hegel, *Dialektik* implies more than a method of knowing. Hegel conceived the history of human inquiry as bound up with a spirit moving through history that included real manifestations of the truth of freedom, or love, or religion. The understanding of spirit in history added to dialectic the conception of necessary movement. Noted Hegel scholar Frederick Beiser states, "When Hegel uses the term 'dialectic' it usually designates the 'self-organization' of the subject matter, its 'inner necessity' and 'inherent movement.'"[20] Beiser emphasizes that Hegel's philosophy is not an a priori method, but rather an account of the inner movement or nature of the subject matter. It is worth noting here that the triadic structure of thesis-antithesis-synthesis, so often cited as the essential feature of the movement of dialectic, has been misattributed to Hegel; it is found earlier in Fichte and Schelling, and Hegel in fact disapproved of it.[21]

Which brings us back to what Buckley means by dialectics. Buckley draws not only on Plato and Hegel, but also on John Dewey's "search for the pattern of inquiry." Apparently aware of the ambiguity and confusion over just what dialectic entails, Buckley describes this dialectical process:

> *To speak of positive assertions, concepts, and arguments as generating their own negations and so constituting or exhibiting contradictions within an initial subject—which is all that is meant by "dialectics" here—is not to suppose that anything finite is not liable to its own finitude, to its own inadequacies and incompletions.*[22]

In other words, like Hegel, Buckley insists that dialectic does not impose an outside method on a given subject matter. The goal is to understand it from within. Buckley makes this point explicitly:

> *The dialectic must proceed not from the external application of determinations from a schema, but as the inner—even organic— progress of the subject under study. Dialectical negation and the negation of the negation must be seen to emerge as the immanent life of the subject reflected in thought.*[23]

Although his intellectual debt to Plato (or Dewey, for that matter) is more explicit than his debt to Hegel, it seems from our survey that despite the reviewers' overplaying of the Hegelianism, they are not altogether wrong— the central thrust of his dialectic appears to entail an inner necessity pointing more to Berlin than to Athens. Nevertheless, Buckley avers:

> *One need not be a Hegelian, an Absolute Idealist, or a Marxist, a dialectical materialist—as indeed I am neither—to recognize that such*

a dialectic can be the development both of the things studied and the process of inquiry into them, that even organic development is into otherness.... This evolving pattern, in which one stage supplants another as mutually incompatible while keeping an organic unity, is made possible, even necessary, by inner incoherence.[24]

Although his critics accused him of imposing a method from without, and more generally, critics accuse dialectical method of doing so, for Buckley, and for Hegel it seems, dialectic essentially involves a discovery of this process from within the matter under scrutiny. The reviewers outlined above fail not so much in ascribing to Buckley a certain Hegelianism, but in misconstruing what Hegel meant by dialectic, as the citation from above points out.

The aim of Buckley's inquiry into atheism was to understand what made possible such a sea-change in modern thought. Rather than begin with the atheists themselves, Buckley began with the theists, in particular the Christian apologists. As Buckley explains, these apologists disseminated the contradiction that the validation of belief in a *personal* god was best confirmed by reliance on *impersonal* evidence for God's existence reflected by the cosmos. This internal contradiction could not stand. Buckley traces the initial cracks and the dismantling of the foundation upon which the house of theism rested.

2. Trajectories of Modernity

Modern secularity and loss of belief presents a vexing challenge to contemporary Christians. This challenge comes into focus against the backdrop of the long Christian attempt to construct a theology of history. The expansion and flourishing of the earliest Christian communities facilitated the construction of a teleological account with the church militant eventually triumphing against pagan or other non-Christian forces. Already in the fourth century the Christian historian Eusebius cited Constantine's conversion and the corresponding elevation of Christianity within the Roman Empire as evidence for Christianity's truth and inevitable triumph. One century after Eusebius, Augustine, especially in the *City of God*, urged his flock to hesitate about such judgments. Although by 390 AD the now-Christian Empire had seemingly rid itself of paganism under Theodosius I, thus fulfilling

Eusebius's manifest destiny, Rome would be sacked by barbarian hordes in 410. Christian theology now had to answer the same question that eighth-century Israelite theology attempted to answer after the collapse of the Davidic throne and the Assyrian invasion. Augustine advises us to be cautious about both triumphs and defeats, for such events do not definitively manifest God's will. The world is fallen. Attempts to bring heaven down to earth are at best mistaken and are more accurately to be read as manifestations of the same sinful *superbia* that motivated the first sin.

Many centuries later, Christian apologists and their interlocutors have tried to understand how a Christian civilization could devolve (or evolve) into a society where belief in God and church attendance experienced a steady decline. A host of worldviews, including secularism, took its place. This secular worldview in particular removed God from the public sphere and replaced such belief with an economy, a religion-less discourse, a nation state, the elevation of instrumental reason, and an account of the good life stripped of any natural teleology. Clearly a massive shift has taken place, and any Eusebian interpretation of events in the formerly Christian West would seem to require an anti-empiricism.

There are two common responses to this situation: the first is triumphant secularism, and the second is reactionary Christianity.[25] According to the former, the Enlightenment ushered in the long, slow march of secularization. A triumphant scientific worldview, coupled with social changes like urbanization that resulted from technological advance, meant that inevitably the West would become increasingly secular. Nothing in the accounts of these secularists would allow for any reversal or stemming of the tide. Enlightenment scholars like Peter Gay, as well as such scholars of religion as Harvey Cox, emphasized the contrast between Christian and secular or Enlightenment worldviews.[26] Of course, the rise of Islamic fundamentalism—highlighted by the 2001 World Trade Center attack—and the political emergence of Evangelical Christianity in the United States provide counter-data to the thesis of inevitability, but do nothing to undermine the fundamentally contrasting worldviews: on the one side: pre-modern religious irrationality; and on the other: modern, secular reason.

We find one incarnation of this contrast in the work of the highly regarded historian of the Enlightenment, Jonathan Israel. In *Enlightenment Contested*, he juxtaposes two irreconcilable worldviews, modern and pre-modern: "From its first inception, the Enlightenment in the western Atlantic world was always a mutually antagonistic duality and the ceaseless internecine strife within it is ... the most fundamental and important thing about it."[27] Although Israel accounts for various strands and stratifications within his general narrative, there can be no question about what lay at the opposite end of Enlightenment, and the political stakes involved therein. Enlightenment promised to bring not only individual emancipation, but transformation of entire societies. Its project, one should not forget, was met with stiff resistance: "Most men had no more desire to discard traditional reverence for established authority and idealized notions of community than their belief in magic, demonology and Satan."[28] Just as efforts to combine traditional theological convictions and religion with the new science and philosophy were doomed in the period under Israel's examination, so too 21st-century efforts at compatibility have no place. The Enlightenment has happened, and there is no turning back. It is worth quoting Israel's concluding salvo at length:

> *It is precisely this continuing, universal relevance of [the Enlightenment's] values on all continents, and among all branches of humanity, together with the unprecedented intellectual cohesion it gave to these moral and social ideals, which accounts for what Bernard Williams called the "intellectual irreversibility of the Enlightenment," its uniquely central importance in the history of humanity. Parenthetically, it might be worth adding that nothing could be more fundamentally mistaken, as well as politically injudicious, than for the European Union to endorse the deeply mistaken notion that "European values" if not nationally particular are at least religiously specific and should be recognized as essentially "Christian" values. That the religion of the papacy, Inquisition, and Puritanism should be labeled the quintessence of "Europeanness" would rightly be considered a wholly unacceptable affront by a great number of thoroughly "European" Europeans.[29]*

What is relevant here is not whether all proponents or historians of the Enlightenment share Israel's viewpoint, but that this viewpoint crystallizes an attitude about the relationship between modernity and Christianity that highlights dissonance and downplays compatibility.

In contrast, many Christian intellectuals have responded in kind to the triumphalism outlined above. Although they juxtapose modernity to Christianity, they do not view the triumph of modernity as necessary, nor do they consider Christianity intellectually inferior. It is impossible to survey all such accounts, and it is equally impossible not to paint with the same inevitably broad brushstrokes used to describe triumphant secularism. Still, efforts can be made to describe this well-trod and many pronged response. One strategy is to pinpoint the location where the train went off the tracks due to a deviation in doctrine or practice. John Milbank's provocative and in many ways illuminating account of modernity drifts in this direction. For Milbank, the point at which things devolved was late medieval nominalism:

> *Now this [late medieval nominalist] philosophy was itself the legatee of the greatest of all disruptions carried out in the history of European thought, namely that of Duns Scotus, who for the first time established a radical separation of philosophy from theology.... The very notion of a reason-revelation duality, far from being an authentic Christian legacy, itself results only from the rise of a questionably secular mode of knowledge.*[30]

One cannot know whether Milbank presents such sharp contrasts for heuristic purposes, or for rhetorical flourish, or because he thinks it properly descriptive. The stridency reaches almost Manichean tones in his concluding paragraph: "It is indeed for radical orthodoxy an either/or: Philosophy (Western or Eastern) as a purely autonomous discipline, or theology: Herod or the magi, Pilate or the God-man."[31]

Certainly a comparison between aspects of modernity, or modern philosophy, provides a sometimes stark contrast with the pre-modern. And there is nothing noble or intellectually superior to underplaying or diminishing these contrasts. One finds a similar juxtaposition in an essay by David Bentley Hart:

> *The only cult that can truly thrive in the aftermath of Christianity is a sordid service of the self, of the impulses of the will, of the nothingness that is all that the withdrawal of Christianity leaves behind. The only futures open to post-Christian culture are conscious nihilism, with its inevitable devotion to death, or the narcotic banality of the Last Men, which may be little better than death.... And we should certainly dread whatever rough beast it is that is being bred in our ever coarser, crueler, more inarticulate, more vacuous popular culture; because, cloaked in its anodyne insipience, lies a world increasingly devoid of merit, wit,*

kindness, imagination, or charity.[32]

Hart presents the contrast between Christianity and modernity as forcefully as possible. To be fair, Hart also enlists Nietzsche and Heidegger in this essay in order to explain how Christianity paves the way for modernity, albeit unintentionally. The citations from Milbank and Hart—two theologians whose breadth of influence would seem to ensure a trickle-down effect of their interpretations and narratives—seem to encourage the same kind of thinking that Jonathan Israel's work encourages. The battle between Christianity and modernity in both instances emerges as a zero-sum game, in which the latter's gain can only mean a loss for the former, and vice-versa.

From a Christian perspective, it is difficult to find consolation in the decrease of the number of believers in Europe and North America. But when one regards modernity itself as an inauthentic development, or as a mistake to correct, then it becomes less likely that one locates the rise of modernity within Christianity itself (not merely within a divergent or heretical branch of it).[33] Buckley's dialectical method rests on the conviction that ideas do not arrive from nowhere. Rather, they are generated in part through the intellectual and heuristic edifices construed by their forbearers. Modernity and the secular age—as mistaken as they may be from a Christian perspective—are best understood when analyzed in conjunction with the Christian culture that birthed them. Precisely at this point the projects of Taylor and Girard become so helpful because of their efforts to account for the emergence of modernity with a method similar to the one Buckley applied to atheism.

3. Taylor and Girard
on Christianity and Modernity

Catholic intellectuals of the highest caliber, Charles Taylor (b. 1931) and René Girard (b. 1923), have attracted legions of followers, scores of detractors, and volumes of commentary. We can only point interested readers toward some of the literature that introduces their thought.[34] Although at this point it may seem pertinent to address how both thinkers locate the relationship between Christianity and modernity, it will prove more illuminating to begin earlier—first with an analysis of how they construe the relation between Christianity and archaic religion, and then with their accounts of the essence of Christianity.

A. Christianity and Religion

In both *A Secular Age* and its much shorter forerunner, *Modern Social Imaginaries*, Taylor develops a theory of religion in order to illustrate the breakthrough of a religious vision central to Christianity.[35] In it he borrows Karl Jaspers's famous distinction between pre-Axial and Axial religions.[36] The former, notes Taylor, is characterized by "a relation to spirits, or forces, or powers, which are recognized as being in some sense higher, not the ordinary forces and animals of everyday" (147). These belief systems engender a set of experiences quite foreign to us. In addition, these forces in early religion are intensely social. God works on the group as a whole, and the group or tribe's consciousness of wellbeing depends on the divine. Archaic religious practice imbues members with a heightened sense of communal belonging or "social embedding." Taylor elaborates, "Because their most important actions were the doings of whole groups, articulated in a certain way, they couldn't conceive of themselves as potentially disconnected from this social matrix."[37]

Consequently, having a proximate and visceral theological experience meant seeing God as intimately bound to this world. It was not always the case that this God was "with us," but to whatever extent God had beneficent intentions, they became manifest in ordinary human flourishing; the pre-Axial God wanted a worshipper to be a king, or to have several sons, or to have a particularly glorious experience in battle (150). In transposing Jaspers's contrast between archaic religions and the subsequent "Axial" religions that emerged between the eighth and fifth century BCE, Taylor sees some continuity between pre-Axial and Axial religion—not the least of which was the role of worship and belief in a ready exchange among the supernatural and the natural.[38] Despite this, the so-called Axial religions, which include Buddhism, prophetic Judaism, and the Vedas, distinguished themselves through "a notion of our good which goes beyond human flourishing" (151). This distinction happens on account of a theological shift, which in the West consisted in the doctrine of creation *ex nihilo*. God went from being contained in the cosmos to transcending it (152). James Alison puts it pithily: "The biblical God is much more like nothing at all than like one of the Gods."[39] Since the notion of human flourishing was so imbedded in theological presuppositions, the Axial shift permitted a corresponding shift in its understanding of human flourishing. Post-Axial human flourishing became disengaged from a more immediate social context. St. Paul flourished, but through a mystical participation in Christ's crucifixion. The martyr Polycarp flourished, but not in a way that many pre-Axial worshippers would recognize.

Given its connection to Judaism, Christianity inherited the Israelite Axial turn. As Christianity came to be the dominant religion in the West, it brought this new religious consciousness with it. Although Taylor does not devote much space to the relationship between Christianity and pre-Axial religion, this relationship comes to play an important role in his account of how modernity and Christianity relate.

For Girard, the dominant matrix to explain pre-Axial religion is the "scapegoat mechanism," which he first articulated in *Violence and the Sacred*.[40] The scapegoat mechanism is humanity's answer to the problem of the violence that stems from the rivalry borne of mimetic desire. Girard claimed that the widespread ritualized killing in archaic societies functioned as a kind of release for the tensions that resulted from a build-up of rivalry. Girard writes, "We can hypothetically assume that several prehistoric groups did not survive precisely because they didn't find a way to cope with the mimetic crisis; their mimetic rivalries didn't find a victim who polarized their rage, saving them from self-destruction."[41] Humanity, says Girard, desperately needed to discover a way to de-escalate mimetic crises, and it found it in the scapegoat mechanism and the subsequent mimetic repetition of this event through what we call ritual. Absent a theory assigning value to ritual, Romantics and Nietzscheans imagine the nobility of primitive, pre-ritualized cultures and therefore see religion as a cultural perversion and fall from a pristine natural state.[42] Anthropological evidence, however, makes such a theory less tenable. Anthropologists and archaeologists have found abundant evidence of sacrifice and ritual at humanity's origins, but as of yet no social contract.[43] This pristine state, purport Rousseau and Nietzsche, has been jettisoned in favor of religion. Girard recalls that both Enlightenment and Romantic philosophies explain the ubiquity of ritual on account of "cunning and avid priests [who] impose their abracadabras on good people." What comes first: the priest or the cult? For Girard, the answer is obvious: "If we simply consider that the clergy cannot really precede the invention of culture, then religion must come first and far from being a derisory force, it appears as the origin of the whole culture."[44]

Although it is easy for modern society to look down its nose at primitive sacrificial ritual and taboos, Girard concludes that these institutions saved humanity from self-destruction. Human culture was built upon sacrificial victims perceived as having broken a taboo: both the Oedipus myths and the founding of Rome attest to this. "Humanity," says Girard, "is the child of religion."[45] At its origins, then, archaic religion is violent and false, yet it paradoxically allows the human species to persevere. Under a Girardian lens the apparent irrationality of incest taboos and cultic bloodletting becomes thoroughly rational.

Before he turned his attention to the Jewish and Christian scriptures, Girard offered a pessimistic take on the human quest for peace. *Violence and the Sacred* states, "The best men can hope for in their quest for nonviolence is the unanimity-minus-one of the surrogate victim."[46] Later, Girard will associate this logic with Caiaphas.[47] Archaic religion and its subsequent religious myths tell a lie necessary for human survival: its violence is necessary. Christianity's revelation consists in taking away the veil from the mythic fabrications that conceal the scapegoat's innocence.

B. Das Wesen des Christentums

Although Charles Taylor says comparatively little about the nature of Christianity, three main points emerge in his distinction of Christianity from generic axial religion. First, Christianity produces an advanced sense of inwardness; second, it contains a reforming spirit that always demands more; third, it sees true religion as selfless love, or *agape*.

To the first point: in *Sources of the Self*, he reads Augustine as a proto-modern figure who, compared to his Greek ancestors, stressed the role of the will in our constitution. As Augustine attests in the *Confessions*, the Platonic maxim wherein the good would be done if it were known does not take into sufficient account the radical perversion of the will generated by original sin and bad habits. In addition, Augustine complements the previous emphasis on divine transcendence with a hitherto neglected sense of God's closeness to us. Taylor writes:

> *Our principle route to God [for Augustine] is not through the object domain but "in" ourselves. This is because God is not just the transcendent object or just the principle of order of the nearer objects, which we strain to see. God is also and for us primarily the basic*

support and underlying principle of our knowing activity.[48]

One sees this push toward inwardness in Augustine's psychological analogy of the Trinity, wherein the pattern of knowing—memory, intellect, and will—is one of the created world's most telling vestiges of the Trinitarian persons. Taylor continues: "Augustine shifts the focus from the field of objects known to the activity itself of knowing; God is to be found here."[49] This emphasis serves as a precursor to the modern self. In jumping from Augustine to Descartes in his account of modern identity, Taylor passes over a millennium of thought because "it is hardly an exaggeration to say that it was Augustine who introduces the inwardness of radical reflexivity and bequeathed it to the Western tradition of thought."[50]

The second distinguishing feature of Christianity comes into view through an examination of Calvinism and its Puritan offshoot. For Taylor, the affirmation of ordinary life comes about primarily due to the reforming efforts that culminated in the Protestant Reformation.[51] No longer was friendship with God bound up with the sacramental system of mediation that infuses medieval Christianity. Instead, each individual was responsible for his own faith, and his commitment to God had to be total. Following Max Weber, Taylor posits that the idea that each person's call in life could be carried out with excellence, together with the democratization of discipline and order, made possible the notion that an entire society could be transformed. In the years between *Sources of the Self* an *A Secular Age*, Taylor apparently became less tethered to the strict correlation of this movement with the Protestant Reformation. His more recent work emphasizes medieval efforts and argues for a more general and less specifically Protestant impulse in Christianity as *semper reformans.*[52] Late medieval and early modern Christians repeatedly attempted to dissolve the radical separation between sacred and profane so that God could be experienced in everyday life. For Taylor, this reforming spirit results from a fundamental tendency or essential quality in Christianity.[53] We feel the effects of this reform in modernity through such derivative religious movements as Prohibitionism and the zeal for physical fitness.

A third feature, perhaps the most central one, is the ethic of *agape*. Exemplified in the story of the Good Samaritan (Luke 10), the unselfish love to which Christians are called extends beyond the basic communal ethic of solidarity. Agape can even disrupt that solidarity, since in an ethic of solidarity the Good Samaritan would have never stopped to help the injured man on the roadside (158; 739-42). Taylor makes two interesting comparative points: first, this loving self-renunciation, which Jesus exemplifies on the cross, differs from Stoic renunciation (17). It does so because, unlike Stoicism, Christianity does not reject the goodness of ordinary flourishing. Second, Christian agape overlaps with the Buddhist doctrines of *anatta* and *karuna* (17).[54] Taylor's repeated appeals to agape and the example of the Good Samaritan, sprinkled throughout *A Secular Age*, support his claim about the centrality of agape for Christianity. In the incarnation and crucifixion of Christ, Christianity posits an identification of this love with God's own being.

According to Girard, Christianity is the great anti-mythology. For the first time, the Hebrew scriptures tell stories of scapegoating from the perspective of the victim. Instead of myths that cover up the founding violence, both of these texts expose the real violence that underlies their mythic superstructure. Besides this negative function, Judaism and Christianity positively reveal that God has nothing to do with violence and that God sides with the victim. In the New Testament, God not only sides with the victim—God *is* the victim. This is the evangelical truth "hidden since the foundations of the world" (Matt 13:35). Jesus' cry from the cross—"forgive them, Father, for they know not what they do"—is based not on a Platonic theory of evil, but on the insight revealed to Judaism about the nature of human culture and the origins of human violence.[55] Girard declares, "The Gospels constantly reveal what the texts of historical persecution, and especially mythological persecutors, hide from us: the knowledge that their victim is a scapegoat [... The Gospel] indicates more clearly the innocence of this victim, the injustice of the condemnation, and the causelessness of the hatred of which it is the object."[56]

The power of the gospel is so revolutionary, and yet the pull in our consciousness towards archaic religion so strong, that the gospel has not really taken root in so-called "Christian" societies. For Girard, this failure does not de-legitimize the gospel or alter its truth. Slowly, however, the gospel works its way through society, and the radical nature of its message about religions has become embedded in the West, although not always in the manner most expected.

C. The Nature and Cause of Modernity

An attempt to understand and explain modernity and secularism has occupied much of Charles Taylor's considerable scholarly endeavors.[57]

Taylor declares it his intent to trace the factors that created the transition from a society in which it was nearly impossible *not* to believe, to a society where belief is no longer taken for granted (1-3). He opens *A Secular Age*, his 2007 *magnum opus*, by rejecting hitherto accepted notions of the secular as its common institutions (the modern state) and practices free of God, or as a more general loss of religious belief and practice. Instead, Taylor argues that secularity best corresponds to an environment where belief is no longer a given, but is conceived as one option among others. For Taylor, it is important that secularism be grasped outside the rubric of what he calls a subtraction theory, according to which a loss of belief is replaced by something like science. This only makes sense if Christian belief is antiquated, like a geocentric model of the universe. Moreover, Christianity is not incompatible with modern science. The lack of any logical incompatibility, as well as the significant number of believing scientists, signifies to Taylor that the subtraction theory falls flat.[58] Far more compelling is to ask why so many moderns failed to see options that would allow for a greater integration, or why these options were not attractive to as many people as could have been.

Although we cannot here recapitulate Taylor's account of the emergence and nature of modernity and of secularism, we can point to a few distinguishing marks in its connection to a Christian past and its current form. One such aspect is the emphasis on ordinary life and human flourishing. Especially as inherited from the Puritan strand, this movement made possible the large-scale application of ascetic discipline that had previously been reserved for the elites. In the new imaginary, this ascetic ideal could spread to all believers, and thus society could be transformed, not simply by common participation in a ritual, but through each individual living a life of holiness and submitting to disciplinary penitence when he fell short. As Taylor traces it, this ascetic zeal became detached from traditional Christianity and mutated into what Taylor calls "exclusive humanism." As he defines it, "Exclusive humanism closes the transcendent window, as though there were nothing beyond."[59] The rest is history—the fitness studio should pay royalties to the monastery.

Additionally, a key feature in Taylor's account is the buffered self, which Taylor connects to the process of "disenchantment" that he borrows from Max Weber and Marcel Gauchet.[60] Taylor contrasts this buffered self with the pre-modern "porous" self (38), which feels itself seamlessly connected to both its social and natural surroundings. We can experience this porous self today only through extreme group activities like attending a sold-out football game or engaging in extreme sports like surfing. That these moments feel so different from our ordinary experiences indicates how buffered the self really has become. As moderns, it is hard for us to grasp how differently we understand ourselves than our pre-modern ancestors. Taylor uses the example of melancholy or feeling depressed:

> *A modern is feeling depressed, melancholy. He is told: it's just your body chemistry, you're hungry, or there is a hormone malfunction, or whatever. Straightaway, he feels relieved.... But a pre-modern may not be helped by learning that his mood comes from black bile. Because this doesn't permit a distancing. Black bile is melancholy* (37).

Modernity no longer imagines an enchanted world, and replaces it instead with a neutral world of matter and motion, which houses people who imagine themselves originally isolated and only secondarily connected to others. They can also imagine moods abstractly and ontologically disconnected from a material substance like a humor. Taylor continues: "For the modern, buffered self, the possibility exists of taking a distance from, disengaging from everything outside the mind. My ultimate purposes are those which arise within me, the crucial meanings of things are those defined in my responses to them" (38). Again, this conception of the buffered self arises as a mutation within the imaginative horizon of the long and winding Christian tradition. Therefore, whatever the shortcomings of the buffered self (and we need not see it as deficient in comparison to the porous self), its existence is not intrinsically disordered or sinful in Taylor's account.

A distinct moral feature of modernity is the concern for all human beings and the need to alleviate suffering. Taylor connects this with the gospel ethic of *agape*. He emphasizes the uniqueness of this quality: "Our age makes higher demands for solidarity and benevolence on people today than ever before. Never before have people been asked to stretch out so far so consistently, so systematically, so as a matter of course, to the stranger at the gates."[61] Here we think of our responses to such natural disasters as the earthquake in Haiti or the hurricane in New Orleans. One would not be surprised to hear that both committed atheists and conservative evangelicals worked side by side in such locales, although each might presume to despise the worldview of the other. The Christian might be motivated by a modified divine command ethic, or have a particular loyalty to his pastor or parish. The atheist scoffs at the impurity of the other's motives, given that the same moral grammar might justify any abuse. For himself the atheist claims a more immanent moral rationality. Of significance for Taylor is that both share a peculiar modern concern for alleviating the suffering of those at the margins.

Although modernity has at its disposal many different "sources," it has been unable to cobble together a synthesis between its two characteristically modern modes of knowing: instrumental rationality and expressive individualism. A worldview based entirely on varieties of scientism—strictly mechanical accounts that reduce morality to pain/pleasure, and neo-Darwinian accounts that derive (albeit not necessarily) an anthropology and a corresponding ethic based on the laws of evolution—fails to appropriate Romantic expressive individualism. Romantics attach profound importance to self-given meaning that constitutes the inner depths of being human. As Taylor argues, most people do not want to face the moral consequences suggested by evolutionary biology: Our lives have no intrinsic meaning and human flourishing is not the purpose of the universe. Moreover, they distrust accounts that effectively read out the self-sacrificial love of a parent for a child from any valid description of reality, as scientistic accounts do. Modern individuals want to find profound meaning in the depths of their souls, or in nature; the religiously inclined want to connect this meaning with the divine. Romanticism exclusive of rationality and modern science, however, seems too much like the leap of faith that religion requires. So it can happen that secular world-views swirl about without ever arriving at a satisfactory synthesis.

Taylor's account of modern secularism is in many ways compatible with Buckley's thesis about the emergence of modern atheism. In describing modern, secular humanism, Taylor writes:

> *Secular humanism also has its roots in Judaeo-Christian faith; it arises from a mutation out of a form of that faith. The question can be put, whether this is more than a matter of historical origin, whether it doesn't also reflect a continuing dependence.... My belief, baldly stated here, is that it does.*[62]

As Taylor describes it, the Christian West made possible a horizon within which secularity was imagined. Although he does not make the case that Christianity "causes" modernity, he does regard it as inconceivable without Christianity—hence the language of *mutation*.[63]

As the transcendence of God emphasized in Western Axial religion created a greater distance between earth and heaven, the terrestrial could be imagined as autonomous and self-sufficient. Rather than regarding secularism, as do Milbank and Hart in the examples above, as a reversal of an upward trajectory, Taylor sees it as a third great stage in religious development, after the pre-Axial and the Axial. In addition, Taylor's genealogy places ideas in a historical setting, as generated not from pure mental ether, but rather through the grit and dirt of an intermingling with social and psychological factors that profoundly complicate any true telling of modernity. Secularity cannot be the opposite of Christendom; instead it is an iteration of it, however unfortunate, wrong-headed, and unself-conscious that iteration might have been.

Taylor's contextualization points to a more tepid assessment of modernity than the boosters and knockers mentioned above. At the 1996 lecture accompanying the Marianist Award at Dayton University, Taylor addressed this point head-on: "In modern, secularist culture there are mingled together both authentic developments of the gospel, of an incarnational mode of life, and also a closing off to God that negates the gospel." His argument strongly expresses the genetic account hinted at above: "In relation to the earlier forms of Christian culture, we have to face the humbling realization that the breakout [modern secularism] was a *necessary* condition of the development."[64] Although lacking Buckley's language of "internal dialectic," Taylor's rendering of modernity, despite its seeming opposition to Christianity, gives an example of this dialectic by showing how Christianity created the environment in which modernity was allowed to come into being.

Girard's description and explanation of modernity is in many ways even more insightful than Taylor's—this despite the fact that Girard concedes a lack of interest in elaborating a theory of modernity.[65] To conclude this section, we will examine three characteristics of modernity identified by Girard: the modern concern for victims, the tendency to self-scrutiny, and the modern belief in the superiority of scientific method. Each of these, according to Girard, is unthinkable without Christianity.

Like Taylor, Girard points out the particular Western concern for victims. Here it is best to quote Girard at length:

> *Our society is the most preoccupied with victims of any that ever was. Even if it is insincere, a big show, the phenomenon has no precedent. No historical period, no society we know, has ever spoken of victims*

as we do.

Examine ancient sources, inquire everywhere ... and you will not find anything anywhere that even remotely resembles our modern concern for victims. The China of the Mandarins, the Japan of the samurai, the Hindus, the pre-Columbian societies, Athens, republicans of imperial Rome—none of these were worried in the least little bit about victims, whom they sacrificed without number to their gods, to the honor of the homeland.[66]

The modern concern for victims arises out of Christianity, which identifies God with the victim. Modern anti-Christian objections to Christian atrocities such as the Crusades and the witch hunts are ironic, for such arguments apply a thoroughly Christian grammar. Girard does not deny that modernity produces victims; the horrors of the twentieth century make such a view untenable. He notes, however, that the modern world "also saves more victims than any previous historical moment ever did."[67] Before Christianity, it would have been unthinkable to use a rhetorical strategy wherein one attempted to identify with the victim. In mythology, the scapegoat is always guilty. In Judaism and Christianity, she is innocent. Siding with the victim or the outsider is so central both to Christianity and to modernity that Girard is able to say that the world is becoming, paradoxically, more and more Christian. Here modernity and Christianity overlap: "We can say [that] we are all believers in the innocence of victims, which is at the core of Christianity."[68]

The proclamation of the gospel, which is the proclamation of the victim's innocence, forces us to look inward in order to understand society's fallenness as represented in the stained or sinful scapegoat. This level of self-scrutiny overlaps with Taylor's buffered self. (I think Taylor would agree that the buffered self is more inoculated from sacrificial ritual than the porous self.) No society has ever been more self-critical than modern, Western society, despite its frequent failings. Both the secular concern for victims, and the desire not to be shaped entirely by one's culture, comes out of and shares this characteristic with Christianity. As Girard puts it, "He [the Christian] is the one who can resist the crowd."[69] Indeed, the very ground of the debate upon which secularity determines the moral legitimacy of Christianity is a Christian one. The new atheists miss this point. Girard responds to this new wave of atheism by highlighting how Christian their anti-Christianity is:

Today's anti-religion combines so much error and nonsense about religion that it can barely be satirized. It serves the cause that it would undermine, and secretly defends the mistakes that it believes it is correcting.... By seeking to demystify sacrifice, current demystification does a much worse job than the Christianity that it thinks it is attacking because it still confuses Christianity with archaic religion.[70]

Like many of the new atheists, Girard also contends that modern science rests at the center of modernity and secularism. He offers, however, an entirely different etiology, which untangles the alleged conflict between science and religion.[71] Girard argues that the zeal for science arises from the Christian attitude about victims. Since victims are chosen arbitrarily and are usually innocent, the gospel teaches the culture to look for different causes. Girard explains:

The scientific spirit cannot come first. It presupposes the renunciation of a former preference for the magical causality of persecution so well defined by the ethnologists. Instead of natural, distant, and inaccessible causes, humanity has always preferred causes that are significant from a social perspective and permit of corrective intervention—victims.[72]

Christianity's proclamation of the forgiving victim's resurrection, in the words of Flannery O'Connor's misfit, "changes everything." Just as we are no longer comfortable with simple theodicies to explain natural disasters, so we are no longer sated by the victimology of old. Girard explains, "The invention of science is not the reason that there are no longer witch-hunts, but the fact that there are no longer witch-hunts is the reason that science has been invented."[73]

It is no surprise that the most popular television dramas are now the most scientific. I am referring to the explosion of CSI (Crime Scene Investigation) series. Christianity has made us vigilant about the culpability of the accused. Hearsay and verbal testimony no longer convince us: we want scientific evidence and DNA. Despite Girard's etiology, it must be conceded that Christians have lost their mettle in this discussion. Voices ignorant of Christian theology and the Christian tradition have too often and too loudly opposed Christianity to modern science and aligned it with modern pseudoscience. But it is Christianity that bred the love of science, the critique of religion, and the suspicion against magic that are the proclaimed virtues of today's secularists.

D. Christian Responses to Modernity

It is never easy to understand the nature and depth of phenomena like secularism, modernity, or the loss of belief: Are they exceptional, passing fads, entirely circumstantial? Or do they signal something bigger, more seismic, more permanent? As each decade passes, it may still be premature to declare a permanent decrease in belief, but one can nonetheless determine that a sizeable majority among educated classes in the West has adopted a secular worldview. Moreover, the old manner by which one came to believe no longer functions.

Michael Buckley addresses the possibility of a post-secular response to atheism in the final two chapters of *Denying and Disclosing God*. If atheism itself results from an "internal contradiction," then can one chart a path to negate the negation of God? Buckley offers a foretaste in the preface, when he promises to use John of the Cross to sublate the projectionists' critique of religion: "The negation of these projections comprises the classical night of the soul, moving beyond the negation of God as projection to the further negation of the negation itself in the affirmation of God."[74]

Buckley reads the nineteenth-century critique of belief in God by Feuerbach and Freud as a critique of a "too-easy" theism. For these thinkers, the God projected by believers was all too human. Buckley points out that their critique runs parallel to a similar critique by "a movement equally aware of the proclivity of religion to become projection" (109). This movement is the apophatic tradition of pseudo-Dionysius, Gregory of Nyssa, and John of the Cross, among others. Buckley centers his retrieval on John of the Cross, the great Carmelite mystic most known for his articulation of the "dark night of the soul." Like Freud and Feuerbach, John admits that our ordinary experience of God is deeply flawed and problematic—according to the Scholastic maxim, *quidquid recipitur secundum modum recipientis recipitur* (160 n.46)—our experience, even the inbreaking of the divine that can come through prayer, is necessarily conditioned by our own limitations. According to John, true religious consciousness does not, however, stop at identifying the fraught nature of ordinary religiosity. Buckley explains:

> *What we grasp and what we long for is very much shaped and determined by our own preconceptions, appetites, concepts, and personality-set. If these are not disclosed and gradually transformed by grace and by its*

progressive affirmation within religious faith, working its way into the everyday of human history and choices, then there is no possibility of contemplation of anything but our own projections (114).

John's crucible of religious reflection forces the student of his method to recognize and disavow the idolatry that often masquerades as worship and to reject the projection that substitutes for the true God.

Buckley's retrieval of apophatic theology as a response to a strand in atheism implies a recognition that at least some atheist critiques have something true and valuable to say. Rather than a more traditional apologetic tactic aimed at prohibiting any entrance to atheism, Buckley suggests that the proper aim "should be less to refute Feuerbachian and Freudian analysis than to learn from them what they have to teach about the relentless remolding of the image of God by religious consciousness" (119). Of course, by the time that most people matriculate out of secondary education, they come to realize that something can be learned from one's opponents. Buckley's account, however, moves far beyond the level of epistemic platitude. Beneath the façade of anti-Christianity, one finds a visage with all the markings of Christianity. His dialectic does not permit a notion of theism and atheism as static, binary terms. The very contradiction upon which modern atheism rests means that the process of understanding this negation will allow the generation of "its own further negation, the negation of the negation" (121). This process is what Buckley intends to accomplish in his appeal to apophaticism and to the mystical theology of John of the Cross. Buckley ends *Denying and Disclosing God* by using data neglected in previous centuries of apologetics: religious experience, examples of holiness, and the critical reflection upon encounters with and by such people.

In a similar vein, Taylor's massive investigation of the cause and nature of modern secularism concludes by examining how Christianity might best respond to this situation. Taylor uses the impasse at which late-modern secularity stands in order to carve out a space for Christianity to flourish. In the final chapter of *A Secular Age*, "Conversions," he also shows how previously unbelieving moderns have found a way to believe within the immanent frame.[75] Beyond reference to important conversions of influential individuals—Walker Percy, T.S. Eliot, Christopher Dawson, Charles Peguy—Taylor points to the Christian attempt to imagine how a Christian civilization persists *without* a return to Christendom. Jacques Maritain earns a privileged place in Taylor's rendering. After his unfortunate association with *Action Francaise*—the monarchist movement founded by Charles Maurras, which sought to restore Catholicism as the state religion—Maritain realized that a recovery could not mean a return. As Taylor explains,

> *[Maritain] sought a unity of Christian culture on a global scale, but in a dispersed network of Christian lay institutions and centres of intellectual and spiritual life .... The central feature of this new culture will be* "l'avènement spiritual non pas de l'ego centré sur lui-même, mais de la subjectivité créatrice."[76]

Taylor distinguishes between converts who condemn the modern order and those who form a loyal opposition (745). As much as the latter converts acknowledge this gain, their Christianity enables them to identify what is lost in a world without Christ. The more authentic navigation of the intersection of modernity and Christianity does not settle for trying to identify a better, earlier order. Rather, "it invites us to a conversation which can reach beyond any one such order.... Inevitably and rightly, Christian life today will look for and discover new ways of moving beyond the present orders to God" (755). Precisely as an instance in which we come to see our previous vision as limited, conversion provides a helpful vehicle for Taylor to move out of the immanent frame.

The examination of different stories of conversion also allows Taylor to introduce the possibility of hope. This hope does not replace optimism, but, as he reminds his readers, the discovery of the truth of God's self-sacrificial love in Christ can manifest the authenticity sought dearly by so many moderns. Moreover, Christianity, especially its Catholic branch, urges its followers to imagine the journey of a wayfaring pilgrim as communal and shared with others: "The Church was rather meant to be the place in which human beings, in all their difference and disparate itineraries, come together" (772). Taylor's final chapter contains perhaps his most impassioned writing and reveals his concern, in the midst of many nuanced points and objections, to articulate the abiding truth of orthodox Christianity.

As we turn to Girard, I would like to suggest that his interpretation of modernity is in many ways deeper than Taylor's. Girard better understands the essence of that from which modernity arises. The qualities in Christianity that form modernity seem in Taylor's rendering like arbitrary offshoots of Christianity. Taylor's hopeful conclusion to *A Secular Age* seems to follow the general arc of *why not?* For Girard, the essence of modernity arises from the essence of Christianity. The essence of Christianity for Girard, as we have seen, is the revelation of the scapegoat mechanism and of the victim's innocence.

Girard makes two important historical points about the implications of the scapegoat mechanism. The first is that Christianity undoes its power, thus paving the way for modernity's unique and singular concern with victims, or in Taylor's terms, Christianity ushers in an inclusivist view of humanity. The second is the historical failure of Christianity for so much of its history. The examples of anti-Judaism, witch hunts, and the Crusades suffice. Despite these failures, Girard points to the correctness of Nietzsche's insight about the absurdity of secularism's anti-Christianity. Nietzsche was right—Christianity has initiated a revolt in morality. Nietzsche was also wrong: "He doesn't see that the Gospel stance towards victims does not come from prejudice in favor of the weak against the strong [the "slave revolt"] but is heroic resistance to violent contagion. Indeed the Gospels embody the discernment of a small minority that dares to oppose the monstrous mimetic contagion of a Dionysian lynching."[77] Nietzsche correctly pinpointed the antithesis—Dionysius versus the Crucified, but he sided with the lie of the former rather than the truth of the latter.

Girard's evangelical hermeneutic allows him to see such modern measures as humanitarian aid, the abolition of slavery and serfdom, and different forms of egalitarianism as evidence for a certain kind of Christian progress that seems counter-intuitive. He notes, "We are not Christian enough. The paradox can be put in a different way: Christianity is the only religion that has foreseen its own failure."[78] Girard then offers us his hitherto dormant eschatology. Although he had made a similar comment in the earlier *I See Satan Fall Like Lightning*, he did so without the apocalyptic conclusions put forth in *Battling to the End* (2009), where he states, "Christian truth has been making an unrelenting historical advance in our world. Paradoxically, it goes hand in hand with the apparent decline of Christianity." Later he states,

> *The fact that our world has become solidly anti-Christian, at least among elites, does not prevent the concern for victims from flourishing—just the opposite.*

The majestic inauguration of the "post-Christian era" is a joke. We are living through a caricatural "ultra Christianity" that tries to escape from the Judeo-Christian orbit by "radicalizing" the concern for victims in an anti-Christian manner.[79]

Whereas Taylor points to the authenticity of Christian converts, who chart a *better* way to be good moderns, Girard points to an incongruence of modern seculars. This incongruence indicates the kind of dissatisfaction with modernity articulated by our "knockers" in the opening section. Despite many indications that Girard would qualify as one of Taylor's "knockers," this is an untenable conclusion. Girard reads modernity as far too Christian in order to read it simply as a mistake or a reversal of a better Christian past.

This evangelical hermeneutic licenses Girard to understand not only modernity, but even atheism, as fundamentally Christian. As Christianity slowly works to dismantle sacrificial religion, it saws off the branch on which historical Christianity rests in so far as it is unable to practice religion free of scapegoating. Secularism and atheism are not simply unfortunate side effects, but rather inevitable results. Girard declares,

Christianity is not only one of the destroyed religions but it is the destroyer of all religions. The death of God is a Christian phenomenon. In its modern sense, atheism is a Christian invention.... The disappearance of religion is a Christian phenomenon par excellence.[80]

In a word, Christianity teaches us how to be secular.

It is hard to let Girard's analysis sink in and not feel that Christianity has the upper hand. Indeed, I would like to conclude pointing out that all three of our authors end their writings on an apologetic note. Although Taylor is the only one of the three who acknowledges familiarity with the other two, Girard, it seems, is the more true to the spirit of Buckley, even if less indebted to him.[81] For Buckley, when one understands modern atheism as a negation, then the steps to negate the negation are clear. For Girard, once it is clear that the skepticism of the anti-Christians "itself is a by-product of Christian religion," then it is a short and swift step to outwit them.[82] Good Christianity continually engages in a kind of brinksmanship, and the bad theology described by Buckley balks at this.

What's Reason Got to Do with It? Examining Contemporary Theologies of Religious Pluralism

Anna Bonta Moreland, Villanova University

At the end of his second book on the rise of modern atheism, *Denying and Disclosing God: The Ambiguous Progress of Modern Atheism*, Michael Buckley suggests that any defense of religious belief that does not begin with personal experience, with a human encounter, is bound to be fruitless. He concludes that "[o]ne will not long believe in a personal God with whom there is no personal communication, and the most compelling evidence of a personal God must itself be personal."[1] If, instead, one turns to other disciplines to provide the foundation of religious belief, one will end up in a process of internal contradictions that inevitably results in atheism.[2] Buckley's book carefully outlines the process of this dialectical development in the modern era.

Although Buckley's comments might seem to elevate the personal at the expense of other modes of being religious, he maintains that a defense of religious belief must include everything that constitutes religion: "the intuitional, emotional and volitional; the speculative and rational; the institutional, historical and traditional."[3] This present essay therefore asks whether those defenses of religious belief that are exclusively personal, experiential, and narrative-based do not potentially pose a risk that, while different from the impersonal rational defenses of religion so common in the 19th century, are every bit as frustrating. Buckley's book outlines the risks of bracketing religious experience. My essay briefly sketches the risks of bracketing the speculative and rational, in this case in the contemporary field of the theology of religious pluralism.

The theology of religious pluralism has been a burgeoning field for the past few decades, but it has become mired in its own terminology, and has largely restricted itself to the area of soteriology. In Christian theological circles, the discussion surrounding the typologies of exclusivism, inclusivism, and pluralism is simply exhausted.[4] This typology is a widely accepted way to categorize the differences in approaches to religious pluralism, developed in the early nineties: Exclusivists believe Christianity is in sole possession of effective religious truth and offers the only path to salvation; inclusivists affirm that salvation is available through other traditions because the God most decisively acting and most fully revealed in Christ is also redemptively available within or through those traditions; pluralists maintain that various religious traditions are independently valid paths to salvation and Christ is irrelevant to those in other traditions, though serving Christians as *their* means to the same end.

On the one hand, the terms are inadequate to cover new positions being developed in this area, and on the other they are entirely too adequate, with those who agree with each other leading isolated conversations. Some have gone so far as to call for a moratorium on the whole project of a theology of religions, in favor of the painstaking and practical work of comparative theology.[5] I sympathize with this impulse, but am still convinced that epistemological questions underlying comparative theology remain both crucial and unresolved. While this is an exploding field, disagreements about the theology of religious pluralism are narrowly centered on the issue of soteriology.[6] This can be clearly seen in the Vatican's reaction to contemporary theologies of religious pluralism in its 2000 declaration *Dominus Iesus*, aptly entitled "On the Unicity and Salvific Universality of Jesus Christ and the Church." I suggest that instead of framing the question around salvation, we focus on truth. For example, we might ask the following question: "What does it mean for the Christology of *Dominus Iesus* to embrace the truth and holiness found in other religions, as famously affirmed in *Nostra aetate*?" Asking the right question together can provide the key to moving beyond current stagnation that surrounds the typology-centered discussion. Reframing the question in this way has three main advantages: a) it preserves the church's longstanding tendency not to overstate what it knows about eternal judgment; b) it widens the discussion of encounter with God to include the whole journey of one's life, not just the final end—beginning with one's natural inclinations and culminating in eternal life; c) it recognizes that despite our differences in faith traditions, we share common human questions that are addressed on a shared journey.

While fruitful work has already been done exploring what holiness in other religions means for Christians, the question of truth in other religions has been neglected, perhaps because we have not yet resolved the epistemological crises brought about by postmodern philosophy.[7] Discussions of holiness or the Spirit's work in other faith traditions can risk sidestepping the question of truth. But this discussion would both clarify current disagreements over the typologies mentioned above and open possibilities for further research.

Accordingly, in this essay I argue that much more attention needs to be paid to questions of truth and reason in the theology of religious pluralism. This suggestion both takes the full impact of *Nostra aetate* seriously and widens our understanding of how people of other faith traditions encounter God. I examine two contemporary theologians who deal with epistemological issues underlying religious pluralism. Whatever their significant differences, the approaches outlined by Gavin D'Costa and Terrence Tilley share similar problems with respect to reason and truth. By identifying these weaknesses, we will bring the cognitive dimensions to the forefront of the theology of religious pluralism.

Gavin D'Costa

In asking what epistemology underlies D'Costa's work on the theology of religious pluralism, it is most helpful to turn to his book, *The Meeting of Religions and the Trinity* (2000), and cull from articles written throughout his career. In this book, D'Costa outlines his constructive proposal of "Trinitarian exclusivism." In its early pages, he sketches out his argument and places it on the larger canvas of contemporary work on interreligious issues. He sees his own work as an extension of Alasdair MacIntyre's project, while at the same time taking seriously Milbank's criticisms of that project. Throughout the book D'Costa adopts Milbank's use of rhetorics (as "conversion by faith" involving out-narration) and MacIntyre's use of dialectics (as "historically contextualized rational argument").[8] Milbank argues that MacIntyre (1) mistakes Thomism for being "dialectically constituted" rather than "rhetorically instilled,"[9] and 2) operates within a foundational belief in rational dialectics. D'Costa defends MacIntyre on both counts. He argues that MacIntyre does not engage in dialectics as a general law, but rather uses dialectics on an ad hoc basis. In the very specific case of Thomas's use of Aristotle, both traditions had a "shared sense of rational argument"[10] that made engagement possible. While D'Costa finds Milbank's method of "out-narrating" different traditions persuasive in some instances, he thinks both dialectics and rhetoric are important methods of engagement. In fact, Milbank's choosing of rhetoric over dialectics replaces "one form of foundationalism... with another."[11]

But in the actual argument of the book and particularly in his criticism of the inclusivist position, D'Costa seems to accentuate Milbank over MacIntyre, the narrator over the dialectician. Rhetoric is given pride of place over philosophy. This is where my questions about his project arise.

How, in his promotion of exclusivism, does he criticize inclusivists? D'Costa argues that inclusivism logically collapses into exclusivism in three particular ways: 1) for both, *really* in the end, the home tradition contains the truth regarding ontological, epistemological, and ethical claims; 2) both hold to the inseparability of ontology, epistemology, and ethics such that truth cannot be separated from the mediator: Christ and his church; and 3) both recognize the tradition-specific nature of their enquiry, but engage in arguments with rival traditions. Despite their resistance to the conclusions of exclusivism, inclusivists implicitly share their presuppositions.

Inclusivists part ways with their exclusivist brethren in affirming that religions other than Christianity are a means to salvation. D'Costa challenges this last claim. In affirming some part of another tradition, an inclusivist necessarily: 1) tears out a part of an organic totality, 2) reinterprets that part, 3) and transforms its original meaning. The new meaning, then, "can *only* [sic] bear some analogical resemblance" to its meaning and use within its original paradigm.[12] D'Costa's examples include not only Sikhism's inclusion of Hinduism and Islam, but also Christianity's inclusion of Judaism, and Islam's inclusion of Christianity and Judaism. Inclusion in all these circumstances becomes radical transformation, although to varying extents. In the end, inclusivists think they are being more inclusive than they actually are—what they choose to include is arbitrary, losing its original meaning and taking on an entirely new meaning in the adoption process.

But, we may ask, is this always and everywhere the case? Perhaps D'Costa's most telling example is that of Aquinas's use of Aristotle:

> *Thomism is not Aristotle perfected, but Aristotle reinterpreted and transformed.... The basic shift from Aristotle to Aquinas requires both dialectics and faith (rhetoric), and an entire paradigm shift.*[13]

D'Costa underscores here that Greek philosophy was neither being affirmed in its own right nor viewed as a legitimate salvific structure.[14] Rather, it was adopted and transformed on an *ad hoc* basis, with no respect paid to that philosophy's native integrity. In a more recent article he argues that

> *there is no reason why Advaita Vedanta should not play the role that*

*Aristotle played for Thomas Aquinas. This process has already begun.
But this process should not be confused with the notion that Advaita
Vedanta per se is 'revelation', just as the early Church did not claim
Aristotle's philosophy was revelation.*[15]

So what happens, then, when one meets a believer from another tradition?
The believer from one tradition affirms those elements within the other tradition that it already holds dear, usually those that reflect the best parts of
itself.[16] This affirmation, in the end, does not truly affirm anything, for it
only affirms the part rather than the whole, and certainly not the tradition
as it understands itself, but "what the alien theologian chooses to prioritize
and select."[17] The method of prioritizing here sounds like it arises out of
personal taste—and a parochial one at that—rather than rational reflection.
D'Costa understands Thomas as an "alien theologian," prioritizing and selecting from Aristotle what resonated with his preconceived notions.

For D'Costa, the act of judging between religions is—in the best of circumstances—like comparing apples to oranges.[18] He does support, however,
a particular version of comparison, that of "judging another religion by the
criteria and standards of one's own tradition."[19] When one encounters believers from another religious tradition, one must allow them to have a "narrative space within Christian theology and practice so that their histories and
stories can be heard without distortion."[20] Our attentiveness to these narratives reflects our openness to both God and neighbor, an openness that can
challenge and even change our own presumptions. But I wonder how it is that
one can preserve a "narrative space" for an alien belief within the Christian
self-understanding but not the "philosophical space" of that same speaker?
How is it easier to safeguard the integrity of another's story than another's
truth claim? Are not the same prejudices at work, regardless of whether we
are listening to a story or a claim to truth? If, for the sake of argument, we
admit that Aquinas picks and chooses from Aristotle on an *ad hoc* basis, then
our own picking and choosing from stories of the Advaita Vedanta do just as
much violence to those stories as Aquinas did to Aristotelian philosophy. It
is not clear why the narrator here is given pride of place over the dialectician.

It is certainly ironic, then, that D'Costa criticizes John Hick's later work
for creating a Kantian divide between our religious language and divine
reality. For Hick there is

no real access to 'the Real.' The ways of analogy and metaphor, for example, are rendered impotent. This inability to speak of the Real or even allow 'it' the possibility of self-utterance leads to the Real's redundancy. Ironically, any detailed and serious interest in the religions of the world is subverted as they are unable to furnish clues about the Real. The color, diversity, difference, and detail are bleached of their meaning, for the Real apparently resists all description and is incapable of self-utterance.[21]

For D'Costa the central problem underlying Hick's theology—and the Enlightenment project as a whole—is that it creates a "fundamental epistemological and ontological rupture that denies the possibility of God's self-revelation in the historically particular."[22] It is curious, however, that the epistemological hurdles that D'Costa sharply dismisses when talking about knowledge of Christ are erected again when addressing knowledge of an alien religious belief.[23] He presents the "color, diversity, difference and detail" of each religion at the cost of judging between colors, distinguishing the details. Parallel charges could be made of D'Costa, that the ways of analogy and metaphor are emptied of their meaning when talking about two different religious traditions. How does D'Costa recognize such barriers of incommensurability between people of different religious belief, while overcoming those barriers when analyzing the human believer and the divine person in whom she believes? In both cases the similarities are affirmed against the background of radical dissimilarity. But the epistemological divide between two believers of different religious traditions pales in comparison between the human person and the God whom she worships. D'Costa, then, claims on the one hand that analogy and metaphor gain us access to "the Real"; but on the other, analogy and metaphor cannot gain us access to the truths of an alien religious tradition. One wonders, however, whether admitting the possibility of negotiating truth claims among traditions necessarily includes adopting the Kantian illusion of a neutral or tradition-free standing point. It is a negotiation that—admittedly—is unceasing, but it is the business of living, of living one's own faith honestly in friendship with those who are committed to other faith traditions.

It is important to note, however, that D'Costa does not always give pride of place to the narrator. He does affirm an inter-religious approach marked by critical interaction, appropriation, and affirmation.[24] One must first learn the other's language such that it becomes one's own second language. Only then can one try to show why there might be internal weaknesses within that tradition that are not fully solved on its own terms.[25] When incorporating insights from alien traditions of belief, the Christian cannot allow herself to assume that these insights are best understood within Christianity, but must rather respect "the genuine otherness of the other; any appropriation takes on a different dynamic by its incorporation within a different paradigmatic framework."[26] I suggest, however, that we must be able to distinguish between more and less appropriate ways to incorporate alien truths into our own tradition. Do not rules of rational inquiry undergird this judgment?

At the same time, D'Costa argues that Milbank too quickly resorts to tactics of out-narration "as if it were possible to narrate without conversation and some point of contact with the 'audience.'"[27] It would have been helpful to have heard some examples here. When should a Christian resort to narrative rather than dialectical inquiry? One is left wondering whether rational inquiry simply establishes the point of contact with the audience, preparing the way for dominance through narrative.

D'Costa's alternative to the Kantian option of a neutral standing point blurs some traditional distinctions that might help clarify his own position. He avoids the seemingly outdated categories of faith and reason. Faith, he replaces with "rhetoric"; reason with "dialectics." But does what seems to be a change in semantics hide an underlying transformation in epistemology? How does he envision the relationship between rhetoric and dialectics? Following MacIntyre and Milbank, D'Costa reminds us that every tradition "requires an element of 'self-committing faith,' for there are no traditions or positions that are self-evident or neutral."[28] But the cure for the Enlightenment illusion of neutrality need not preclude one from rationally deliberating among religious traditions.

D'Costa does not often address the category of "human reason." When he does, however, he outlines its instrumentalist role: it is able to help the believer understand her faith. I want to argue that it is not just that human reason is used in *ad hoc* apologetics or as a way to gain a point of contact with an audience. Rather, human reason can be used as a tool—one tool among many, to be sure—to address believers of other traditions. One need not fall into the Enlightenment trap, creating some fictional "neutral space" within which this dialogue occurs. The conversation is difficult and messy.

But we can and do share the ability to engage in rational discourse in dialogue with those who represent traditions alien to our own.

I find D'Costa, in the end, more able to recognize stories of holiness in other traditions than claims to truth. Truth claims cannot be properly heard from one tradition to another since the meaning of the claim becomes unrecognizable in the process of transplanting it from one tradition to another. Upon close investigation, even stories of holiness cannot be clearly recognized. D'Costa's ecclesial commitments lead him to claim that other religious traditions cannot be *de jure* paths to salvation. The Christian concept of "sainthood," for example, cannot incorporate holy men and women from other traditions, as "sainthood" is as ecclesially-bound a term as "revelation."[29] It is not clear, then, what status the models of holiness from other traditions have in ours. D'Costa's greatest contribution lies in overcoming the Kantian illusion of a neutral standing point in the theology of religious pluralism. But I will argue that while his ecclesial commitments rightly keep him from affirming other traditions as *de jure* paths to salvation, his epistemology should be able to recognize truth and holiness in alien traditions.

Terrence Tilley

Terrence Tilley's position on the theology of religious pluralism arises from a career-long battle against the "philosophical disease of modernity" and in favor of "practical epistemology."[30] At the heart of his eight books lies a fervent commitment to the position that theological problems are best resolved in the arena of religious practices rather than theoretical beliefs. This pragmatic theological approach aims to dissolve the problems of theodicy (1991), the rationality of religious belief (1995), the challenge of religious diversity (1995 and 2007), the construal of tradition (2000), and the problem of history (2004).[31]

While the shadow of Kant looms large in D'Costa's work, in Tilley's work we find the shadow of David Hume. Tilley seeks an alternative to defending religious belief from modern skepticism. He does not accept the terms of argument inherited from modernity, and seeks instead to develop an alternative method, one that is decidedly *un*systematic and firmly rooted in the religious practices of particular contexts. Despite this avowed lack of system, however, the patterns and principles of his approach can be pinpointed through an examination of his work. Tilley frames the problem of religious diversity as one of the three major interrelated problems that have been the subject matter of much modern philosophy of religion, the other two being the reasonableness of religious belief and the problem of evil. His approach to religious diversity grows out of both his practice of narrative theology and the way he understands religious commitment. We must examine each in turn.

In 1985 Tilley develops a full, fundamental narrative theology for Christianity that preserves the centrality of stories to Christian living, and renders doctrines "derivative." This book contributed to a growing field in narrative theology at the time. The last chapter in the book is the most provocative and relevant for our purposes, as it reveals by what standards one can call a story true.

Instead of rewording "old propositions into new systems" in the way of traditional dogmatic theology, narrative theologians retell the Christian stories in ways that make them intelligible to particular contexts.[32] Doctrines that used to make claims about the truth of Christianity become here "live or dead metaphors... extracted from stories."[33] This way of understanding doctrine as metaphor has surprising results:

> [T]here is good reason for difficulty in showing doctrines to be true. Metaphors are not true—nor are they false. They may be found "good" or "bad," "effective" or "ineffective," "powerful" or "weak," "live" or "dead," but not "true" or "false." Hence, it should be no surprise that it is so difficult to find doctrines true—they may not be the proper items to examine.[34]

Rather than arguing whether this or that *doctrine* is true, narrative theologians examine the truth of Christian *stories*. The truth or falsity of a story can be assessed to the extent that it (1) represents the world; (2) is coherent by corresponding to the facts as we understand them; (3) shows ways of overcoming self-deception; (4) shows how to be faithful to others; and (5) provides a model for constancy in trying to tell the truth.[35] Consequently, no single story can be absolutely true for everyone always. Each story is context-dependent and must be evaluated as such. According to this kind of pluralism, other people "may tell stories different from mine, yet as true as mine."[36]

Several questions of a Christological, ecclesiological, and doctrinal nature immediately arise. While no one story is necessarily better than another, and there is no single Christian story, Tilley maintains that to be a disciple is to conform one's story to the story of Christ.[37] But it is hard to pinpoint how the story of Christ's life, which is contextually bound to the practices—religious, cultural, or political—of ancient Israel, could possibly govern *my* story. It is also not clear where the ecclesial boundaries lie in this approach. How does *my* story become *our* story? How do we arbitrate disagreements in this area? Finally, how do these stories govern what we believe to be true about ourselves, our world, and our God? The Christology at work in this narrative theology needs to be more clearly delineated. Tilley might object that this delineation happens in *living* rather than in *thinking*. But he has not yet addressed how theology differs from living a religious life at all, if it primarily consists in the retelling of stories.[38]

While the theoretical dimensions of narrative stories were underdeveloped at this early stage in Tilley's career,[39] he takes this theme up again ten years later in his 1995 book, *The Wisdom of Religious Commitment*. This study attempts to do for the problem of the rationality of belief what *The Evils of Theodicy* (1991) attempted to do for the problem of evil: the solution lies not in the construction of a better theory, but rather in the appeal to engaging in better practices. Defending the rationality of religious belief, then, is not a matter of "*scientia* and certainty," but rather of "*praxis* and *phronesis*."[40] Coming to hold doctrinal beliefs here is constitutive rather than foundational; reasoning and evidence are internal to the faith, not its external foundations.[41] The tradition of *scientia* that began with the thirteenth-century scholastics, who tried to build a comprehensive *summa* or system of Christian beliefs, ended in the bloodshed of irreconcilable conflict of the beginning of the seventeenth century.[42] Tilley contends:

> *A viable alternative to the fading modern, individualistic, academic, externalist practice of religious epistemology is not to make a fideistic choice or leap of faith. Rather, the alternative is to engage in practical religious 'epistemology,' the shared practice of seeking the wisdom of a religious commitment, to abandon the academic practice of unengaged jousting in mainstream philosophy of religion, and to enter into one of the shared religious practices of a committed seeking of the Truth valorized by Pascal in the wake of Montaigne.*[43]

Pascal represents for Tilley a pivotal movement away from theoretical foundations in Christian theology and toward a way of living, a religious practice as foundational for theology.

What makes a wise religious commitment? Tilley maintains that our wise practices and commitments will inevitably be different, but he does lay out some markers that reveal what makes an "unwise" commitment. Traditions are to be avoided if they are irrational, if they value disembodied beliefs, if they are irremediably oppressive, triumphalistic or absolutist, if they obstruct practices of renewal or silence the voices of those on the margins of the tradition.[44] The answer to the question of whether one has chosen a wise religious commitment ultimately lies in the living out of that commitment. The paths chosen may be irreducibly different.[45] The challenges posed by religious diversity cannot be theoretically resolved, but must be practically dissolved.[46]

While people will surely make different choices about which religion deserves commitment, the practices across different traditions may be analogous "so that we may come in different ways to different forms of endless happiness and joy, if not to the same belief."[47] It is difficult to know what to make of this claim. Are the different forms of endless happiness simply incommensurable? If they are incommensurable, then is there a relationship, in the end, between the term "happiness" in each of these forms? What is clear, however, is that truth claims have no place in this view of salvation history. Finally, what would these forms of endless happiness look like if they were cut off from the belief claims of the faith tradition?

Tilley's critics have accused him of claiming that philosophy of religion cannot be done from a position other than that of a religious believer, that an outsider cannot offer a critique of a particular religious practice.[48] In response to his critics, Tilley clarifies that philosophy of religion is not a "neutral game": "everyone who plays the game is a committed believer in a formal sense, but the material content of that belief varies."[49] Insofar as a person has ultimate commitments, those commitments can be judged as wise or unwise, prudent or imprudent. Such ultimate commitments need not be religious in nature.

Tilley's critics have also accused him of not attending to the "plausibility of the transcendent referent of religious commitment."[50] Anthony Godzieba maintains that the "practical question of 'to which tradition should I belong?' is always preceded by the truth-question posed to that tradition: does this religious tradition have a *telos* beyond the community which is invested in that tradition?"[51] Tilley finds the truth question unanswerable. We might have warrants for our beliefs that we can draw upon when challenged, but

we cannot make those beliefs true. We cannot show them to be true. Theoretical answers or intellectual proofs are feckless. They cannot show that
what one seeks is *the truth*. The only way to address the truth question is to
point to unwise practices and to engage in the practice

> *[of] recognizing the beauty, wisdom and goodness that we together can
> generate if we will to be prudent. There is no guarantee, no warrant,
> not in theory or practice, that there is any Truth. But to engage in
> the wise shared pursuit of Being, of being rightly related to and
> constituted by that than which nothing greater cannot be conceived,
> is the practical answer.*[52]

While I agree that there is no *guarantee* that Truth exists (I wonder what
that would even look like), I would have to point out as well that just as
there is no guarantee that truth exists, there is no such guarantee for beauty
or goodness or wisdom or any of the transcendentals. But we do recognize beautiful things, and loving people and truthful friends—the practical
answer, as Tilley affirms, directly leads back into the theoretical answer. I
would add that just as we distinguish between better and worse friends, we
should be able to distinguish between better and worse arguments or warrants for belief—in fact, we do so all the time. Tilley's approach unnecessarily makes truth less accessible than beauty, goodness, or wisdom.

If *The Wisdom of Religious Commitment* developed the theoretical dimensions to the narrative theology outlined in *Story Theology*, Tilley's 2000
book *Inventing Catholic Tradition* more fully develops how he understands
religion as an enduring set of practices. These practices endure if they include (1) a vision or belief, (2) a set of attitudes, and (3) patterns of action.[53]

Tilley's approach deemphasizes doctrines (*tradita*) as the way generations inherit tradition, on the one hand, and accentuates the living out or
practice (*traditio*) of the tradition, on the other. Tilley thinks the privileging of the former over the latter has led to serious errors. Practice always
precedes rules; change in practice causes change in rules; the repetition of
a rule only makes sense in the context of practice. The example he offers is
the Catholic understanding of the Real Presence. He uses speech-act theory
to lay out his argument. The verbal token "Real Presence" can remain
unchanged while its meaning radically shifts. The philosophical category
of transubstantiation might have fully expressed how medieval Europeans
understood "Real Presence"; it is not clear that contemporary invocation

of that philosophical category makes sense anymore. In a later article Tilley incorporates liturgical practices in this analysis. Twentieth-century liturgical innovations have led Catholics to understand the Eucharist as a ritual meal more than as a divine sacrifice: "[n]ew patterns of ritual behavior reshape the participants' attitudes as new significances of the doctrine of the Real Presence emerge and the 'meaning' of the linguistic token changes."[54] The tradition, then, is passed on in the sets of practices engaged in by Christian believers. Individual believers learn what to believe by practicing the faith, just as architects or basketball players learn by practicing with those who are expert in their art.

While practice certainly shapes theory, I wonder whether—as is implied by Tilley's work—practice determines theory. To take his example of liturgical practice and the meaning of the Eucharist, it is certainly the task of theologians to ask whether something that is true about the Eucharist—namely, that it represents Divine Sacrifice—has been lost through contemporary liturgical practice. Simply pointing to liturgical practice leaves the issue unresolved. Regardless of where one falls on this issue, the question itself moves beyond Tilley's idea of theological practice. As Kathryn Tanner maintains:

> *Agreement with other Christians is not so much the ideal as agreement with God. Faithfulness to the past is therefore viewed not so much as faithfulness to what people in the past believed and did as faithfulness to what they were trying thereby to witness to.*[55]

It might be, then, that liturgical practice today weakens rather than simply changes our understanding of Real Presence. But this is a question that demands—at least in part—a theological argument.

The natural question that arises here is that of doctrinal development. Tilley suggests that doctrinal development is more fiction than reality: "We have found that there is not (and I would argue there cannot be) a theoretical criterion of constancy of tradition."[56] Instead of doctrines, he argues in favor of principles that make the tradition recognizable, while at the same time offering flexibility for varying intellectual positions. Traditions, then, are constantly being invented. We have seen how Tilley's approach to the theology of religious pluralism grows out of how he applies his narrative approach to the practice of theology.

While Tilley's pragmatic method resists categorization, he is also explicit about his method. In responding to critics a few years ago, for example, he identified himself as an "epistemological nonfoundationalist."[57] Religious practices need not be justified by some foundational principle. The reasonableness of these practices can only be shown through engagement in those very practices. There is no neutral theory to which one can appeal for arbitration purposes. While different religious traditions are fundamentally incommensurable, members of different traditions can talk to each other about something that concerns both (his example is neighborhood crime).[58] There is no need to seek a foundational common ground before the conversation begins. Instead of assuming that theory grounds practice, as do foundationalists, Tilley presumes that theory is a reflection of practice.[59]

I share some of the questions critics of Tilley's approach have raised. While it may be true that theory grows out of practice, when faced with the need to adjudicate between different practices it is not enough to refer back to excellent practitioners, for each tradition surely lays claim to such persons. Truth questions do not simply grow out of religious practices. Anyone who has been involved in programs that prepare those seeking to convert from one tradition to another knows that to answer the question "to which religious tradition should I belong?" one cannot simply point to religious practice. Very real intellectual knots can lie at the heart of this question that need be addressed on their own terms. One of the richest Christian conversion stories, Augustine's *Confessions*, profoundly exhibits this insight. Practice, of course, affects these theoretical questions, but it does not determine them. Tilley's practice-centered approach to theology is certainly a viable way to move beyond the biases and rationalist moves of Enlightenment theology, the fragility of which he rightly exposes. Often we define our theological commitments by what we react against. I wonder, however, whether Tilley has left adequate room for any sort of theoretical justification for a commitment of faith, or whether he necessarily smuggles in this justification in his regulative principles.

Throughout their theological work, both Tilley and D'Costa have consistently argued against foundationalism. Indeed, foundationalism has become a dirty word in contemporary theology. But I wonder whether in the move from foundationalism to non-foundationalism, something valuable is lost. One need not be a foundationalist to maintain that dialogue with people of other faiths can take shape because we share certain fundamental characteristics as humans. Tilley insists that one need not prove that God exists in order to pray. I would add, however, that if someone catches us in prayer, we must, in the spirit of 1 Peter 3:15, always be ready to give an explanation to anyone who asks us for a reason for our hope.[60] This explanation may well involve pointing to prudent practice, but it should include theoretical justification as well. D'Costa and Tilley also both correctly reveal that a neutral standing point from which to judge between traditions is a fiction. But what if philosophical questions that we all share *qua* being human inevitably lead beyond themselves? We ask them together—in religious communities, interfaith discussions, or secular conversations—and we come to somewhat similar and somewhat different answers. But what unites us is the journey of inquiry, not some foundation of philosophical conclusions. If we look to the way Thomas Aquinas engaged in theological inquiry, we find some helpful moves—specifically his theological use of analogy—that might help us break through the impasse between foundationalists and non-foundationalists.

Concluding Considerations

I have argued that if the church is to maintain with *Nostra aetate* that truth and holiness can be found in other religious traditions, it needs an epistemology to make sense of this claim. I have shown how two leading contemporary theologians, however different their methodologies, share a common epistemological weakness, namely that neither provide enough place for the cognitive dimension of the theology of religious pluralism. I have not yet shown, however, what this more robust epistemology could look like.

I am increasingly convinced that the path to a robust theology of religious pluralism lies in the work of analogy—where one sees the resonances of one's home tradition in alien traditions against the background of radical difference. In comparing traditions, analogy arises as a possible candidate to negotiate similarity and difference. Working out the movement of these analogies is the work of comparative theology, and its possible outcomes are varied and multiple. I might become fully converted to another tradition; I might reside in an area of "multiple religious belonging," as Catherine Cornille and others have defended.[61] But I might also affirm my own Christian convictions in a new way. Christ should always be at the center of anything we have to say to our friends in other faith traditions. As Leslie Newbigin claims, "The starting point for my meeting with those of other faiths is that I've been laid hold of by Jesus Christ, to be his witness."[62] Losing this aspect of inter-religious dialogue makes it increasingly difficult for the encounter to be inter-religious at all; instead, it becomes simply amorphous. What analogy enables us to do is to maintain the unity of truth in Christ on the one hand, and the diversity of its expression on the other. It is not just a linguistic tool. It has an underlying metaphysics of participation. It maintains unity in difference in a way that I find lacking in the works of both D'Costa and Tilley.

The exhortation from Peter above, demanding us to give an account of the hope that is within us, leads directly into my own argument. Peter commands the early Christian community to give an account—in the Greek an *apologion*—for the hope that is within us. I suggest that narrating our "apologias" is a primary way to encounter those of other faith traditions. But this encounter cannot stop here. For our conversation to develop, we need to move from "apologia" to "analogia." In "apologia" we speak words "from" or "out of" our narrative, but in "analogia" we are taking words "up" from our narrative and seeing how those words cohere in other religious traditions.

This movement of analogy could help refine the inclusivist position, since analogy's main advantage is that it preserves the radical dissimilarity at work in the relationship, whereas the inclusivist position incorporates— some would say colonizes—a foreign concept within one's home tradition. I suggest that analyzing the way Thomas Aquinas employed analogy could advance this discussion.

Applying Thomas's understanding of analogy to the area of religious pluralism admittedly involves moving his work into new territory. Aquinas uses analogy primarily in the arena of Divine Names. He puts analogy to Christian theological use to balance two main commitments: 1) God is inconceivable mystery, and 2) we speak truthfully when we make claims about God. Analogy steers a middle course between univocal and equivocal language.[63] The risks of these other two options are severe: in univocal language, we reduce God to one creature among others in the universe; in equivocal language, our God-talk becomes mere babble.

Aquinas distinguishes between metaphor and analogy here to show that while all language is wrapped in human clothing, some ways that we talk about God reach farther than others.[64] When we say, analogously, that "God is good," we understand that goodness applies to God in an utterly perfect way, a way unknown to us. But we believe that goodness in God is related—analogously—to goodness in humans. So our words, while not able to capture the whole meaning of how God is good, captures *something* of what this would mean. Goodness as we understand it is a pale shadow of how good God is, but if it has only the relationship of shadow to statue, then it nonetheless reflects *something* true about God, however vaguely or imperfectly. Analogical language is crucial for Aquinas because he does not follow the tendency of agnosticism of his predecessors pseudo-Dionysius or Maimonides. He wants to maintain truth claims amidst radical difference when speaking about God.

To move this theological practice into a secondary sense of analogy, one that recognizes true resemblances among religious traditions amidst the backdrop of radical difference: that, I suggest, is the task of the theology of religious pluralism. There is an implicit faith here that some of our words can have purchase across faith traditions, an implicit faith that we are all on a similar quest—not that a quest can be reducible to some common denominator, but that the quest is framed in human terms, with human questions that inevitably reach beyond themselves. It is no longer the case that we share this journey only with those of our own faith tradition. To make sense of the journeys of our neighbors, friends or spouses, to be companions along the way with them, we need to draw upon something like analogy that recognizes similarity in difference—not arbitrary, not fictional, but true similarity in difference.

In following Thomas we cannot lose sight of both our hierarchy of authority and an organic understanding of truth. We believe that truth is One, that all knowledge is related to and culminates in Jesus Christ. This belief should lead us to seize deposits of knowledge outside our tradition while recognizing at the same time that the source and summit of our knowledge is Jesus Christ. The fact that our friends in other religious traditions will not share that same understanding of truth does not obliterate our ability to recognize truth in their traditions. The dynamics of coming to know the truth in Christ take shape throughout one's life, beginning with one's fundamental human questions and culminating in the beatific vision. The *preparatio evangelica* tradition, of which Thomas is a part, should not be discarded as condescending to other traditions, or as arcane. There is much work to be done in resurrecting this tradition. There are seeds of the Gospel in other traditions. These do not just constitute natural knowledge. If the church means what she says when she claims not to reject anything that is true in other traditions, then she must have a way to recognize that truth, an epistemology that can incorporate this claim. Neither D'Costa nor Tilley's epistemologies have fully done this. If the church means what she says when she claims not to reject anything that is holy in other traditions, then it must recognize that holiness arises from an encounter with divine grace. The work of the Spirit is not bound by the church. That is why Augustine warned his contemporaries against presuming to divide cleanly who makes up the City of God and the City of man. Fruitful theological work in this area is already well underway.

Admittedly, these final considerations call out for a more detailed study on how to apply Thomas's theological use of analogy to the arena of religious pluralism. I suggest that such a study would remedy the weaknesses besetting D'Costa and Tilley's epistemology, and create a way to make sense of the Church's affirmation in *Nostra aetate* that other religions can provide places of encounter with truth and holiness. *Dominus Iesus* restricted itself to pointing out certain errors in current theological research. But this research only addresses how salvific grace reaches non-Christians. At the same time, the Declaration reaffirmed the wider position of *Nostra aetate*, and called for further work in matters that are of "free theological debate." [65] Outlining how analogy could be used in the theology of religious pluralism would respond to the call in *Dominus Iesus* to work out these unresolved questions.

This work responds to Fr. Buckley's call in *Denying and Disclosing God* to expand the breadth of religious apologias, but in the new context of radical religious pluralism. It also responds to new theological trends that, instead of bracketing the personal, bracket the speculative and rational. While this essay has only offered a preliminary sketch of what such a theology would look like, it has, I hope, demonstrated the need for such constructive work.

Transposing Richard McKeon's Philosophic Pluralism into a Theological Key

Dominic Doyle, Boston College

WHEN CONFUSED BY THE SHEER diversity of philosophical and theological views I encountered in graduate studies, I would often repair to Michael Buckley for guidance through the thicket. One of the many things that struck me in those conversations was Buckley's ability to engage the breadth of theological and philosophical opinion with critical generosity. In conversation and classroom discussion, students had modeled for them—and were held accountable to—rigorous standards of close reading and serious reflection upon highly divergent texts. Students were left in no doubt that they should show they understood a text before they criticized it, and they consequently learned to respect and understand genuine differences between texts, rather than superficially dismiss positions other than their own. This was a demanding yet ultimately charitable model of learning, because it allowed the integrity and the voices of many different authors to come through without the distorting lens of one's own preconceptions and preemptive judgments. As Buckley was fond of saying, the result of this close reading and formal analysis is that the author becomes your teacher.

Buckley's rigorous acceptance of pluralism stemmed in part from his doctoral work with Richard McKeon, who founded the interdisciplinary Committee on Ideas and Methods at the University of Chicago, and who trained or influenced thinkers as diverse as Susan Sontag, Wayne Booth, John Cobb, Richard Rorty, and Marshall McLuhan. His approach was the antithesis of a "lazy pluralism" of one who, overwhelmed by the sheer range of views and the difficulty of making any coherent sense from them, capitulates through an imprecise or weak grasp of the differences between them with vague yet politically advantageous appeals to diversity. One of McKeon's lasting legacies was a comprehensive argument for the viability of multiple philosophical positions. It is this exacting yet generous reading of intellectual difference that I learned from McKeon, as mediated to me by Buckley—a reliable guide, since McKeon regarded him as the one who best understood his work.

As someone who has benefited enormously from Buckley's training, I would like to share what I have learned from his approach and explain why I find it to be so helpful and clarifying, especially for the student of theology overwhelmed by the variety of methods and positions he or she faces when entering graduate work seriously. The specific goal of this essay is to explore and expand the use of McKeon in theological reflection. I approach this goal by addressing the following three questions. [1] What are the basic elements of McKeon's coordinates of inquiry, the four fundamental categories by which any philosophical text may be analyzed? [2] How does the first coordinate, selection, account for some of the major differences in emphasis in theology? [3] How does the second coordinate, interpretation, yield a more finely-grained picture of more nuanced differences in contemporary theology? If this essay brings the reader to read McKeon's work and to reflect on the merits of his critical acceptance of pluralism for theology, it will have served its goal of assisting in the process of making some sense of the bewildering diversity in theology today.

An Overview of McKeon's
Four Coordinates of Inquiry

To render philosophic pluralism intelligible, McKeon isolated four coordinates of inquiry: selection, interpretation, method, and principle. These coordinates were laid out, in dense fashion, in McKeon's essay "Philosophic Semantics and Philosophic Inquiry." They formed the basis of his procedure for interrogating the wide diversity of positions that the history of Western philosophy presents. Buckley lucidly summarized lucidly the basic meanings of these four terms at the beginning of his *At the Origins of Modern Atheism,* in his introductory description of some of the key analytic tools he uses in his now-classic study of the emergence of modern disbelief.[1] To indicate the value of this approach, Buckley said the following:

> *These coordinates allow a series of questions to be leveled at any tractate, speech, argument or discursive expression, and a subsequent relationship to be drawn between one text or inquiry and another, without either reducing every philosophy to a single true philosophy or regarding all positions as of equal worth because each represents a different perspective. To ask questions governed by these coordinates is to look for the values given to certain variables in every discourse.*[2]

So what are these four variables, and how does each vary? What follows is an introduction to the area each variable treats and the different values or options that can be given to each variable. Since I will be expanding on the first two of these variables in more detail below, I only offer here a short summary.[3]

Selection is what the inquiry is about, its fundamental subject matter. It can focus upon being (metaphysics), knowing (epistemology), or doing and the communication required to get things done (ethics and grammar/rhetoric). *Interpretation* determines what counts as the evidence by which propositions can be made about the area selected. Specifically, it concerns the view of reality that allows something to be predicated of the subject matter. Does the real diverge from appearances, either by underlying them or transcending them, or does reality merge with appearances, by constituting either the essence of what appears or the limited perspective we actually see?

Method indicates the way or procedure by which those propositions are forged into a coherent argument that yields reliable conclusions. This patterning of inquiry may be operational, by imposing a matrix upon the subject matter, as in Galileo's initial distinction between primary and secondary realities in his investigation of nature. Or a method may be dialectical, as it [1] finds incompleteness or contradiction in the subject matter that threatens (or causes) its collapse into incoherent fragments, and then [2] negates that inadequacy in order to [3] resolve the fragmented parts into a more secure synthesis. Plato's dialogues or Hegel's understanding of world history fall under this method, with its ambition of universal, synoptic comprehension. Alternatively, a method may be logistic, as it analyses the whole into its constituent parts, since the whole is only the combination of its parts. Similarly, in the realm of logical analysis, since a conclusion is conditioned by a premise, it is the premise that requires careful examination. Democritus's attention to atoms, Newton's focus on the mathematical principles of nature, or computer programming's building from fundamental binary options are examples of this method. Finally, a method may be characterized as problematic, in that it arises in questions and perplexity, and, in contrast to the universal method of dialectics, adapts itself to the particular subject matter and different problem at hand. As Aristotle says, "a carpenter's interest in the right angle is different from a geometrician's."[4]

Principle, the fourth and final coordinate, unites the many parts of an inquiry to give it its integrity. Although I will not be dealing with this coordinate in this essay, the following summary sketches some of the different values that can be given to this final variable: a comprehensive principle, by which a single source integrates all the elements of an inquiry; a reflexive principle, that is similar in nature to the subject matter under investigation; or a simple principle, that is nothing but the parts of the whole.

These four coordinates of inquiry—selection, interpretation, method, principle—guide the student overwhelmed by the vast array of philosophical positions by giving a clarifying conceptual map or operational matrix by which different thinkers can be understood in their integrity and diversity. According to Buckley, they "provide not a way of categorizing an author or his work arbitrarily, but of asking questions about a work which brings out its unique procedure. 'With their aid, contrasts or corroborations can be asserted, and the real issue of disagreement can be separated from verbal contradictions or philosophical complementarities.'"[5] With these introductory comments in mind, I will now focus on the first two coordinates, selection and interpretation, in order to explore how McKeon's insights there can be applied to theology so as to make some sense of its pluralism.

Selection

The first coordinate *selects* the fundamental subject matter that gives an inquiry its unifying focus and overarching concern. Figure 1 charts the three basic options within this variable "selection" and lists the consequent positions in first philosophy, ethics, and the naming of God. This section will unpack the positions laid out in the chart in order to show how they shed light on theological pluralism.

Figure 1: How the different options for the coordinate "selection" alter the ordering of philosophy, the framing of ethics, and the naming of God.

Selection	1st Philosophy	Ethics (theological)	Naming God
[1] Being	Metaphysics	Virtue (faith, hope, love)	*Ipsum esse subsistens*
[2] Knowing	Epistemology	Duty (divine command)	Holy Mystery or Wholly Other
[3] Doing/ Speaking	Pragmatism	Responsibility (social grace)	Liberator

The variety in possible foci of selection can be expressed by the following three fundamental questions that initiate and determine the nature of an inquiry. [1] What is? [2] How do we know what is? [3] So what? Or, to expand on this rather terse formulation of the driving question for the third option, "how do we express what we know and act accordingly?" The first emphasis deals with being, the second with knowing, and the third with doing and speaking. Depending upon which of these fundamental foci is selected, different areas of philosophy will serve as architectonic, as the overarching "first philosophy" by which other concerns are ordered and deemed secondary.

1. Being

If a thinker operates with the selection "being," then the first philosophy will be metaphysics, the study of being *qua* being. The kind of ethics that accompanies this selection will be a virtue ethics, since it examines the kind of good character a person wishes to become, rather than agonizing over the rightness of particular acts in dilemma situations. The focus is on being, not acts. Actions are examined as the means by which a person conforms him or herself to what is: in particular, to the yardstick of the good person who embodies moral excellence.

In theological terms, this selection will understand God as self-subsistent being. Indeed, Aquinas asserts that *HE WHO IS* is the most appropriate name of God, citing Yahweh's reply to Moses in Exodus 3:14.[6] God is the unrestricted source of being that exists in and of itself, and from whom all finite created being derives. Correspondingly, theological ethics in this selection will center around the theological virtues by which the human person is united to God's being. Thus, Aquinas's *Secunda secundae*, which treats the particular ways in which the human creature returns to the Creator, begins with the three theological virtues of faith, hope, and love, which order the totality of human moral life toward God. The principal theological virtue, charity, unites the believer with the divine source of being, or, in one of Aquinas's favorite scriptural verses, makes her a "sharer in the divine nature" (2 Peter 1:4).

2. Knowing

But being is not the only fundamental selection that can be made. Answering the question "What is?" is not easy. Great minds have labored over this question only to give complicated and contradictory responses, not least to the most basic questions such as the existence of God and the nature of the soul. So, according to the second option within selection, one must first examine the antecedent structures of knowing by which we come to make any claims at all about reality. This is the reasoning for selecting a quite different fundamental mode of reflection, one that begins with knowing, not being. Its first philosophy will be epistemology, the study of how we come to know anything at all and the examination of the conditions of the possibility for making assertions about what is. A classic example of this selection is Immanuel Kant's first critique, the *Critique of Pure Reason*, which promises a Copernican revolution by asking not how our thoughts conform to objects, but how objects conform to our *a priori* modes of thinking.[7] The process of our knowing, not the structure of an object's existence, is the critical and prior issue. How we know conditions what we know.

In this turn to the subject, it is (at least for Kant) those *a priori* categories and processes of thought that impose intelligibility on an otherwise unintelligible manifold of sense intuition. Correspondingly, the approach to ethics in this selection will focus upon the self-legislating subject whose intrinsic, non-heteronymous sense of duty imposes moral order upon the otherwise unruly passions and unintelligible inclinations. The difference between the ethical systems of the first and second selection are captured nicely in the following quite different use of similar imagery: whereas Aristotle reckoned the process of acquiring virtue as "just like somebody straightening a warped piece of wood,"[8] Kant believed that "nothing straight from the crooked timber of humanity may grow."[9] Kant thus appealed instead to a noumenal encounter with duty that alone would correct phenomenally wayward paths.

In theological terms, the corresponding ethic and naming of God admits two options, depending on how limited our knowing is said to be. If, following Kant, strict limits are imposed upon our knowledge that cut off any natural understanding of God, then understandably God will be named "Wholly Other," as in the early theology of Karl Barth, who claimed, in the preface to the second edition of his commentary on Romans: "If I have a system, it is limited to a recognition of what Kierkegaard called 'the infinite qualitative distinction' between time and eternity..."[10] Given the consequent futility and hubris of any human attempts to know such a wholly other God, the *analogia entis*—a critical tool in the metaphysical selection—becomes in the epistemological selection "the invention of the anti-Christ."[11] Correspondingly, in this epistemological sub-selection that strictly limits natural openness to the divine, the theological ethic will favor a divine command theory, for nothing more clearly lets the believer know what the wholly Other God wants them to do. Karl Barth even renames theological ethics accordingly: "What is called ethics I regard as the doctrine of the command of God. Hence I do not think it right to treat it otherwise than as an integral part of dogmatics..."[12] Obedience to noumenal duty replaces cultivation of human excellence, and divine command overshadows theological virtue.

But one may select knowing as fundamental and not share Kant's strictures on the limits of knowledge. In theological terms, a less restrictive epistemology will yield a different naming of God and theological ethic. The transcendental Thomist tradition questions Kant's insistence on the limits of knowledge, and argues instead that to know a limit is in some way to have already transcended it, essentially following Hegel's critique of Kant: "Something is only known, or even felt, to be a restriction, or a defect, if one is at the same time *beyond* it."[13] Heirs of this tradition, such as Karl Rahner, argue that the human mind possesses a natural dynamism that is open to the divine. The infinite is experienced in the finite as the encompassing horizon that gives it its intelligibility. Thus, when it comes to naming God, this non-restrictive epistemology sub-selection will not see God as "wholly Other." But neither will it follow Thomas and name God as the self-subsistent cause of being from which all else derives. Rather, it will describe God as the source and goal of human transcendence. Rahner's term "holy mystery" is a good example of the renaming of the divine within this mode of fundamental thought, for in this phrase God is primarily designated with reference to the human subject—the term of a person's transcendence—and not independently of the human in terms of the self-caused cause of being.[14] Not unsurprisingly, the proofs for God's existence—the attempt to objectively establish the existence or being of God—are relegated to the conclusion of Rahner's discussion of "The Knowledge of God," since "we do not need to discuss in any great detail those assertions which are the elaboration of a more original knowledge."[15] As Rahner maintains,

> *A theoretical proof for the existence of God, then, is only intended to mediate a reflexive awareness of the fact that man always and inevitably has to do with God in his intellectual and spiritual existence…. The point of the reflexive proofs for the existence of God is to indicate that all knowledge… takes place against the background affirmation of the*

holy mystery, or of absolute being, as the horizon of the asymptotic term and of the question ground of the act of knowledge and of its 'object.'[16]

For Aquinas, by contrast, the proofs that establish God's existence come first (the *prima pars'* question two "*an deus sit?*"), followed immediately by a long examination of the nature of God's being (qq. 3–11, since "*cognitio de aliquo an sit, inquirendum restat quomodo sit, ut sciatur de eo quid sit*"). Only after this elaboration of what God is (or, more accurately, is not) does Aquinas treat, in one question, how we know God (q. 12 "*quomodo deus a nobis cognoscatur*"). The reversal in the order of presentation from being to knowing demonstrates the shift in fundamental selection from Aquinas to Rahner.

3. *Doing and Speaking*

The third and final option within the coordinate of selection focuses neither on being nor on knowing but on doing and speaking. Metaphysical and epistemological theories do not answer the question "How, then, should we live?" And those theories themselves must use language, and, in doing so, invite scrutiny of the words that shape and condition their ideas. Furthermore, if those inclined to prioritize epistemology criticized metaphysics for trading in irrelevant and unanswerable obscurities, then they should take care lest the same charge be leveled at them. For epistemology has generated multiple and contradictory theories—from idealism to empiricism to skepticism—that compete to build or deconstruct a reliable bridge between mind and world. But while these disputes go on—and they do tend to go on—most people find it quite obvious that we are more or less reliably aware of the world around us, without needing a prolegomenon for objective and epistemologically sound criteria for knowledge. The pertinent question is not "How can I ground my knowing?" but "What should I be doing?" When this becomes the driving question, epistemology cedes its place as first philosophy to pragmatism.

With this change of focus comes a renewed attention to language, for language is the means by which people are moved to get things done. In political life, language is the medium by which any society understands the common history that binds it together and articulates the future goals that move it forward. "Words and deeds," to use the phrase of the consummate philosopher-politician Cicero, deserve our attention before any grand meta-physical or epistemological theory.

In more radical ways, language is said to play an even deeper role than that of motivating action and articulating already-known goals. Language does not just mediate, it actually conditions how and what we know. For Heidegger, the "world is worded," and language is the "house of *Dasein*," that unique human mode of being in the world. If language deeply shapes the way we experience our place in society, then sustained attention to the way ideas are described can remove inaccuracies and prejudices embedded in linguistic habits. Analysis of categories such as race and gender makes plain how even seemingly innocent and time-honored uses of language rein-force differentials in power and sustain prejudice.

When selection takes this pragmatic and linguistic turn, its ethics will shift from duty to responsibility. Duty is often presented as cutting through the bonds with others, and is even deemed less worthy if it derives from affection or partiality to others. As Buckley was fond of singing in one of his impromptu renditions of burlesque opera: "Oh duty, duty, duty, thou art no beauty, beauty, beauty!"[17] Responsibility, on the other hand, calls to mind the *response* that one human being feels towards another. In Levinas's phenomenological account of moral experience, it is the face of the other that stirs our ethical reflection. Intrinsically social, this ethical framework does not privilege the excellence of virtue, nor demand the rigor of duty, but instead awakens and nurtures a sensitive response to others, especially others in need.

The God of this selection may best be called "Liberator," the One who hears Israel's cry and responds with a promise of freedom, and who expects Israel in turn to respond to that covenant in which faithfulness to God is shown through responsibility for others. Liberation theology, picking up on the broader story of Exodus more than the existentialist Thomist's focus on Exodus 3:14, names God not in terms of who he is in himself, but what he does for his people. And whereas the epistemologically conditioned names for God derived from the way humans may or may not know God—i.e., as either the enveloping horizon of "holy mystery" or the "wholly other" beyond any human contact—the pragmatically conditioned naming of God is a functional designation, since it derives from the actions God performs, not the way he exists or is (un)known.

"Liberator" summons up the unavoidably social and relational nature of God's involvement in human history. Correspondingly, the task of theology—the reflection upon this God—becomes, in Gustavo Gutiérrez's phrase, "critical reflection on praxis,"[18] that is, reflection on informed action in the world. This theological approach breathes life into suppressed or spiritualized political metaphors in the bible, such as "Kingdom" and "Exodus." The ethic that flows from this selection will focus upon social grace and its relationship to justice. It will likely stimulate greater interest in ecclesiology, as the shared experience of grace connects with the great social and political questions of poverty, injustice, and emancipation.[19] In fact, the very experience of grace leads the believer to share in the interruptive movement of liberation that released Israel from slavery.

Interpretation

If the first coordinate—selection—identifies the fundamental focus of an inquiry or text, the second coordinate indicates the basic *interpretation* of reality that allows statements to be made about the subject selected. The second coordinate of interpretation therefore concerns one's position on what Plato called "the really real," as distinct from the apparently real. It gets at what is truly the case, as distinct from what custom or first impressions assume to be the case. This coordinate therefore deals with the fundamental philosophical distinction between reality and appearance. The relationship between reality and appearance may involve them either diverging, when appearances are at odds with reality, or merging, when reality is in some way disclosed in and through the appearances. McKeon offers four possibilities for how to construe this fundamental relationship between reality and appearance. The following diagram sketches these basic options.

Figure 2: The different options within the coordinate "interpretation."
Since this coordinate deals centrally with the relationship between reality and appearances, I have labeled the axes of this chart with reference to the two basic ways in which that relationship may be construed. The vertical Y axis treats those instances in which reality and appearance diverge, whereas the horizontal X axis treats those instances where reality and appearance merge.[20]

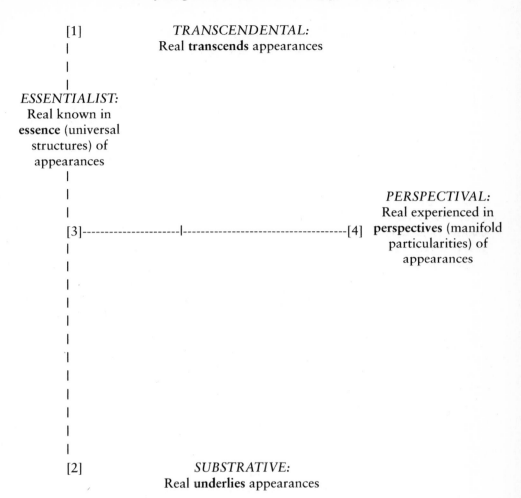

[1]   *TRANSCENDENTAL:*
                          Real **transcends** appearances

ESSENTIALIST:
Real known in
essence (universal
structures) of
appearances
                                                          PERSPECTIVAL:
                                                          Real experienced in
[3]--------------------|----------------------------------[4] **perspectives** (manifold
                                                          particularities) of
                                                          appearances

[2]   *SUBSTRATIVE:*
                          Real **underlies** appearances

In the first two possibilities, reality and appearance *diverge*. Reality is inter-preted as either [1] transcending appearances (e.g., Plato's Forms or Kant's noumenal realm) or [2] underlying them (e.g., Democritus's atoms, Freud's unconscious, Dawkins' selfish gene). Thus, an unseen reality is the final explanation for the ordinary commonsense world of appearances. These appearances take on a derivative quality, as they are interpreted either as transient, imperfect hints of an eternal, unchanging realm or epiphenomena of an unconscious, material substrate.

In the other two possibilities for how reality and appearance relate, one can interpret reality as *merging* with appearances either [3] essentially (e.g., Aristotle's substances or the phenomenological tradition) or [4] perspectivally (e.g., Heraclitus's flux, Joyce's stream of consciousness, Derrida's deconstruction). Thus, the real is *either* grasped and known in the general structure or intelligibility ("essence") of what appears, *or* the real is simply encountered and experienced in the irreducible, particular perspectives of ever-changing, manifold appearances. In this fourth, perspectival interpretation, to abstract any concept or universal essence is to recede from concrete, existential reality into mere nominalism, i.e., having reality only in name. Because it deals with concrete existents, McKeon calls this interpretation "existential," and it is perhaps what Scotus is getting at with his notion of *haecceitas* ("thisness"), a key term in Gerald Manley Hopkins' description of his poetic attempts to convey the singular, unrepeatable uniqueness of a thing or a person. By contrast, for the third, essentialist interpretation, this poetic sensibility fails to advert to the patterns that are in fact common to many particulars. In Bernard Lonergan's view, the one who grasps and communicates a concept experiences that abstraction as enriching, as it sees the intelligibility immanent in the data and communicates that insight through concepts.[21]

How can diverse theological positions today be understood in light of McKeon's account of these four interpretations of reality?[22] What follows are some suggestive, broad-stroke examples. I offer them not as tidy answers but as stimulants to your engagement with, and theological reflection upon, the fact of theological pluralism and the possible relevance of McKeon's matrix for a better understanding of that fact.

#1. Transcendental. Any theology that believes God is creator must accept the basic truth of interpretation #1 that the ultimate referent in theology transcends the world. Insofar as a theological system gravitates to this pole of interpretation, it will tend to find its theological home in platonist-influenced theologies, such as Augustine's, that emphasize the transience of the world and the pilgrim nature of Christian identity. Contemporary examples include Pope Benedict XVI, who considers himself "decidedly Augustinian."[23] For example, in his first two encyclicals, he has presented imperfect human love as but a fleeting glimpse of the unchanging perfection of divine love (*Deus caritas est*) and sharply contrasted idolatrous secular hopes with enduring eschatological hope (*Spe salvi*).

#3. Essentialist. But if God is creator, then creation must exhibit intelligibility, the essential structure of which the human mind, made in the image of God, can grasp. And if the mind no longer readily sees how nature's design proves God's existence, then it must turn inward to the essence of the human instead. In one version of the modern turn to the subject, the structures of human knowing and willing are presented as "open upwards" to God, in Rahner's language.[24] Thus, the essence of the human is *a priori* dynamism for God. What appears in creation can therefore "merge," or more accurately, unite with the divine essence, as argued in Rahner's classic essay "On the Theology of the Incarnation."[25] In this theological transposition of the #3 essentialist interpretation of reality, the focus falls on the doctrine of the Incarnation, on the participation of secular hopes in eschatological hope, and on the sacramental goodness of creation (e.g., in the Vatican II document *Gaudium et spes*).

#4. Perspectival. But what do the pleasing generalities of the argument for human openness to God say about the vastly differing perspectives of concrete individuals—in particular, between the powerful and the powerless, and their grossly divergent access to the goods of creation? If "humanity is the grammar of the Incarnation" (Rahner), then what is the vocabulary that God uses to speak the eternal Word into human history? Clearly, in his ministry, Jesus sided with a particular perspective. His life and the manner in which he sacrificed it gave shape and substance to the encounter of divine love with different perspectives: for the suffering, compassion and solidarity; for the contrite, mercy; for the unrepentant, judgment and a call to conversion, and so on. The ensuing conversion or resistance to conversion gives rise to the fundamental tension between the opposed perspectives of the Kingdom and the "anti-Kingdom" (Jon Sobrino), in which, respectively, either "the last shall be first" or, as Philip Roth memorably said in a different context, "the ruthless screw the dispossessed." The theology of the cross captures the dramatic collision of these irreconcilable perspectives, holding within its tensive symbol both divine love and human sin. Memory becomes a critical battleground for suppressing or keeping alive the disappeared voices and disfigured experiences of oppressed lives (Johann Baptist Metz). As advocacy and liberation theologies insist, perspectives matter; and (as seen in their insistence on the preferential option for the poor) the perspective that matters most to God is of those whose human dignity is denied.

#2. *Substrative*. The fourth and final interpretation is not strictly theological, in the sense of dealing with specific claims of revelation, for it considers the material substrate (e.g., economic modes of production/consumption; unconscious and instinctual bases of consciousness). When it is the sole focus of an inquiry, it becomes reductive. How, then, is this substrative interpretation relevant for theology? Its significance lies in the negative consequences when theologians overlook or deny its explanatory power, and reach instead for theological explanations when sociological or evolutionary ones would do. If theology fails to incorporate some (non-reductive) version of these explanations, it will give increasingly detached and other-worldly accounts of human behavior or church organization, the implausibility of which invites the "revenge of the lower" that explains faith as neurotic projection or rejects church as yet another configuration of social power. This substrative interpretation can also moderate the rhetorical flights that sometimes come with the #3 perspectival interpretation. For it is not uncommon to see the passionate advocacy of a particular perspective degenerate into "prophetic license" that overstates its case, and thereby impedes a fuller understanding of underlying economic realities. For example, assertions such as Jon Sobrino's claim that "the accumulation of a few is what generates the death of others" overlook the complex and more ambiguous nature of wealth creation.[26]

Conclusion

The goal of this paper has been to show how McKeon's analysis of philosophical pluralism can assist contemporary theology's understanding of its often bewildering diversity. Transposing McKeon's philosophical coordinates to theological inquiry facilitates understanding and dialogue between very different ways of doing theology, and distinguishes serious theological disagreement from superficial difference in emphasis or terminology. It allows the theologian to locate herself on a broad and comprehensive map, to better understand alternative positions, and thus to see her own work as part of a collaborative effort for the good of the Church.

St. John of the Cross
and Interreligious Dialogue

CHRISTIAN S. KROKUS, UNIVERSITY OF SCRANTON

IN THE PAST DECADE OR SO, the works of St. John of the Cross (1542-1591) have assumed increasing prominence in the writing and teaching of Michael Buckley. As Grant Kaplan noted earlier in this volume, in his book, *Denying and Disclosing God*, especially in the chapter on "Atheism and Contemplation," John of the Cross represents for Buckley no less than a proper Christian response to the polemics of nineteenth- and twentieth-century atheists. His painstakingly close reading and clear analysis of St. John's poetry and commentary as well as his marvel at the accuracy of the saint's comprehensive description of the soul's journey toward God—an accuracy Buckley has verified through his long experience as a spiritual director—has been evident to anyone fortunate enough to study John of the Cross with him. He offered courses on the sixteenth-century Spanish mystic and Doctor of the Church nearly every semester of his final years at Boston College, and he continued to do so regularly when he arrived at Santa Clara University. In fact, it is in the classroom where many of Buckley's students, both graduate and undergraduate, have come to embrace his contagious enthusiasm for the Mystical Doctor. This essay is indebted both to that enthusiasm and to Buckley's interpretation of the saint's writings, but it applies the work of John of the Cross in a direction that Buckley himself has not emphasized, namely interreligious dialogue.

Introduction

The most obvious way to enlist John of the Cross in contemporary interreligious dialogue would be simply to study his own words explicitly devoted to the topic, but unfortunately there are few, if any, such words. It simply was not his question. In fact, with a few notable exceptions, it was not the explicit question of any Christian theologian until the early- to mid-twentieth century. Addressing Christian faith in the context of religious pluralism is one of the pressing challenges of our time, however, and a proper response to that challenge demands that one turn to the leading lights of the

Christian intellectual tradition, even if that means adapting insights from the past in creative new ways.

How to do so with John of the Cross? Some scholars search for parallels, similarities, and convergences between his writings and those of spiritual masters in other religious traditions.[1] Some researchers seek evidence of actual borrowing from other religious traditions in his writings.[2] Both approaches are worthwhile and potentially complementary. To demonstrate Islamic and/or Jewish influences in the vocabulary, practices, and images of a fully orthodox, Trinitarian, Christocentric Doctor of the Church would provide concrete historical evidence—resulting from the latter approach—that elements of another religious tradition can possibly be appropriated by the Church in authentic and meritorious ways—a hypothesis generated by the former approach; a full treatment of John of the Cross and interreligious dialogue would certainly draw on both of these aspects. A third option focuses on the intention and content of John's writings themselves, namely a description of the journey of the soul toward union with God, and it asks what insights might be drawn from John's treatment of that journey by persons engaged today in interreligious dialogue or its corresponding theological disciplines, e.g., theology of religions and comparative theology.

Such is the approach of this essay. After a brief treatment of how mysticism is often applied to interreligious questions, this essay turns directly to the work of John of the Cross, focusing almost exclusively on the *Ascent of Mount Carmel* and the *Dark Night of the Soul*, for there one finds, contrary to what practitioners of interreligious dialogue often seek in mystical literature, namely an apophatic conception of God that leaves room for other interpretations of the Absolute, a thoroughly Christocentric notion of the soul's relationship to God. One also discovers, however, that the particularity of St. John's approach need not discourage dialogue, for the virtues cultivated along John's path—especially the virtue of "holy envy"—can translate into generosity toward seekers in other traditions. Because John's description of the journey is so Christ-centered, and particularly because the Catholic theological tradition has acknowledged his work as a standard of mystical theology, it may be that his work can function as a heuristic lens for discerning the work of Christ in the members and elements of other religious traditions.

Mysticism and Interreligious Dialogue

It has become relatively common among Christian theologians and others interested in interreligious dialogue to invoke the work of mystics as a useful tool. Paul Knitter notes that those who employ a "mystical bridge" to affirmation of religious pluralism do so because they feel "the deeper a person enters into the religious experience that is made possible through her own particular religion, the more aware she will be that what she is experiencing cannot be limited to her own religion—and the more openness and sensitivity she will have to recognizing the same mystery in other religions."[3] Knitter's own endorsement of the mystical bridge focuses on the fact that "[s]tated simply and provocatively, according to the mystic-theological traditions within all religions, absolute claims can be made only in a qualified manner."[4] In other words, the genius of the mystic is to remind us (who often forget) that "God names a mystery that is incomprehensible" and Ultimate Reality is "just as much (or more) 'beyond' as it is 'here'—just as transcendent as it is immanent."[5] As such, it is the recognition of the "*ineffability* of God or Truth" and the "*non-absoluteness* of their own claims and beliefs" that should impel representatives of particular traditions to the table of interreligious dialogue.[6] Raimon Panikkar added to the second edition of *The Intra-religious Dialogue* a "Mystical Model" of religious pluralism that is first and foremost grounded in "silence," a silence that maintains "unity and… harmony" among competing truth-claims. He also asserted that the future of dialogue would require a movement from *inter*-religious to *intra*-religious dialogue, that is, "from dogma to mysticism."[7] In other words, for Panikkar too, the mystic's critique of overly determined formulae concerning God reminds one that the ongoing dialogue, quest for understanding, and silence rather than answers are of paramount importance.

Some elements of John's program, especially his emphasis on faith, resonate with such an approach, but other elements, especially his insistence on the necessity and uniqueness of Christ for enjoying union with God, complicate the ways that his work might profit contemporary approaches to dialogue. Therefore, in order to assess both the opportunities for and the obstacles to the task at hand, one should review briefly the outline of John's description of the soul's ascent to God in *The Ascent of Mount Carmel* and *The Dark Night of the Soul*.

The Soul's Ascent to God

The Ascent of Mount Carmel and *The Dark Night of the Soul* are two treatises centered on one poem, *The Dark Night* (*Noche oscura*), which Buckley refers to as an art-object, the fruit of John's religious experience.[8] The treatises contain the poem itself as well as extensive commentaries that describe in painstaking detail the journey of the soul toward union with God. They describe the twofold process of purgation, active and passive, of the two parts of the soul, sense and spirit, that is required for enjoyment of union. Ostensibly, *Ascent* covers the active purgation while *Dark Night* treats of the passive, but in actuality there is overlap, and together they describe not two nights but several moments in one night or movement of purification: "In actuality these three [or four] nights comprise only one night."[9] As John writes at the beginning of Book Two of *Ascent*, the movement from purgation of the senses to purgation of the spirit to union is like the transition from dusk to night to dawn.[10]

In *Dark Night* 2.11.4, John makes the following astounding statement:

"One might, then, in a certain way ponder how remarkable and how strong this enkindling of love in the spirit can be. God gathers together all the strength, faculties, and appetites of the soul, spiritual and sensory alike, so the energy and power of this whole harmonious composite may be employed in this love. The soul consequently arrives at the true fulfillment of the first commandment which, neither disdaining anything human nor excluding it from this love, states: You shall love your God with your whole heart, and with your whole mind, and with your whole soul, and with all your strength [Dt. 6:5]."

The statement is astounding because it suggests that only after moving through the nights of sense and spirit is the person ready for and capable of honoring the first commandment, the same commandment one has likely heard since the earliest days of one's youth. This is why Iain Matthew argues that to love the Lord with all one's heart, mind, soul, and strength is practically impossible, for "we do not possess all our heart, all our soul or all our strength"—at least not prior to purification.[11] For John, in order to love God it is necessary that the person first be brought into integrity. The senses must be united with the spirit. The intellect, will, and memory must be purified and oriented toward God.

This process involves nothing less than the radical detachment of the soul from all creatures, whether physical or spiritual. As John writes,

God and creatures are contraries, but "love effects a likeness between the lover and the loved."[12] Thus the more one loves creatures, whether according to physical appetites, or to a wandering imagination, or even to one's ideas about God, the less probable becomes union with God: "By the mere fact that a soul loves something, it becomes incapable of pure union and transformation in God; for the lowness of the creature is far less capable of the height of the Creator than is darkness of light."[13] The soul must be stripped of all attachments. Then, and only then, can God, through a passionate and consuming love, so concentrate the desire and affection of a person that it might be said that he/she properly honors the first commandment. Only then can God bring this integrated and purified subject into union with Himself. It is precisely St. John's emphasis on detachment, especially from one's ideas about God, that seems to recommend itself to interreligious dialogue.

Detachment as Key to Interreligious Dialogue?

In the night of the spirit, the intellect, memory, and will of the adept (those who are spiritually advanced) are purified in both the active and passive stages. This night, which Michael Buckley reminds us "is far more terrible and demanding than the first," is also referred to as the "night of faith."[14] If the night of sense was primarily about transforming one's motivation from a desire for anything besides God to a desire for God himself, particularly in Christ, the night of faith purifies "support systems and security: the concepts, the systems of meaning, the symbolic structures by which reassurance is forthcoming." Buckley continues: "What functions critically here for John is the infinite distance between human concepts or experiences and the divine, and it is this gap that will suggest religious development," for "through faith," which is where the soul must place his/her trust, "one moves into utter mystery, what is incomprehensible and unimaginable; 'for however impressive may be one's knowledge or feeling of God, that knowledge or feeling will have no resemblance to God and amount to very little.'"[15] In the sentence immediately preceding the one Buckley quotes, John reminds the reader that "if the soul in traveling this road leans on any elements of its own knowledge or of its experience or knowledge of God, it will easily go astray or be detained because it did not desire to abide in complete blindness, in the faith that is its guide."[16] Simply put, "God's being cannot be grasped by the intellect, appetite, imagination, or any other sense; nor can it be known in this life. The most that can be felt and tasted of God in this life is infinitely distant from God and the pure possession of him."[17] Finally, "those are decidedly hindered, then, from attainment of this high state of union with God who are attached to any understanding... Consequently they must pass beyond everything to unknowing."[18] Or, as Buckley puts it: "Whatever knowledge one has does not move into the objectification of God but passes through objectifications, contradicts their adequacy, and in faith 'reaches God more by not understanding than by understanding.'"[19]

This is precisely why the night of faith is so terrible. In the passive night of faith, God removes the security that at least one has a proper understanding of God. The paradox is that unknowing or not understanding, which seems and feels like a lack of security, is actually an invitation to a deeper security. Commenting on the verse *In darkness and secure*, St. John notes that only by letting go of one's attachment to particular conceptions or ideas about God is one freed "from vainglory, from pride and presumption, from an empty and false joy, and from many other evils. By walking in darkness the soul not only avoids going astray but advances rapidly, because it thus gains the virtues."[20]

One could make the case that such a radical unknowing, or radical not-understanding, prohibits one from judging the truth claims of other faith traditions. Detachment from one's ideas about God, or recognition of the inherent limitations of one's ideas about God, or affirmation that "what can be felt and tasted of God in this life is infinitely distant from God" should give one pause before claiming triumphantly that "my understanding of God is superior to yours!" Our finite, temporal, imperfect language, even our expression of religious doctrine, always and necessarily falls short of the infinite, eternal, and perfect reality of God. There is no doubt that John would concur with Knitter and Panikkar about the value and necessity of recognizing the limitedness or "non-absoluteness" of one's understanding of ultimate reality, but one must be careful not to overextend the scope of his reservations vis-à-vis personal understandings of God. There is no evidence that he would endorse the same sort of reflexive criticism at an institutional, that is, ecclesial level.

Particularity of Christ and Church

The prescription for the soul in the grip of the dark night of spirit is faith. First and foremost that means faith in God, faith that it is God who has invited the soul into this terrifying process, faith that it is God who awaits the soul in the dawn that succeeds this terrible night, but it also means concrete faith in the particular teachings of the Church and faith that the Church was established and is guided by Christ Himself. As Iain Matthew writes, "John says, faith, faith, faith, faith—and we say, 'What *is* this faith for which we sacrifice everything else? The answer: Jesus Christ."[21] For example, at the beginning of Book Two of *Ascent*—the beginning of the active night of faith—John, introducing his commentary on the second stanza of the poem, reminds the reader that one must darken the intellect, that is, not trust his own knowledge of God, but instead lean "on pure faith alone." The soul must ascend "the secret ladder," which "represents faith, because all the rungs or articles of faith are secret to and hidden from both the senses and the intellect. Accordingly the soul lived in darkness, without any light from the senses and intellect, and went out beyond every natural and rational boundary to climb the divine ladder of faith that leads up to and penetrates the deep things of God."[22] The soul cannot trust what it knows by nature or by reason, but it can trust the articles of faith.[23] The soul must adhere to the teachings and to the authority of the Church, no matter how attractive new ideas or new presentations of old ideas may be:

> "Since there are no more articles to be revealed to the Church about the substance of our faith, people must not merely reject new revelations about the faith, but out of caution repudiate other kinds of knowledge mingled with them. In order to preserve the purity of faith, a person should not believe already revealed truths because they are again revealed but because they were already sufficiently revealed to the Church. Closing one's mind to them, one should rest simply on the doctrine of the Church and its faith that, as St. Paul says, enters through hearing [Rom. 10:17]."[24]

A cynical view of passages such as those might suggest that John was merely placating would-be ecclesial investigators who would otherwise be suspicious and critical of his project, but really he simply reiterates the need to denude one's intellect and to trust God alone who reveals Himself to and through the Church.[25] Throughout the "night," one continues to attend Mass, to read Scripture, to visit with one's spiritual director, etc., each an opportunity to be weaned from attachment to one's own understanding in favor of God's self-revelation.

Another reason the Church, and especially the particularity of what the Church teaches, cannot be secondary or peripheral to the ascent is that the journey toward union with God and the terrifying detachment that journey entails, ultimately, is a participation in the passion of Jesus Christ. Christ is central, sometimes thematically, sometimes unthematically, but always central to the process. The only permissible desire in the active night of the senses is "perfect observance of the Lord's law and the carrying of the cross of Christ."[26] In the crucial chapter thirteen of the first book of the *Ascent*, John offers the method for entering the night of sense: "First, have habitual desire to imitate Christ in all your deeds by bringing your life into conformity with his. You must then study his life in order to know how to imitate him and behave in all events as he would. Second, in order to be successful in this imitation, renounce and remain empty of any sensory satisfaction that is not purely for the honor and glory of God. Do this out of love for Jesus Christ." After stressing the importance of inclining oneself to the more difficult, the more distasteful, etc., John explains the motivation one must have: "Do not go about looking for the best of temporal things, but for the worst, and, for Christ, desire to enter into complete nakedness, emptiness, and poverty in everything in the world."[27] Interpreting Matthew 7:14, John suggests that Christ is the gate through which one enters the journey toward union with God.[28] Later, discussing the active night of faith, he clarifies that in fact the entire journey—i.e., not only the beginning or the "gate," but the entire night in its several modes—is a participation in the passion of Christ. He comments on Mark 8:34-35 by criticizing those who think "denial of self in worldly matters is sufficient without annihilation and purification in the spiritual domain," accusing them of avoiding the necessary bout with spiritual dryness and of having "a spiritual sweet tooth." These people are effectively "enemies of the cross of Christ."[29] On the contrary, "a genuine spirit... leans more toward suffering than toward consolation," for it "knows that this is the significance of following Christ and denying self."[30]

Lest one imagine one's self-denial independent of its Christian foundations, John demonstrates the relationship between our purgation and the passion of Christ: "Because I have said that Christ is the way and that this way is a death to our natural selves in the sensory and spiritual parts of the soul, I would like to demonstrate how this death is patterned on Christ's, for he is our model and light. First, during his life he certainly died spiritually to the sensitive part, and at his death he died naturally," and "second, at the moment of his death he was certainly annihilated in his soul, without any consolation or relief, since the Father had left him that way in innermost aridity in the lower part. He was thereby compelled to cry out: *My God, My God, why have you forsaken me?* [Mt. 27:46]"[31] He continues: "When they are reduced to nothing, the highest degree of humility, the spiritual union between their souls and God will be an accomplished fact. This union is the most noble and sublime state attainable in this life. The journey, then, does not consist in consolations, delights, and spiritual feelings, but in the living death of the cross, sensory and spiritual, exterior and interior," and for this reason "Christ is little known by those who consider themselves his friends. For we see them going about seeking in him their own consolations and satisfactions, loving themselves very much, but not loving him very much by seeking his bitter trials and deaths."[32] Edward Howells confirms the Christocentric dimension of the ascent when he points out that in the *Spiritual Canticle* "the final union of the soul with God is a union 'corresponding' to the hypostatic union," and that "it is only once the soul begins to recognize itself as Christ-like in union that it sees the purpose of its suffering."[33] Christ is the entrance to the night; his passion and death are the night itself, and his resurrection and divinity are the dawn that follows the night. Buckley writes: "In this purification of desire and of awareness, the critical influence for John is Christ," for "the contemplative evolution is an assimilation into the love of God through the progressive possession by the Spirit that configures the soul to Christ."[34]

John exhibits a robust confidence in the teachings of the Church about Christ, about the Incarnation of God in the historical Jesus, and about the revelation of the Word in Jesus. For example, in chapter twenty-two of the second book of *Ascent*, where he warns against the desire for spiritual communications from saints, angels, or even God Himself, he writes: "Those who now desire to question God or receive some vision or revelation are guilty not only of foolish behavior but also of offending him by not fixing their eyes entirely on Christ and by living with the desire for some other novelty. God could answer as follows: If I have already told you all things in my Word, my Son, and if I have no other word, what answer or revelation can I now make that would surpass this? Fasten your eyes on him alone because in him I have spoken and revealed all and in him you will discover even more than you ask for and desire."[35] He continues, even more forcefully: "One should not, then, inquire of God in this manner, nor is it necessary for God to speak any more. Since he has finished revealing the faith through Christ, there is no more faith to reveal, nor will there ever be," for "when Christ dying on the cross exclaimed: *Consummatum est* (It is consummated) [Jn. 19:30], he consummated not these ways alone, but all the other ceremonies and rites of the old law"; that is, "anyone who desires to commune with God after the manner of the old law is walking in vain."[36] In just a few paragraphs, although the context deals with private revelations, John dismisses the possibility of a revelation subsequent to Christ, possibly in reference to Islam and to the Qur'an, as well as the efficacy or legitimacy of worshipping God according to the "old law," certainly in reference to Judaism, all of which provides little incentive for dialogue among the Abrahamic faiths. As noted at the beginning of the essay, John uttered very few words about other religious traditions, and it turns out that the few he did write (if in fact these statements refer to Judaism and Islam) are not particularly encouraging. John is thoroughly Christian, thoroughly Christocentric, thoroughly confident in the teaching authority of the Church, and although it was not addressed here explicitly, thoroughly Pneumatocentric and therefore thoroughly Trinitarian. Authentic spirituality requires participation in the passion, death, and resurrection of Christ. Real union with God is participation in the divinity of Christ. The path demands utter and complete obedience to Christ. As Iain Matthew puts it, "John reasons like this: I know that what I am saying seems to be stretching things, so I want to show that it comes, not from me, but from Christ."[37]

Possible Contributions to Interreligious Dialogue

In light of John's definite and explicit affirmations of key Church doctrines, faithful obedience to Church authority, and conviction that the authentic journey toward union with God is a participation in Christ, one begins to wonder whether the Mystical Doctor in fact contributes anything at all to contemporary Christian reflection on the question of religious pluralism. He does, but less in terms of a Christian theology of other religious traditions, and more in terms of a particular attitude that might successfully be employed by Christians in faithful engagement with those traditions. Concretely, he provides an example of how to hold in tension both the truth of Christian doctrines about God, Christ, and Church—not as one of many equally inadequate options, but simply as true—together with the realization that one's understanding of those truths is always limited, finite, and an inadequate objectification of the divine reality. In other words, his work reminds one of an important distinction between truth—i.e., that which we know—and understanding, which always falls short in the case of the divine realities we know.

A faithful Christian affirms that God has spoken the final and fullest Word in Jesus. He knows that Jesus is the only way to the Father. He knows that the spiritual journey toward God, if authentic, begins with the imitation of Christ and consists of a participation in the passion and death of Christ, and he knows that real happiness, true fulfillment consists in participation in the hypostatic union, the joining of divinity and humanity in Christ. All of this he knows. Nonetheless, he recognizes in his dialogue partners, or at least in the shining examples—one might say the "saints"—of their traditions, real examples of holiness, real embodiment of the virtues, an authentic display of the kinds of qualities John teaches follow from an authentic surrender to the purification of the dark night. Could it be that Christ, Whom the Christian knows is the vehicle by which the virtues and eventually divinity is conferred onto true seekers, is at work in the saints of these other traditions? Could it be, while he trusts in the truth of Christ and in the authority and ability of the Church, founded by Christ as it is, to communicate the truth most fully, that he does not fully understand exactly to what extent and how Christ is at work in other religious traditions or how those traditions figure in the divine plan for history? In other words, a Christian engaged in interreligious dialogue should exhibit both a conviction about the truth of Church teaching and also a kind of agnosticism about the ways that God, through Christ, is working in and through participants of other religions.[38]

John's teaching in *Dark Night* on "holy envy" pushes one even further, namely to assume the best of the other and to be most critical with oneself, for once the soul "recognizes the truth about its misery"—i.e., its sinfulness—and once the soul "commune[s] with God more respectfully and courteously"—i.e., the soul is now aware of the infinity and incomprehensibility of God—then "the thought of [its] being more advanced than others does not even occur in its first movements, as it did before; on the contrary, [one] realize[s] that others are better."[39] Instead of criticizing, explaining away, downplaying, or ignoring examples of holiness in others—a vice John calls "spiritual envy"—converted souls "become sad at not having the virtues of others, rejoice that others have them, and are happy that all others are ahead of them in the service of God, since they themselves are so wanting in this service."[40] It is not too far a stretch to employ this virtue of "holy envy" in interreligious dialogue, so that Christians recognize, celebrate, and even desire the holiness they sometimes see in practitioners of other religions.[41]

Catherine Cornille, citing the virtue of humility as a condition for authentic interreligious dialogue, has recently endorsed this approach, although without explicit reference to John. She points out that "many of the early pioneers of the East-West dialogue (Henri Le Saux, Bede Griffiths, and Thomas Merton) were monks. And the inter-monastic dialogue has become one of the most enduring and fruitful forms of interreligious dialogue."[42] This is explained in part by "shared monastic emphasis on poverty and renunciation, silence and contemplation, [and] other monastic values such as hospitality," but most likely it is also the "cultivation of humility that generates a greater attention and receptivity to the truth of other religions."[43] Drawing upon Bernard of Clairvaux's *The Steps of Humility and Pride*, Cornille encourages among participants in interreligious dialogue what she calls "doctrinal humility," a twofold act of humility "toward" doctrine and "about" doctrine.[44] While Christian spirituality normally cultivates humility "toward" doctrine, that is, obedience to the teaching authority of the Church even when one's understanding of a particular doctrine is lacking, Cornille suggests that spiritual or mystical training also lends itself to cultivating humility about doctrine, that is, realizing that all teaching about God falls short of the reality of God. Cornille cites official Church documents (e.g., *Dei verbum, Mysterium ecclesiae, Dialogue and Proclamation, Redemptoris missio*) as well as the efforts of important twentieth-century theologians (e.g., Rahner, Balthasar)[45] and the fruits of official dialogues (e.g., Monastic Interreligious Dialogue)[46] as lending legitimacy to the latter type of doctrinal humility. In terms of the topic at hand, humility "toward" doctrine corresponds with John's emphasis on recognizing and accepting the absolutely central role of Christ in authentic spirituality, while humility "about" doctrine corresponds with his insistence on the failure of finite intellects to comprehend the fullness of divine reality. "Holy envy" demands that one assume the best about his interlocutors' path, at least where it does not obviously contradict Church teaching.

Conclusion: Beyond Dialogue, Toward Theology

In 1926, Pope Pius XI named St. John of the Cross a Doctor of the Church under the title of "Mystical Doctor," and most (if not all) of the prominent Catholic theologians working in the early to mid-twentieth century in the disciplines of ascetical and mystical theology turned to John of the Cross's description of the purgation of the soul and its union with God as normative for the tradition. For example, for Maritain the importance of John of the Cross rivals that of Thomas Aquinas: "To our mind, St. John of the Cross is the great Doctor of this supreme incommunicable wisdom, just as St. Thomas Aquinas is the great Doctor of the highest communicable wisdom. It is in function of the delicate and admirably instructive relations existing between the Doctor of Light and the Doctor of Night that we shall... examine certain aspects of the spiritual teaching of John of the Cross."[47] For Garrigou-Lagrange, "none has better described these crises which mark the transition from one spiritual period to another than St. John of the Cross."[48] Maréchal cites John Ruysbroeck and John of the Cross as "particularly exact authors" when it comes to describing the unity of the mystical life.[49] Guibert lists John of the Cross among the acceptable sources for conducting "spiritual theology."[50] Finally, Poulain only employed "the word mystic in the restricted sense in which St. Teresa [of Avila] and St. John of the Cross employ it," because "it is the one in most common use in the Church."[51]

Buckley also uses John of the Cross in an authoritative manner when, toward the end of *Denying and Disclosing God*, he argues that the negation of atheism depends on a proper appropriation of "such constituents of Christian life as the lives of the saints, the life of prayer, the abiding call to holiness, the committed practices of justice and compassion, the interaction and effective love within the community, the beauty and symbolic world of liturgy, and so on—in short... all of the categorical manifestations of the holy in the interchanges that constitute personal histories and experience."[52] It is this "fact of sanctity" that reveals the authentic pursuit of God even in places as unexpected as the lives of Jacques and Raissa Maritain, Simone Weil, and Edith Stein in their pre-Christian periods.[53] And it is John of the Cross's brilliant explication and demonstration of the "fact of sanctity" that reveals authentic movements toward God also in the most ordinary of lives, for he *throws into bold relief what is the experience, in various degrees and infinite varieties, of many deeply good people. What appears at first sight as a rare or highly specialized experience of mystical development "writes large" the outline by which the surrender that is faith evolves into its fullness in many lives. Any serious following of Christ leads by way of the reversals of concepts or disappointments of expectations, the sacrifice or the suffering—by way of the deconstruction of an initial understanding of God—into the loving awareness that God is beyond concept, beyond management, and beyond form. There is in Christian living an abiding purification from expectations and projections that social workers or mothers of families or dedicated teachers undergo— must undergo if they are to continue faithful to the God who dwells in light inaccessible, whose incalculable reality is embodied in Jesus, and whose draw they feel within their own spirits.*[54]

It is precisely by studying St. John's "theology, which is essentially an experiential process with its description, its negative analyses, its stages of development, and its prescriptive counsels," that one comes to recognize religious development in other extraordinary and ordinary Christian lives.[55] John's work functions heuristically; it provides something for which to look.

Does one encounter the "fact of sanctity" among non-Christians? Buckley thinks so: "[O]ne can find similar narratives of being brought before the reality of God by the witness of holiness in the deeply religious traditions of Judaism and Islam."[56] Joseph Maréchal, the Belgian Jesuit philosopher, psychologist, and theologian, thinks so too. He was introduced by the great Catholic scholar of Islam, Louis Massignon, to the example of the tenth-century Sufi saint, mystic, and martyr, al-Hallaj, who practiced severe renunciation motivated by love of God and neighbor and who was executed by crucifixion for having claimed "I am the Truth" at the pinnacle of his experience of God.[57] Maréchal was so overwhelmed by Hallaj's sanctity that he judged Hallaj "must have drawn upon himself the merciful predilection of that Jesus who is not only the human masterpiece of divine grace, as Hallaj believed, but 'the Author and Finisher' of that grace."[58] He then asked: "Would it not be worth the trouble to seek, more attentively than ever, with exact science and wholly evangelic charity, for the 'stepping-stones' which God has probably provided by his grace in these vast religious milieu?"[59]

What exactly would constitute an "exact science" for determining the grace and presence of Christ in other religious traditions? As *Dominus Iesus* indicates, it is notoriously difficult to say how exactly "the salvific grace of God—which is always given by means of Christ in the Spirit and has a mysterious relationship to the Church—comes to individual non-Christians, [for] the Second Vatican Council limited itself to the statement that God bestows it 'in ways known to himself.'" The text continues: "Theologians are seeking to understand this question more fully. Their work is to be encouraged, since it is certainly useful for understanding better God's salvific plan and the ways in which it is accomplished."[60]

Given the weight that his description of the spiritual path carries in the Catholic tradition, perhaps one can move beyond agnosticism about the ways that Christ is operative in other religious traditions by using John of the Cross's program as a lens through which one begins to detect and to name the activities of Christ among members and elements of other traditions. The logic for doing so would run something like this. There is precedent in the Catholic tradition for taking John of the Cross as normative on the soul's journey toward union with God. There is precedent in contemporary theology (such as with Buckley) for applying John's work as a heuristic device for discovering and naming authentic movements toward God in the lives of ordinary Christians. The Church has affirmed the possibility of Christ's grace working in individual members of other religious traditions, and John of the Cross insists that authentic movements toward God are in fact evidence of conformity to the life, passion, death, resurrection, and finally divinity of Jesus. Therefore, when examining other religious traditions, one might focus on the "saints" of those traditions. One might seek evidence of a twofold process of purgation (active/passive) of the soul (sense/spirit) in the life of a non-Christian "saint." One might look for evidence of detachment from all creatures, physical and spiritual. One would be especially keen to detect surrender to God, "death" to senses and spirit, self-sacrifice, "reversals of concepts or disappointments of expectations, the sacrifice or the suffering," and inclination "more toward suffering than toward consolation." One would look for "deconstruction of an initial understanding of God" and "awareness that God is beyond concept, beyond management, and beyond form." The presence of these attributes among members of other traditions could suggest to Christians—and surely this is a theological claim—that the Spirit and grace of Jesus is at work in these extraordinary lives. There of course remains the problem of squaring this discovery with John's insistence on explicit obedience to Christ and Church, but perhaps that is best worked out in concrete study. One might begin, for example, with al-Hallaj and ask how it is that a Muslim could enjoy a life so conformed interiorly and exteriorly to the life of Jesus. One would inevitably be led to al-Hallaj's sources, the Qur'an, the life and example of Muhammad, devotion to the Qur'anic Jesus, and constant prayer, fasting, and almsgiving. One could then ask whether Christ is present not only within the extraordinary life of al-Hallaj (or other non-Christians) but also within aspects of Islam (or other religions), which produced such an extraordinary life. Carrying out such a concrete application would entail an entirely separate and exhaustive study; therefore one hopes here only to have pointed in a fruitful direction and to have shown that John of the Cross might gainfully be appropriated by those engaged in interreligious dialogue. At the very least, he teaches the disposition toward God and neighbor that makes inquiry into the life and path of one's interlocutor not only possible but necessary.

Part Three:

NEW DIRECTIONS IN CATHOLIC HIGHER EDUCATION

Beyond Education for Justice: Christian Humanism in Catholic Higher Education

JOSEPH CURRAN, MISERICORDIA UNIVERSITY

Justice as the New Humanism

IN *THE CATHOLIC UNIVERSITY AS Promise and Project: Reflections in a Jesuit Idiom,* Michael Buckley describes the Catholic and Jesuit University's education for justice as a kind of "new humanism." This new humanism replaces a humanistic education that may have formed students to appreciate the achievements of human culture, but did not in fact make them more humane. Buckley describes a humanistic education that sensitizes students to the suffering of the poor and marginalized, and provides them with the skills and knowledge to ameliorate or eliminate that suffering. Many Catholic and Jesuit universities currently use service learning, community based learning, and immersion trips to advance this very goal. In this chapter, I will examine Buckley's description of education for justice as the new humanism and compare it to some examples of this kind of education taking place today. This comparison will demonstrate that these efforts at education for justice are in fact based on a broader set of Christian virtues, including mercy and hospitality. Not only do these virtues offer a more accurate description of the effect of these educational efforts—they also offer a more robust Christian and Catholic vision without sacrificing the ability to find common ground with other faith traditions—a quality that makes justice attractive as a basis for the Catholic identity. Education for mercy, justice, and hospitality through service also has inherent dangers, as it involves the university in the personal moral formation of students, a project that most Catholic universities, particularly theology departments, have avoided since the 1950s. I will argue that what has typically been called "education for justice" is more accurately described as education for mercy, hospitality, and justice through service. Not only does theological language more accurately describe what is being done in this kind of education—serious theological reflection and analysis also steers this process away from some possible pitfalls. Finally, the role of theological reflection in education for justice helps to define and secure the place of theology in undergraduate education.

Buckley uses a chapter in *The Catholic University as Promise and Project* to describe the commitment to the work of justice made by the 32nd General Congregation of the Society of Jesus in 1972, and how this commitment has directed Jesuit efforts in higher education. Following the spirit of *Gaudium et spes* (1965), the Congregation required every Jesuit apostolic work—including universities—to be judged by service to faith and promotion of justice. For education, the documents of the Congregation specifically refer to the "conscientization" of those who might be able to change social conditions, as well as the need to give special attention to the poor and oppressed.[1] Buckley understands the call for conscientization to mean that "the university, as such, can and should foster in its faculties and in its students a profound and educated concern for a just social order."[2] This commitment is the contemporary manifestation of the university's traditional commitment to the Renaissance humanist tradition, which was rooted in an attempt to "humanize" students by exposing them to the great accomplishments of human culture.[3] This new approach seeks to humanize students by forming them to a "disciplined sensitivity to human misery," a "humane sensibility and educated awareness" of the suffering of the poor and the miserable condition of the oppressed people of the world.[4] Humanism, broadly understood, has always driven the university to ask questions of human significance. Today, we number among these some fundamental questions about human misery: Why do so many people in the world live in crushing poverty? What must be done to eradicate this condition? Unfortunately, the academic culture of the university tends to isolate students and teachers from the reality of this poverty and suffering; these questions are often not even considered.[5]

A humanist education focused upon the great cultural and intellectual achievements may form students who appreciate these accomplishments, but who are inured to human suffering and uninterested in eliminating or alleviating that suffering. The answer to this problem is a humanistic education that intentionally develops students' sensibility to human suffering and injustice, and instills in those students a desire to act to relieve that suffering: "Humanistic education must develop an educated awareness that includes a profound sense of human solidarity and a spontaneous sympathy for human pain."[6] Such an educational project is not a matter of partisan politics since it is directed by the Christian understanding that the Kingdom of God requires the establishment of a just social order. It is not simple indoctrination, since this education would both expose students to suffering and give them the critical and analytical tools to understand its root causes, effects and dimensions, and not merely rehearse ideologically driven interpretations.

Classical education strategies may be used to develop this humane sensibility in students. Initially, courses would concentrate upon making students aware of the fact and reality of human suffering. These would be followed by courses in disciplines that could educate this awareness—e.g., economics, political science, and other social sciences—and finally by courses that engage in theological and ethical reflection. The study of literature moves from appreciation to criticism to aesthetics; in a similar manner engagement with social concerns should proceed from awareness to analysis to moral evaluation. The social sciences provide the tools of analysis. Philosophy and theology, with their attention to the values that inform all of human life, provide the basis for moral evaluation. This approach treats the social sciences as the "social arts," courses that serve in a humanistic curriculum to focus and educate students whose enthusiasm and heightened awareness of social problems would make them eager consumers of such courses.

Buckley's analysis of the need for a new humanism and his proposal for the development of a curriculum based upon this humanism assumes that the desired outcome of Catholic higher education is a person who both knows and cares about the suffering of other human beings and is committed to reducing or eliminating that suffering. It also assumes that the first step—the creation of an awareness of human suffering—will lead in turn to sympathy, solidarity, and the desire to change the conditions that cause that suffering. Subsequent courses would direct that initial impulse to effect social change by giving students the tools and knowledge that would allow them to do so.

The Catholic University and
Education for Justice in the 21ˢᵗ Century

Reflections on the nature and identity of Jesuit and Catholic higher education since the publication of *The Catholic University as Promise and Project* suggest that Buckley's desired outcomes and assumptions are widely shared, even if his approach has not be adopted in detail. The commitment to justice has been affirmed and advanced by a series of mission statements, meetings, publications and public pronouncements by church and educational leaders. Prominent among these are Jesuit Superior General Peter-Hans Kolvenbach's speech at Santa Clara University in 2000, "The Service of Faith and Promotion of Justice in Jesuit Higher Education." As a principle guiding the mission of a Catholic University, justice offers the advantage of being at once consistent with the values and principles of the Catholic tradition and also accessible and intelligible without reference to specifically Catholic or Christian warrants. Particularly in undergraduate education, Catholic universities have embraced the promotion of justice and the conscientization of students to a degree that even Buckley might find surprising. The way in which this has often been done—immersion or service-learning experiences—suggests a slightly different paradigm from Buckley's, however, while also providing an even more prominent role for the academic study of theology.

To clarify, Buckley does not define justice, although he makes it quite clear that justice has to do with "a deeper and more pervasive commitment to the wretched of the world."[7] Both Buckley and Kolvenbach follow the 32nd General Congregation in describing the work of the promotion of justice as at least including "conscientization," which for Buckley corresponds to the cultivation of an awareness of suffering and also a moral responsibility to respond. To achieve this in students, Buckley argues that the University must reduce its distance from human suffering, and therefore make exposure to human suffering part of the education of its students.

In his speech at Santa Clara, Kolvenbach emphasizes that this heightened awareness of human suffering must result in action. He describes the "promotion of justice" as a careful and systematic program directed at making the world more just by eradicating or reforming unjust conditions and social structures:

> *Since Saint Ignatius wanted love to be expressed not only in words but also in deeds, the Congregation committed the Society to the promotion of justice as a concrete, radical but proportionate response to an unjustly suffering world. Fostering the virtue of justice in people was not enough. Only a substantive justice can bring about the kinds of structural and attitudinal changes that are needed to uproot those*

sinful oppressive injustices that are a scandal against humanity and God. This sort of justice requires an action-oriented commitment to the poor with a courageous personal option.[8]

The University forms students who are willing to make a commitment to justice because they have been educated in solidarity for the whole world, a solidarity that is learned through "contact, not concepts."[9] According to Kolvenbach, the Congregation intentionally avoided using words like "charity, mercy or love"—words "unfashionable" in 1972—in an attempt to be more "incisive."[10] Charity, mercy, and love suggest individual actions to alleviate individual cases of suffering, with no commitment to challenging the unjust structures or conditions that may cause suffering. The Society of Jesus was committed to changing unjust social structures, and the language of mercy does not seem to support that commitment as strongly as the language of justice.

Buckley and Kolvenbach share a conviction that the promotion of justice requires cultivating in students a commitment to transforming the social order so as to reduce the unnecessary suffering of human beings that is a result of unjust practices and social structures. This commitment, in practice, involves orienting individual members of the University community to a greater awareness of and commitment to changing the plight of the poor and suffering. A more detailed knowledge of justice would be required to determine which social structures and cultural attitudes are in fact unjust and how they should be reformed or replaced. Classes in the social sciences, philosophy and theology that follow and build upon courses that acquaint students with the world's suffering would offer such a detailed education in justice. But these are preceded by courses or experiences that raise students' consciousness of suffering and excite their sympathy for those who suffer.

Many universities that have chosen to promote justice do so by first bringing students into direct contact with people who suffer the grinding effects of poverty. This is done through service-learning classes, immersion experiences and extra-curricular service requirements. These experiences make students aware of the massive suffering of the poor and marginalized—a suffering that students may not even have been aware of. Students meet people who are poor and vulnerable, form relationships with these people, and come to care about them. As a result of these experiences, students know about the existence and extent of human suffering caused by injustice, and because this knowledge is personal and relational, they care about this suffering and are willing to work towards its end. These are precisely the orientations and commitments outcomes described by Buckley and Kolvenbach as necessary components of any education for justice.

If we turn now to the implementation of the strategies sketched out by Buckley and Kolvenbach, we find that many Catholic universities have embraced a number of different types of experiential learning, bringing students out of the classroom to have a personal encounter with the poor. Kristen Heyer describes one such experience in a class taught at Loyola Marymount University—community based learning that "combines organized service activities with guided reflection and critical analysis to enhance both the academic objectives of the curriculum and the social needs of the community."[11] These courses expose students to the suffering of people living near the university through service placements. The experience is meant to counter student apathy about social issues and encourage students to see the need for serious theological and ethical reflection on these issues. Students work in settings that encourage them to form relationships with marginalized people; classroom assignments require reflection on these experiences and the integration of these experiences into classroom learning.[12] The placement experiences of students in Heyer's classes has encouraged them to think about problems from an interdisciplinary standpoint, bringing to bear what they have learned in courses in different disciplines as they consider problems of injustice. Ideally, this kind of course can become a moment of synthesis that encompasses the entire university education. Buckley envisions course content that would make students aware of the existence and extent of human suffering; Heyer describes how direct contact with marginalized people in the context of a theology course can also establish this awareness, perhaps even more effectively than in Buckley's initial vision.

Stephen Pope describes a similar process in more detail in his description of immersion experiences. Like Heyer, Pope has taught in Boston College's PULSE program, which combines basic education in philosophy and theology with a ten-hour per week community service component, much like Heyer's community-based learning.[13] In addition to his involvement with PULSE Pope has also participated in and described a campus ministry-run immersion trip to El Salvador. Such trips demonstrate the importance of direct and personal encounters with the poor and marginalized in the education for faith and the promotion of justice.[14] Like service learning, immersion trips proceed from the assumption that contact encourages solidarity more than concepts. Pope describes in some detail the transformative experience of the immersion trip in which he participated, a Boston College campus ministry trip to El Salvador. Trips like this are not valued primarily for the direct service or aid that the students may render to the poor and marginalized—the concrete work done by a handful of students in a week or ten days is hardly enough to make a significant impact in the ocean of misery that the trips reveal. Rather, the primary purpose of the trip is to transform the students into people who care about the suffering of the poor and will return from these trips inspired to act to reduce the suffering of poverty, not only immediately upon their return, but throughout their lives. Immersion trips are predicated on the assumption that this transformation is more far-reaching and important than any work done on the trip, and will ultimately lead to a more just world.

Unfortunately, a trip that concentrates so much upon the effect on the traveler runs the unintended risk of devolving into a kind of "poverty tourism" that projects disrespect for those visited. I have also known students to return from such trips with a misguided gratitude for the comforts and luxuries of their own lives, or with a depressive sense of their own impotence in the face of massive suffering. Neither of these attitudes contributes to a strong desire to transform the world to reduce poverty. Guiding and challenging students who go on immersion trips with careful intellectual reflection can prevent these undesirable outcomes. This reflection must also allow students to ask questions critical of the entire enterprise, so that it is not seen as being in the service of any single political ideology. For example, Pope describes how the Boston College campus ministry trip to El Salvador specifically develops students' skills, including "active listening, paying attention, asking appropriate and thoughtful questions and taking seriously the words and self-expression of one's hosts."[15]

Pope offers a detailed account of how such trips encourage personal transformation on three levels. Social transformation consists in an awareness of the scope of global injustice and a sense of personal responsibility, a transformation best facilitated through face-to-face encounters. This transformation ideally changes the way that students regard their own cultural context and opportunities, which includes but is not limited to recognizing the ways in which they are privileged socially and economically. Students also experience a moral transformation that leads them to act more responsibly. Pope describes how the experience of an immersion trip has led some

students to more careful moral reflection in their personal and sexual relationships, as the habits of reflection, critical thinking, and considering the
consequences of one's actions (or inaction) spill over into other aspects of
their lives. Just as service learning courses provide an opportunity for syn-
thesizing what students have learned in the classroom across their university education, immersion trips provide an opportunity for moral synthesis,
leading to more thoughtful moral behavior.[16]

Finally, Pope describes a spiritual transformation that includes both a
heightened sense of the sacred and a deeper understanding of Christian life
"as animated by faith, hope and charity," as a result of meeting and forming a relationship with people who live lives of Christian hope and charity
in circumstances of dire injustice.[17] These changes are affective as well as
cognitive, as powerful emotional experiences take place alongside thoughtful and rigorous reflection. Students who go on these trips are converted to
a life of deeper solidarity with marginalized people. They may feel guilty
about their privileged status, but this is not the point of the trips—the point
is to make them into people who will work to change the world.[18] They
learn that individual acts of mercy and kindness are a necessary but not
sufficient response to the massive suffering of poverty. As a result of these
trips, some students have enlisted in the Jesuit Volunteer Corps, changed
their career paths or chosen different fields of graduate study as they move
toward professions and lifestyles that are more likely to transform the social order.[19]

It is worth repeating that there is no pretence, for either Pope or Heyer,
that the service rendered to the poor and marginalized people by the students involved in these programs is the primary purpose of the programs.
They do not, of course, discount the positive effect of the work. But the
primary goal of the service learning courses and immersion experiences as
they are described in both cases is the transformation and education of the
students ostensibly doing the service. In this regard, these programs privilege Buckley and Kolvenbach's desired outcome—a person who is aware of
the massive suffering caused by poverty and injustice, who cares about the
people who undergo that suffering, and who is committed to reducing or
eliminating that suffering by reforming unjust social structures and conditions.

In each of these cases, students witness and interiorize the suffering of
marginalized people. They form relationships with poor people that will

result in what Buckley described as a "disciplined sensitivity to human misery," a "humane sensibility and educated awareness" of human suffering.[20] For the introductory informational courses in Buckley's revised humanist curriculum, these programs substitute the raw power of direct contact with the poor and suffering. Heyer's description of community-based learning suggests that one thoughtful and well-structured theology course may at least initiate progress toward the goal of educating students to be more sensitive to and aware of human misery. Pope's analysis of the effect of immersion trips on students demonstrates that such powerful experiences can be lifted beyond a kind of emotional manipulation through the use of careful reflection and critical thinking. Heyer and Pope recognize, however, that a series of powerful emotional experiences does not a university education make. The experience is therefore analyzed and understood through careful reflection that is based upon theology, philosophy and social science.

I have shown that "education for justice" may be more accurately described as a process that produces a person who has been made aware of the suffering caused by poverty and social injustice, who cares about those who endure this suffering, and who manifests a commitment to act to relieve that suffering. I would argue that this process, at least as we have described it so far, has very little to do with justice as such. The outcome sought is a more just world, but the process begins with the cultivation of mercy—one of the "unfashionable" words that were deliberately excluded from the statements of the 32nd General Congregation.

Education for Mercy

According to Thomas Aquinas, mercy is the love that responds to the distress or suffering of another person.[21] Because they cultivate mercy as a re-action to the suffering of poverty, service learning, immersion trips, and other experiences guided by the outcomes described above demonstrate that the preferential option for the poor is alive and well on Catholic university campuses. Instead of direct institutional action to transform the social order and reduce the suffering of poverty, the preferential option for the poor in this case is a systematic commitment to forming students who will themselves be more likely to make choices and evaluate their own status and opportunities in light of the reality of poverty and its attendant suffering. In other words, one meaningful way in which universities make the preferential option for the poor is by forming students who themselves make the preferential option for the poor. But what is meant by the preferential option for the poor?

Defining the preferential option for the poor has always been problematic. For the institutional church, it has functioned as an imperative which directs the church's pastoral work to benefit the poor.[22] The preferential option is intended not only to direct the pastoral actions of the church itself, but also to evaluate the actions and obligations of individuals, institutions, and governments. The Catholic Bishops of the United States have written that the preferential option should be used "to assess lifestyles, policies and social institutions in terms of their impact on the poor."[23] Theologians have argued that the preferential option constitutes a hermeneutical privilege of the oppressed, and requires that theology be done from the standpoint of those who suffer unjustly in poverty. In light of this diversity of opinion, David O'Brien suggests that Catholic universities may undertake the preferential option in three distinct manners. First and foremost, it is a theological statement about God's love of and commitment to the poor. Second, it is for scholars a hermeneutical principle "demanding that one self-consciously examine things from the standpoint of the poor."[24] Finally, it is a moral imperative that makes demands, although O'Brien concedes that "it is far from clear exactly what those demands are."[25] O'Brien describes various activities at Holy Cross University as manifestations of the University's commitment to the preferential option for the poor, including service days and service-learning experiences, common enough at Catholic and non-Catholic universities.

I would argue that the immersion trips and service learning experiences described above demonstrate that the university makes the preferential option most radically by educating students to make the preferential option themselves. These experiences lead students to reevaluate the world and their place in it in light of the massive suffering of poverty; this corresponds to O'Brien's description of the preferential option as a hermeneutic principle. Direct experiences of the suffering of poverty may lead students to undertake direct action to alleviate the suffering of poverty, to study how their chosen disciplines of study affect structures of poverty, or to engage in more responsible moral behavior in other areas of their lives, and in this manner the preferential option for the poor functions for students as a moral imperative. Finally, these experiences facilitate a spiritual transformation that leads students to reevaluate their relationship with God and with the Christian community; this corresponds to O'Brien's description of the theological dimension of the preferential option. The process produces students who have made a preferential option for the poor, and whose future actions will be shaped by this fundamental choice.

In these examples, students are encouraged to make the preferential option for the poor through mercy, that is, a love of compassion in response to the suffering of another. The relationship between the reaction of mercy and the preferential option is so important that Jon Sobrino has suggested that mercy is simply another name for the option for the poor. In "The Samaritan Church and the Principle of Mercy," Sobrino argues that mercy provided a basic structure and orientation for the life of Jesus. Therefore, mercy should provide the basic orientation and structure for the life of the church as well. Sobrino describes mercy as having to do with compassion, but not being limited to it. He recognizes that mercy can have inadequate, even "dangerous" connotations.[26] Mercy may be associated with individual works of mercy that do not address the injustice that is the root cause of the suffering of poverty. Therefore, mercy must not be understood as focusing on the alleviation of individual needs at the expense of a commitment to changing unjust social structures,

> *By the principle of mercy, we understand here a specific love, which, while standing at the origin of a process, also remains present and active throughout the process, endowing it with a particular direction and shaping the various elements that compose it.*[27]

That specific love called mercy results from interiorizing the suffering of another human being; this is the moment "at the origin" of the process to which Sobrino refers. Allowing another person's suffering to penetrate one's own heart is "the first principle and foundation" of mercy.[28] For Jesus, this reaction to suffering shapes his entire life and directs his actions. Mercy is a form of love, but it is a specific kind of love, a love that responds to suffering (for Sobrino, particularly unjustly afflicted suffering). Jesus offers the Good Samaritan as the ideal human being because he reacts with mercy to the suffering of the beaten man and in so doing acts to eliminate his suffering. The Good Samaritan is willing to be taken out of his way and is moved by the plight of the victim.

Sobrino argues that the church, in order to be guided by the principle of mercy, must be "de-centered," that is, must locate itself with those who suffer unjustly, must "set off down the road where the wounded lie."[29] To respond to suffering, of course, one must encounter suffering. The first step in Buckley's curriculum of the new humanism, Heyer's community-based learning and Pope's immersion trip all provide that encounter in an intentional and structured way.

For Sobrino, the Principle of Mercy is simply a restatement of the preferential option for the poor to which the institutional church is committed.[30] The preferential option is often stated or defined as a principle guiding public or institutional policy and pastoral choices, as in the documents of the first meeting of the Latin American episcopate or in the US Catholic Bishops' pastoral letter on the economy.[31] For Catholic higher education, the option for the poor is frequently understood as a measure of institutional commitment to eliminating the social injustice that causes poverty and through service and direct action. But I would argue that the preferential option on a personal level must begin with a personal transformation, a conversion, to caring about the suffering of others through contact with those who suffer. The resulting orientation or disposition to alleviate that suffering, a disposition which guides one's actions and moral choices, can be thought of as a *personal* preferential option for the poor.

Encouraging students to make a preferential option for the poor through a conversion to mercy is a complicated matter. Such a project places the university precisely in the business of the moral formation of students, an endeavor that was abandoned amid significant criticism in the middle of the last century. I would like to examine some of the inherent problems of such a project, offer some remedies for these, and finally suggest a broader and more holistic approach to education for justice that established it even more firmly within the Catholic and Christian tradition.

Catholic Higher Education and the Moral Formation of Students

In 1955, John Tracy Ellis famously challenged the state of Catholic higher education in the United States, pointing out that religious instruction at Catholic colleges and universities was focused upon moral training at the expense of intellectual development.[32] This critique presaged a sea-change in the structure and focus of theology in Catholic higher education. Departments became more professionalized and offered more intellectually challenging courses. At the same time, theology or religious studies departments became more important as representatives of the university's Catholic identity, as other academic units, especially philosophy departments, became more intellectually diverse.[33] Graduate programs in theology and the changing nature of theological education itself led in turn to theology and religious studies departments reflecting more intellectual and confessional diversity.[34] The movement towards teaching specialized and intellectually challenging undergraduate courses is at odds with the reality that most Catholic university students in the United States today know very little of the basics of their religion, and many of the students are not in fact Catholic.[35] Students are less catechized than ever, but theology in the university has moved decisively away from a pre-Vatican II emphasis on catechesis.[36]

As we have seen, education for justice begins with encouraging students to be empathetic, to witness and be transformed by the suffering of others, and to experience a moral conversion into the kind of person who seeks to change the world to alleviate the suffering of others. So Catholic higher education has not abandoned moral formation, but it has instead embraced a new set of moral values and a different kind of moral formation, one more widely accepted in our increasingly fragmented religious environment. Through experiences that allow them to form relationships with people who are suffering, students are encouraged to become people who care about the suffering of others enough to work to reduce or eliminate that suffering. A moral transformation takes place, one based upon contact which develops sympathy for those who suffer.

I consider this a worthy project but believe that Ellis's critique of the previous concern with moral formation in Catholic higher education should be kept in mind. These experiences should be conducted and analyzed with intellectual rigor. Stephen Pope's analysis of the theological and anthropological dimensions of the transformation and conversion wrought by these experiences is a helpful model. It is not enough to expose students to suffering and expect a worldview-altering transformation to result. Only serious and rigorous intellectual reflection will help students to interpret their experience and direct their future actions. As Pope's treatment of the immersion experience demonstrates, theology is uniquely equipped to provide such analysis and also provide guidance in designing and following up on these experiences; Heyer demonstrates that theology classes at the introductory and more advanced levels provide an ideal setting for service learning. Theology here is not necessarily a formal architectonic discipline which orders the place or interaction of other disciplines within the university; theology is the discipline that provides the vocabulary and concepts that will help students to understand the life-changing experiences that the university is more and more frequently encouraging—even requiring—them to undergo. Theology can help a student to make sense out of an experience of mercy and to understand it as such, and also to make the connection between that experience and the reevaluation of one's place in the world, including a commitment to working for a more just social order. An experience of the suffering of the world that is unaccompanied by sufficient theological analysis is unlikely to produce the desired outcome of the fully conscientized student. An experience of the suffering of the world that is mediated by theological reflection, however, will produce a student who is more compassionate and more theologically and religiously literate.

Catholic Identity and Education for Justice: Brief Reflections from a Mercy Idiom

I have shown that what has commonly been called "education for justice" begins with education for mercy. Catholic universities have often made the preferential option for the poor by forming students, faculty, and staff to make a personal preferential option for the poor, in the spirit of liberation theologians like Sobrino and Gustavo Gutiérrez, whose theological method and scholarship have been decisively influenced by their relationships with those who suffer in poverty. These observations lead me to make some practical suggestions regarding the relationship between justice and Catholic identity in institutions of higher education.

For institutions with growing numbers of non-Catholic faculty, staff, and students, justice offers significant advantages as a value informing Catholic identity because it is a value or virtue that transcends individual faith commitments and does not depend exclusively upon religious warrants. Buckley, Kolvenbach, and the other participants in General Congregation 32 recognized that the language of justice is a powerful tool to be used in the service of reducing the misery of human beings living in poverty. The language of justice, however, provides an incomplete account of what Catholic universities are in fact doing as they form students to be committed to alleviating the suffering of poverty and transforming the social order. Mercy, as Jon Sobrino states, is at the origin of this process, and continues to guide the process of educating a more humane student. Analysis of these experiences must therefore attend to the theological meaning and religious value of mercy.

I teach at Misericordia University, founded and sponsored by the Religious Sisters of Mercy. Discussions of identity and attempts to include identity in curricular and other institutional commitments rarely mention justice and service apart from mercy and hospitality. These four charisms of the Sisters of Mercy together encompass a range of values that are central to Catholicism without being exclusively Catholic. Hospitality, like mercy, is rooted in the recognition that all human beings have dignity. Hospitality encourages action, and action directed at those who need help—strangers, those on the margins of society, the excluded. Like justice, it is a practice rooted in Christian values and the affirmation of the dignity and value of God-created human life, but its practice is not dependent upon Christian warrants. Like mercy, hospitality responds to human relationships and human contact, and accounts for the role that these have in promoting and reinforcing ethical behavior.

Christine Pohl has described some of the unfortunate consequences of the identification of hospitality with institutions and civic entities rather than the home and small community.[37] The practice of hospitality has become less frequent and personal, and more difficult. Pohl also suggests, however, that hospitality may be practiced not only by welcoming a stranger into one's home or place, but by recognizing in that stranger a human being with dignity, and by identifying with the suffering of that person.[38] Hospitality requires dealing directly with a person and treating that person with respect; simply addressing physical needs is not sufficient.[39] These service learning experiences and immersion trips which place students in contact with marginalized people and encourage them to form relationships based on mutual respect are exercises of hospitality as much as they are exercises in justice and mercy. Hospitality emphasizes the human dignity of the person being helped, and this is a helpful counterweight to any paternalism or lack of respect that may be suggested by mercy, which has been too often identified with pity.

Hospitality also embraces the Ignatian notion that love is found in deeds and not words:

The practice of hospitality forces abstract commitments to loving the

*neighbor, stranger and enemy into practical and personal expressions
of respect and care for actual neighbors, strangers and enemies....
Claims of loving all humankind, of welcoming "the other" have to be
accompanied by the hard work of actually welcoming a human being
into a real place.*[40]

In the case of the education for justice, that real place into which the stranger is invited is the University itself. The effect of experiences that expose students to the suffering of the poor, the marginalized, and the vulnerable is to invite the experience of the poor, the lived reality of poverty into the University's curriculum and research. This understanding of hospitality is not an abstraction; we have seen how these experiences lead to real transformations and moral choices.

In this age of outcomes assessment in higher education, it would be interesting to know if university graduates who have done service learning, gone on immersion trips, or had other experiences meant to foster solidarity with the poor are in fact more likely to engage in activity that transforms the social order and reduces the suffering of poverty. This would be difficult, at best, to determine. In the meantime, I would argue that undergraduate education is better served by an intentional and rigorous theological analysis of the experiences that often initiate and inform what we have called education for justice, and that this entire educational enterprise is better and more accurately understood as education for mercy, hospitality and justice through service.

Theology as Architectonic Wisdom in the Catholic University: Promise and Problems

BRIAN W. HUGHES, UNIVERSITY OF SAINT MARY

CATHOLIC THEOLOGIANS WHO WORRY ABOUT the academic nature and future of theology in the Catholic university understand many of its problems. The fragmentation of knowledge, the pervasive utilitarian ethos of the academy, the incoherence in the various sequences of undergraduate theology requirements, the general suspicion by colleagues about theology's value, and the unpreparedness of students for college rigor coupled with their breathtaking religious illiteracy are just a few.[1] It does not help the situation of Catholic theology to know that institutional Catholicism is doing a poor job of nourishing the lives of its members. According to the 2008 Pew Forum U.S. Religious Landscape Survey, "Catholicism has experienced the greatest net losses as a result of affiliation changes. While nearly one-in-three Americans (31%) were raised in the Catholic faith, today fewer than one-in-four (24%) describe themselves as Catholic." The survey also reveals that less than half of all U.S. Catholics finish *or even attend* an institution of higher education.[2] Given these statistics, many theologians might wonder if theology really makes any difference at all in the broader church aside from its contributions to the small number of students—Catholic or not—who take university theology courses.

If this portrait gives good grounds for realistic pessimism concerning theology's prospects within the Church and university, Terry Eagleton sketches the deeper problem for theology's relevance within contemporary culture at large.

> *The advanced capitalist system is inherently atheistic. It is godless in its actual material practices, and in the values and beliefs implicit in them, whatever some of its apologists might piously aver.... A society of packaged fulfillment, administered desire, managerialized politics, and consumerist economics is unlikely to cut to the kind of depth where theological questions can even be properly raised, just as [it] rules out political and moral questions of a certain profundity.*[3]

119

Eagleton touches on a critical point here: the cultural (and academic) marginalization of theology makes it difficult to raise questions of depth and meaning on a broader scale. When the issue concerns Catholic theology's place and contribution to the nature of a Catholic university, we cannot accept such questioning within the limited confines of a class. Theology must somehow reach beyond the course, beyond the specialization of its professors, and reach the university community more deeply. In this way, theology might be better positioned to focus academic attention on the vital questions at the intersection of Christ and culture.

In this chapter, I want to explore different ways and challenges to how theology might accomplish this goal. The first part examines Michael J. Buckley's argument for Catholic theology as an architectonic wisdom. Next, I will show how Edward Farley's work to recover theology as a personal sapiential *habitus* builds upon Buckley's proposal, giving Buckley's argument more concrete contours and detail. Finally, I will examine a serious challenge to Buckley's vision advanced by Gavin D'Costa. Unlike Buckley and Farley, D'Costa does not believe theology can fulfill its promise within the contemporary secular or Catholic university. He argues for a post-liberal Catholic university as the best context in which the conditions for theology and its practitioners will flourish. By selecting Farley and D'Costa, my aim is to take seriously Buckley's proposal by demonstrating its possibilities and challenges.

Theology as Architectonic Wisdom

Michael Buckley advances an important argument for serious academic and practical consideration: theology needs to be an architectonic wisdom in the Catholic university. As such, theology would become more vital as a discipline, serve the theological education of students more deeply, and strengthen the identity of the university as Catholic. Theology as architectonic wisdom comes out of Buckley's key premise about the Catholic university. He writes: "The fundamental proposition that grounds the Catholic university is that the academic and the religious are intrinsically related, that they form an inherent unity, that one is incomplete without the other."[4] This proposition itself builds on Buckley's view of the transcending intellect, which to reach completion must ever press beyond the limits of knowledge, raising further questions that expand toward a more comprehensive understanding of reality.[5] Human intelligence never remains satisfied with one area, field, or piece of knowledge, but desires to push questions into larger frames of reference and coherence. In the end, such questioning unavoidably raises topics of ultimacy, meaning, purpose, and God. This dynamism of the human intellect allows the Catholic university to be paradigmatically the union of knowledge and the divine, the relationship between human culture and the ordered reflection upon faith.[6]

The challenge for any Catholic institution of higher education will be the integration of the religious and the academic. One major expression and interest of Buckley's concerns the nature, function, and place of theology within such institutions. As indicated above, Buckley calls for theology to become an architectonic wisdom. By this term, he does not mean some quaint or antique role for theology to be "queen" of the sciences once again, holding a consensus of master and issuing pronouncements of orthodox approval or censure upon other departments, studies, faculty and students. Such an imperial view, though it might be what theologically ignorant figures such as Richard Dawkins and Christopher Hitchens imagine theology to strive for, has nothing to do with Buckley's proposal.[7] For Buckley, theology as wisdom must be in vital contact with university disciplines. Contact, however, does not mean imposition or control. By contact with other disciplines, Buckley's view of architectonic is perhaps better understood as unrestricted engagement. In part, the notion of architectonic calls for a re-envisioning of theology's genre from specialty field (such as Patristic theology or Second Temple Judaism) or predominantly clerical knowledge to a hermeneutical habit of mind. As Buckley puts it,

> *Theology... must not be seen as one science among others, self-contained in its own integrity and adjacent to the other forms of disciplined human knowledge. It is more like a place, a place within which the critical thought and developed habits of reasoning in the arts and sciences are encouraged and their ineluctable movement toward questions of ultimacy taken seriously. Such questions of ultimacy are not simply about interlocking content, but are even about the absolute commitments entailed by serious teaching and inquiry themselves. This is theology as an architectonic wisdom rather than as a particular* Wissenschaft, *theology as one wisdom within which disciplines are distinct but not separate.*[8]

The important point here is that theology is one unified matrix of critical thinking rather than several different but related branches of knowledge. Knowledge can always be further analyzed and segmented, sometimes by specialized vocabulary or historical partitions. Nevertheless, within the dynamism of human intelligence, the need for larger frames of reference spurred on by integrative questions naturally seeks connection, relationships, and mutual coherence. The deeper implication for theological study and for theology's place in the university is that in its own compositional nature, Christian theology, whether defined as reflection on religious experience or the self-understanding of the Christian mysteries, is and must be interdisciplinary. This is precisely why Buckley holds so strongly for the presence of the liberal arts within the undertaking of theological reflection. History, philosophy, language, and interpretation are university disciplines in their own right. Such skills are already present, however, when one starts theological study and never remain absent from the scope and depth of questions, topics, and issues that theology takes up. Buckley would like to see renewed attention to the underlying patterns of hermeneutical emphases that take place in the doing of theological inquiry.[9]

Another implication of theology as architectonic extends beyond undergraduate or graduate courses. If good theology contributes to the identity of a Catholic college or university, this character cannot be simply the responsibility of the theology or religious studies faculty and department. The entire university must in some real way support the discussion of topics, questions, and forums that somehow connect to theological and religious questions of ultimate meaning, value, purpose, and concrete transformation for human betterment. On a curricular level, Buckley cites the initiative of Santa Clara University to focus courses

> *in the arts and sciences and professional schools together around a single topic [war].... The integrative function of theology here was twofold: to raise and press in critical Socratic fashion a question of common and urgent importance; and to contribute to a common effort that both traced something of war's pervasive presence within every aspect of human experience and moved to the resolution of some of its many issues. In this way, theology provided for common critical reflection among all the university disciplines, accomplishing a collaborative reflection unachievable by any of these disciplines taken separately.[10]*

Several outcomes follow. First, theology more directly engages with different types of knowledge, argument, and evidence from across the spectrum of human understanding. This would be a positive development since theologians are primarily rewarded and advanced for their increased specialization, particularization, and publications of one narrow way of understanding a dimension of a particular subject matter. Graduates of master's and doctoral programs are trained to be specialists in the image of their distinguished teachers who are primarily narrow researchers themselves.

Second, Buckley's concern here is about the temptation, and all too often the reality, of Catholic theology falling victim to "fad or prejudice or ideology" that can occur when reflection becomes too insular and abstracted from possible correctives that other disciplines might bring.[11] Correctives that might come from other disciplines such as biology, physics, business, sociology, and psychology help good theology in confronting contemporary issues of concern to human beings. Buckley touches on the order of topics or procedure concerning the derivation of theological questions that, in the university and interdisciplinary context, can become questions of common engagement and serious inquiry. In other words, what should the focus of theology be? There is no single answer given the inevitable and healthy pluralism alive within the rigorous examination of issues that emerge from human experience. For Buckley, the vital questions for theological exploration must emerge from the problematic of our own 21st-century context. This is not to say that specialized studies in, say, late seventeenth-century French spirituality are unimportant in a university education, but such studies particularize and deepen what must be primary in a common learning experience that draws different groups together since the problems will be common: What should be done about the growing number of unemployed persons in America? What should civic duty be towards the environment, given the present and future effects of climate change? How should we view and treat the immigrant, or the prisoners at Guantanamo Bay? Who should be helped by health care and where should government dollars be spent most effectively? What should citizens and churches be doing about the growing misery of the poor in the United States and in third world countries? Where is God in all this? All such questions when raised touch on subjects of freedom, justice, human society, the nature of community, the common good, health, purpose, the nature of human dignity and fulfillment. All these topics and so many others intersect with knowledge, principles, and values embedded in different but related disciplines, including the wisdom of theology.

As an architectonic, one could envision theology proceeding to do at least two things, according to Buckley. Within a multi-disciplinary seminar, talk, or sequence of courses, wherever diverse members of an academic community gather, the implications of any aforementioned question can be related to God or the church or Christ, on the one hand. On the other hand, theology can judge the humanitarian/spiritual/moral effects of given lines of argument or the conclusions of public or foreign policy decisions.[12] Buckley is convinced—with Karl Rahner—that theology must not begin with the questions, symbols, or doctrines so past and removed from human experience today.[13] Theology must start with the desires, problems, and situations that call out for explanation, solution, and clarification, ones that people struggle through today. In either approach, the more deeply the Catholic university pursues questions vital to humanity, the greater its contact will be with that mystery Christians call divine.

The issue of human desires and problems and situations, however, raises an important question: How might teachers and students who want to do theology closer to their own contextual experiences proceed? Buckley does not provide a theoretical framework for how to connect the various human situations with the elements of the Christian tradition. Indeed, even his proposal for the "theological arts" remains formal and removed from a more applicable framework for the doing of theology at different levels. It is precisely here that the work of Edward Farley becomes important. His understanding of theology and its hermeneutic modes offers a compelling way to structure theological study today.

Theological Hermeneutics and the Genre of Wisdom

Buckley's proposal is more an ideal than a concrete set of curricular prescriptions. His proposal considers the broad sweep of the entire Catholic university or college community. Still, though, he mentions theology in reference to graduate and undergraduate students, what he means by *audience* is relatively undeveloped. What one finds in Buckley's argument is the necessity for different theological arts to be developed and used to refine the sources of theological engagement with the vital questions of faith and culture. Who could accomplish this, and how such a theological education might proceed, are issues left untreated. Obviously, there is a difference between doctoral students in theology and typical undergraduates who will likely take only the minimum required theology courses. Edward Farley's work on the nature of theology and theological education offers a way to fill in some of the spaces Buckley's vision leaves undeveloped. Two, in particular, merit attention. The way that theology becomes a sapiential knowledge is the first. Second, Farley discusses theological education for different groups of students.

First, we need to explore theology's genre more specifically. Buckley wants to retain the term "architectonic." This effort is deeply problematic for Farley. In the medieval sense of the term, *architectonic* had a dual meaning. It could refer to theology as a sapiential habit of mind (knowledge of God and the things of God) or it could mean a discrete body of knowledge, a faculty science. This is what we think of as "science" today. For Farley, this latter meaning came to dominate what scholars designated as "architectonic," leading to efforts by theologians to arrange theology atop the pyramid of progressive theological encyclopedias, seeking ways to justify the inclusion of this body of knowledge amidst courses of university study.[14] Schleiermacher's outline for theology is the best-known example, along with that by Johann Sebastian Drey.[15] One could justify theology within the university or a course of studies by placing it alongside law and medicine as a professional area of knowledge necessary for practical undertakings.[16] By defining theology as a professional undertaking, theologians like Schleiermacher and others turn theology into discrete specialty fields and pedagogical areas (e.g., systematics, Bible, ethics, church history) that comprise clergy education. In each case, the term or goal of theology was practical care of souls and service to institutional church life.[17] Consequently, Farley thinks the older and more correct meaning of "architectonic" is too freighted with the modern sense of science to be of any value. Theologians who use this term and refer to it in the legacy of science—as discrete bodies of knowledge—actually move further away from the richer meaning of theology as *one science*. These theologians seek some configuration of *sciences* in hopes of satisfying what theological study comprises. Without the unity of a personal sapiential *habitus*, the different divisions that mark theological faculty make the subject matter and the unity of theology deeply unclear.[18] For this reason, Farley drops the term entirely.[19] He argues that one of the major problems with theological education is the shift in the understanding of theology from a unified hermeneutic or personal *habitus* of wisdom to a more specialized paradigm of diverse sciences and pedagogical areas. For theology to be vital within the university, however, it must be broader. He writes:

> *What I propose is a... way of thinking about theological study which neither reduces it to clergy education nor partitions it into sciences. It conceives theology to be a certain kind of reflective, interpretive activity, and its natural structure or pattern to be constituted by modes of interpretation. It follows from this conception that theological study can occur in church congregations, clergy schools, and universities. As a pedagogy, theological study disciplines modes of interpretation, and it does that by availing itself of the full resources of scholarship for the inquiry into its subject matter, the Christian faith.*[20]

This fascinating history and argument of how theology changed from one unified wisdom to discrete specialty fields unfolds in his important book *Theologia*.[21] Consequences of this shift, which still persist in the vast majority of Protestant and Catholic divinity schools, seminaries, and university faculties, include the suppression of foundational hermeneutic modes that comprise theology and which cause incoherent theological formation. Toward overcoming these problems, as shown below, Farley proposes that theology be reconceived outside the categories of science, pedagogical area, and specialty field.

Theological Reflection Beyond Specialty Field

Sciences, especially in the modern sense, are discrete areas of scholarly investigation, intellectual activities of rigorous empirical methods and research. They are focused abstractions upon the human and natural world that can be further differentiated into physical, social, mechanical, and functional sub-fields and sub-disciplines. Each science has its respective methods and what counts as criteria for sound advancement. As the success of the different sciences depends upon a rigorous focus and deeper levels of analysis with all of their specialized vocabulary, however, there is what Farley calls the "tragic character" of inevitable "distortion of its (science's) object." He states:

> *Any abstracting act necessarily suspends consideration of the total concrete entity, its total contact and environment and its essential*

unrepeatability over time. Any specific entity—an enzyme, a rural village, a human emotion—occurs as a synthesis of aspects and dimension and in a vast web of relations. To pursue any cognitive problem—for example, why the crime rate in a rural village has increased by twenty percent in one year—is to place in suspension most of the entity's contents and relations. The tragedy lies in the essentially unresolvable tension between the abstracted or focused aspect and the synthetic (concrete) character of what is under consideration.[22]

Correctives to the distortion can, he argues, simplistically be understood as parts to wholes. Better grasp of a phenomenon occurs when one is conscious of viewing something from a perspectival emphasis that is not total. Each dimension of reality requires supporting perspectival emphases to understand it more accurately within larger and larger contexts of meaning and greater patterns of interconnection.[23]

As I move toward discussing Farley's proposal of foundational hermeneutic modes as structuring theological study, it is important to understand how sciences relate to pedagogical areas and disciplines. A pedagogical area, for Farley, "is a corporately pursued subject matter that exists within some larger arrangement of subject matter that reflects the aims of teaching. High school teachers of English occupy a pedagogical area and so do teachers of auto mechanics, real estate, and business finance in technical schools."[24] Pedagogical areas are broader than sciences, though they may be "based" on them. A discipline connects a pedagogical area to scientific research and scholarly inquiry. The "aims of pedagogy and the aims of science" are combined in a particular discipline.[25] Farley provides a good example of the difference, noting that "middle-school biology is a pedagogical area but not a discipline. Graduate school, research-oriented biology is a discipline."[26] For Farley, disciplines connect "instruction, teaching, learning" but they are not defined by a particular configuration of subject matters.[27] Why these distinctions are important concerns the audience that would be expected to understand and participate in theology as a sapiential habit of mind or one "architectonic." Commentators on the state of Catholic higher education, Catholic identity, and the place of theology rarely—if ever—identify the ways theology can be understood in relation to science, discipline, or pedagogical area.[28]

Yet the main problem with the current state of theology as divided and practiced throughout higher education is its transformation from discipline to specialty field. For Farley, the specialty field displays several features that make it neither discipline nor science. I will highlight three of them: professionalization, the university reward system, and a narrow empirical paradigm of knowledge.[29] Professionalization is a gradual, historical process that establishes normative criteria, standardized training, credentialing, and accrediting through socially recognizable organizations (such as the guild, the state). In graduate programs, professionalism is everywhere. One normally finds standard sequences of courses across denominational programs, including similar distribution requirements, scholarly languages requirements, comprehensive exams, professional societies, annual conferences, and peer reviewed publications. All of these dimensions enforce explicit or implicit norms of who is judged to be scholarly, what passes for good scholarship, and thus satisfies accepted standards for academic competence. Theology's specialty fields are most present in graduate programs, which train the young scholar-to-be in the accepted canons of content, scope, paradigms, and current methodologies. The university reward system functions to promote those who successfully navigate the professional hoops and produce research judged sound by the invisible group of scholars that determine a field's standards. Doctoral students and entry level and tenure-track professors must define ever-smaller areas in which to publish and thus become recognized enough by similar authorities to receive tenure. The professionalization acquired during graduate studies mitigates against achieving the breadth one might expect a degree in theology or religion to bestow. The problem is that the requirements for landing scholarly positions and thriving in the university department depend not on breadth, but upon ever more specialized research and publication. Though standards for survival and promotion in higher education appear similar, they vary in practice from institution to institution. Teaching-intensive institutions privilege teaching and service while larger, more national ones favor faculty research, grants, and publications. Nevertheless, for scholars who write in each context and not merely teach, the focus of one's research, due to pressures of time, family, committees, and other forms of university service, inevitably continues and promotes the specialized research started in graduate school.[30] Scholars have little time for much else. In the end, writes Farley, "the reward system encourages the scholar-teacher to begin in and remain in a specialty field: it affords little or no chance to explore broader territories, alternate paradigms, or the contours of the discipline itself."[31]

The next feature, narrow empiricism, can refer to the ongoing scholarship produced in and encouraged by the narrow work undertaken in graduate school and supported by the rigors of obtaining, maintaining, and advancing one's academic career. The effects of narrow teaching and even more specialized research mean that most departments of theology and religion are staffed by specialists—not by those who actually practice a discipline, a science, or even a pedagogical area (though their courses fall under them, e.g., Bible).[32] These specialists are nurtured by the dominant narrow paradigm that reigns in the academy. In large part, the success of one paradigm of reality, that is, the quantitative-measurable model presupposed by the "physical and engineering sciences" have come—due to their stunning scientific and technological achievements—to dominate as the overall model for reality generally, rather than being understood as one paradigm among others (e.g., religious, literary, aesthetic).[33] Indeed, as Felix Wilfred rightly observes, "The information society tends to think that the quantitative profusion of information amounts to quality and value, and that the *production of more data is equal to greater truth*—a delusion to which theology and religious studies are in danger of falling prey."[34] Another effect of the empirical sciences' success in higher education generally is surely the multiplying and accreditation-driven assessment outcomes that proliferate across undergraduate course syllabi. Instructors are increasingly required to link assignments with specific departmental and course outcomes that can be measured and quantified into statistics for accreditation reports, agencies, licensure boards, and the like. The problem with this empirical model not simply for teaching but for the humanities generally is that one cannot quantify or statistically measure the quality of a liberally educated mind through rubrics, grades, or idealized outcomes. They only tell part of the story. The rise of the assessment obsession in the academy is one effect of the narrowing focus of the empirical paradigm spread out, collected, quantified, and implicitly assumed to be what counts as knowledge in the academy.[35] What John Henry Newman spoke of so compellingly as the philosophic habit of mind was never, for him, the conclusion of quantitative or scientific analysis and thus demonstrable through repeated experiment and verification. Farley would agree:

Humanistic scholarship reflects the paradigm when it construes its subject matter as discrete units—say, the images of color in a novel, the cluster of publicly visible facts and occurrences that form the surface of a past event. When the paradigm becomes an ontological paradigm, a paradigm of reality itself, its paradigmatic character will go into hiding. When reality is taken to be revealed in abstracted units of explanation, the complexity and dimensionality of reality will be excluded by a methodological decision.[36]

The complexity and dimensionality of a subject matter or a thing suffers not from what intensive focus reveals, but from what intense focus excludes and conceals. To some degree, the intensive focus and promotion of a particular form or perspective at the expense of others is natural. As Nicholas Lash wittily observes, "We worship things as naturally as we breathe and speak. But that is the problem—untutored, we set our hearts on *things*: on forces, elements, ideas; on people, dreams, and institutions; on the world or on some item of its furnishing. We are spontaneously idolatrous."[37] This is the deeper issue of suppressing the dimensionality of knowledge and of the rise of uniform interpretation due to the empirical paradigm.[38]

The distortion effected by the nature of specialized inquiry as such also means that an intelligent attentiveness to alternative perspectival emphases provided by the other disciplines and specialty fields becomes harder to achieve. Two consequences follow for Farley. A subject's genuine multidimensional reality (e.g., historical, aesthetic, religious) becomes suppressed since a specialty field brackets other dimensions in order to pursue its line of inquiry. "With the suppression of dimensions," writes Farley, "disciplines are redefined as ways of organizing specialties of one-dimensional inquiry. Eliminated or discredited in the university are teaching areas that have the character of perspectival emphases; these include philosophy, religious studies, and the fine arts."[39] Second, this narrowing means that the question of something's "truth" becomes obscured. Farley defines knowledge as "the experience of being laid hold of by evidencing realities."[40] The empirical paradigm of knowledge that reigns across the different departments, disciplines, and specialty fields, however, tends to see the issue of "truth with a descriptive and phenomenological interest in their subject matter."[41] Students in religious studies and theology courses are infrequently called on to consider the implications of a claim of whatever doctrine, idea, or situation as being true and thus as having a real claim upon their lives. Instead, it is far more common for students to be asked for Geertzian thick descriptions or to repeat conclusions by specialists about the particular details of a religious tradition, historical event, ritual, or ethical practice. Assessment or evaluation that challenges one's assumptions and values gives way in practice to historical and phenomenal description.[42] Indeed, attempts to advocate or touch on questions of truth are risky in the current political climate of higher education. One example should suffice.

Kenneth Howell, adjunct professor at the University of Illinois, Urbana, and director of the Institute of Catholic Thought of the St. John's Catholic Newman Center, was presenting the Catholic teaching on the morality of homosexual acts in an introductory course on Catholicism. In a review email to the class, he wrote that, "Natural Moral Law says that Morality must be a response to REALITY.... In other words, sexual acts are only appropriate for people who are complementary, not the same." A student complained to the head of the religion department that Howell's email constituted discriminatory "hate speech." Shortly thereafter, Howell was fired from his teaching job in the university's department of religion after nine years there. He is appealing the decision, arguing that his email and pedagogy is protected by academic freedom.[43] This example shows, though it tends to be in the extreme category, that when professors touch on the truth of a moral or theological position, it can prove problematic in different ways.

Foundational Theological Hermeneutics

Farley's main contribution to the discussion about the structure of theological study is to recover the (earlier) meaning of theology as reflectively interpretive activities of the believer.[44] He also shows a way to refine Buckley's desire for theology to be restored as an architectonic within the Catholic university. There is, for Farley, a theological coherence and unity within what he argues to be elemental modes of interpretation. These modes of interpretation are nothing else than self-conscious ways of thinking towards different situations.[45] They can be seen as interconnected reference points, for the aims of theological understanding do overlap with aims of a liberal arts and university education: human beings aim to understand their concrete situation, to assess and judge the reality so interpreted, and finally to take action. The narrowing distortions of the specialty field can be corrected by focusing on how theology attends to one's more basic interpretation of situations. In addition, the surrounding political and economic influences that constantly alter shifting curricula within departments and embed cultural presuppositions of bias, idolatrous tendencies toward self-securing, power, gender, and race can more easily be identified as dimensions of theologically inflected interpretation. As types of interpretations, Farley grades some of these modes as more central than others.[46]

Human life, as concretely lived in the day-to-day, is a series of successive situations. Each situation—work, family, study, sport, a class, a meeting, waiting in traffic—involves ways of understanding the multi-dimensionality of that situation. A bank transaction involves factors such as social and cultural dynamics with the teller, mathematics, future or present purposes, the location, and other people. Situations are never singular experiences but a multitude of composite dimensions—if one is trained to see them. Yet the experience of the bank transaction is not life separated into sequential, discrete units of time or data but an integral whole. The situation is unified. Normally, people focus on a few dimensions of any situation, but there are always potentially more. Academic disciplines, analogously, break up the unity of experience into pedagogical areas that can be scrutinized. Mathematics, sociology, and architecture rigorize and further focus attention on what is available for interpretation in some situations.[47] Ordered learning disciplines and rigorizes the interpretative activity of the person who is naturally "normative, reality-oriented, interrogative, curious, and assessive."[48]

The situation of faith is a more particularized way of interpreting situations. Still, it is, for Farley, "a comprehensive mode of existence." "He describes it this way:

> *Christian faith, at least in its ideal expression, means existence—social and individual—in the mode of redemption.... Redemption is to the Christian unthinkable without the historical event, community, and tradition in which redemption is communicated and mediated (ecclesia); without the imagery and vision of the goodness, fragility, corruption, and hope of the human condition under the transcendent (gospel); and without a praxis-oriented existence, an existence in and toward the world in modes of obligation, forgiveness, and liberation (faith). Ecclesia, gospel, and faith become dimensions of the situations in which the Christian believer exists.*[49]

When he elaborates a bit more, Farley explains that the elemental modes of interpretation essential within faith are a distillation of interpenetrating and interdependent dimensions from this matrix. There are three: the interpretation of "the events and texts of tradition"; the interpretation of truth and reality under the gospel; and the interpretation of the tradition, truth and reality oriented towards action.[50] The strong point, for Farley, is that all of these are elemental modes that are "primordially present in faith."[51] These modes of themselves do not indicate a specific program of theological study or a precise series of courses departments might offer. They are more dimensions of Christian life in interpreting the multitude of real situations that emerge. Yet, Farley does not leave the structure of theology limited to these three specific dimensions of Christian faith. That would bracket these modes, bringing back precisely the problem of abstracted views becoming ever more refined and divided until we return to the contemporary academic morass of the empirical paradigm and the dominance of the specialty field. For this reason, two more modes of interpretation are included alongside the specifically Christian ones: the interpretation of one's primary world and then "vocation." First, interpreting situations encompasses the lifelong education of the person in navigating the contours of the various human conditions that break into concrete situations: joy, hope, pain, loss, friendship, business transactions, marriage, school, play, community. In the broadest sense, this mode is how human beings interpret the "world." All the ordered learning offered in the university can contribute to this mode as to the others. Second, "vocation" is Farley's label that draws out the deeper religious dimensions to one's "primary occupation." This mode of interpretation touches on the human person engaged in long-term focused activities, commitments, and attention and the broader hermeneutic of interpreting situations as such. It is precisely these two other primary modes of interpretation—world and work—that offer the distinctively Christian way of self-understanding and action. These modes provide the necessary assistance of ongoing correction (humanities, sciences, etc.) and relevance (career, job). In short, world, vocation, tradition, truth, and practice comprise the fundamental theological modes that constitute *theologia* as a personal *habitus*. There is here a discernible progression from the wider and broadest hermeneutical framework to the more specific. The advantage of Farley's analysis and description is its palpable unity and coherence. His selection of modes is also standard and applicable across varied Christian institutions.

A Post-Liberal Challenge: Secularization, Catholic Identity, and Theology

Alongside other postliberal thinkers such as Stanley Hauerwas, John Milbank, and Alasdair MacIntyre, Gavin D'Costa calls for a new, post-liberal form of the Christian university as a necessary alternative for the teaching and study of Catholic theology. His argument is wide-ranging, treating issues of secularization, the history of the decline of Protestant and Catholic religious identity, the proposal for a theological religious studies, and a new vision for relating theology to university disciplines within this new "post-liberal" Christian university. Given that I cannot take up all of D'Costa's proposals, my focus takes up two major claims: first, that theology (and by implication, an architectonic possibility) requires an alternative Christian university; and second, his interpretation of how prayer conditions the practice and teaching of theology.

Having read Buckley's account of theology as an architectonic wisdom, its need for a form of theological arts, and his call for a vital matrix of guiding questions that emerge from human knowing and longing, D'Costa might question: Where have the supporting conditions of theology as wisdom gone that would make it not just architectonic but Christian? Where is the church, prayer, liturgy, and cultivation of virtue?[52] This concern for an identifiable religious matrix for proper theological reflection arises out of D'Costa's conviction (with MacIntyre and Milbank) that the modern streams and assumptions of enlightenment liberalism have so secularized higher education in the United States and elsewhere as to make the teaching and the practice of theology within the modern university virtually impossible.[53] The current number of Christian institutions in the United States— where one might suspect theology goes on as opposed to the discipline of religious studies done in secular institutions—are in large part "dying," losing their religious and theological character.[54] Christian identity at Christian research universities typically consists of liturgy, pastoral ministry, and the work of social justice. Yet concerning such elements, D'Costa comments: "These features are very important, and I think they are a vital element of a Christian university, but they are not enough to constitute a Christian university."[55] For D'Costa, theology as it currently exists not just in secular universities but in Christian ones as well "is in danger of being assimilated to modernity."[56] As evidence of this threat, he holds that there is practically no difference between the methods and procedures of religious studies and that of theology. Echoing Farley's criticism of the empirical paradigm and of the specialty field, and Buckley's view of an architectonic form of theological integration, D'Costa argues that "there is very little evidence of any Christian vision affecting the different disciplines, either in their intellectual practices or procedures, or in their being related to theology or philosophy in some sort of holistic manner."[57] Because of this assimilation, theology (and philosophy) is unable to show "the *telos* and unity of the different disciplines." In large part, he reiterates Farley's critique of fragmentation, professionalism, and utilitarianism.[58] Consequently, part of D'Costa's proposal is an alternative "vision of theology."[59] He writes that "good, intellectually rigorous, theology within the university can only be done within *the context of a praying community*, not just nourished by prayer as if an optional and private extra, but also *guided* and *judged* by prayer."[60] I will return to this point shortly. First, we need to understand D'Costa's interpretation of secularization.

D'Costa's reading of theological education's winding history somewhat parallels but is less nuanced than Edward Farley's.[61] I will provide only an abbreviated overview, since more detail would require another essay. Theology begins as one integrated wisdom whose practice enjoyed, from the patristic age through the medieval, an ecclesial context (church or monastery), an agreed-upon goal as the glorification of God, and the common pursuit of destined union with God through Christian holiness. This holiness was grounded in a plurality of traditional practices, prayers, and styles of worship that furthered the individual end and common social good. After the dissolution of the medieval synthesis, the Aristotelian divisions of the sciences became more determinedly autonomous while theology became more fragmented, cut off into specified areas of dogmatics, morality, and spirituality which then became more isolated from one another and from the lived experience of Christian religiosity.[62] After the Reformation and during the seventeenth century, prayer and contemplation and the pursuit of Christian virtue become further removed from the ecclesial context of doing theology, with the explosive success of and interest in the natural sciences. Citing major points from Buckley's treatise on atheism, D'Costa narrates the assimilation of theology into the scientific methodologies that helped spawn the roots of modern atheism. Theologians gave over the grounds and evidence for God from religious experience and biblical revelation to philosophy and physical mechanics.[63] If one adds the new Enlightenment turn towards subjectivity and the emergence of a scientific ideal of normative objectivity freed from confessional appeals, theology ultimately finds justification in the modern university through its association with professional training and practical ends—this was Schleiermacher's conclusion in the *Brief Outline for the Study of Theology.*

This academic and theological settlement—which contributed to a shift of theology into divinity schools and seminaries in the Protestant religious history from the eighteenth to the twentieth centuries—D'Costa sees as "corrosive" and a high point of university theology's secularization.[64] It is not long before the 19th-century study of the history of religions grows into the modern notion of a non-confessional academic discipline: religious studies. He interprets this deeply truncated history of theological education as progressive decline.[65] One major change from the medieval university to the modern (which D'Costa locates paradigmatically at the University of Berlin) was how "the Enlightenment university began the process of translating theology into its own philosophical, natural scientific, or social analysis modalities." Such a shift, for D'Costa, entailed the "ascendance of alien methods and disciplines as the definitive interpreters of scripture, tradition, and authority."[66] The pragmatic pressures of market forces and political and philosophical settlements and interests have no reference to an overarching vision of reality that unifies the knowledges of the modern university. This history charts the development and triumph of secularization:

> *The foundations of the universities took place in a universe with a sacred canopy, whereby people understood their practices to relate to an organic and cosmic pattern participating in the nature of reality. The reality was divinely created for the good of men and women, for the flourishing of human society, and for participation in truth and love. The modern university, with some exceptions, in contrast, develops its programs and practices without any reference to a sacred canopy.*[67]

Let me summarize D'Costa's reading of the various currents that largely comprise secularity. Without the unifying and integrating sacred canopy, various streams of liberal Enlightenment ideas converged to initiate the impossible situation of theology's "Babylonian captivity."[68] These currents include: the scientific idea of neutral objectivity, the privileging of universal reason and freedom over particular faith traditions, the abandonment of *paideia* in favor of "critical, orderly, and disciplined" research, the reduction of theology to phenomenological description, the modern disdain for traditional or sectarian narratives, and a total rejection of human teleology and Aristotelian science.[69]

Towards a Post-Liberal Christian University

Before the secularizing forces of the Enlightenment, one could not conceive of doing theology without faith. Schleiermacher, one of the founders of the University of Berlin, did not even conceive of a theologian without some clerical office and duties. Today, personal or ecclesial faith matters little for scholars of religious studies and theology, since faith adds nothing to scientific methodologies and serious scholarship. D'Costa wants not only a different setting and location for Catholic theology to be studied and practiced, but also traditional epistemological perquisites on behalf of those who would study, teach, and learn it. Before we turn to these epistemological requirements, a few words about the key source for what "post-liberal" and "Catholic" mean institutionally.

The blueprint for D'Costa's post-liberal university—its spirit and character—turns out to be the Catholic university according to John Paul II's Apostolic Constitution *Ex corde ecclesiae* (1990).[70] As such, there is little change in having the typical departments of knowledge, degrees, competent faculty, students, university liturgies, administrators, courses, classes, grades—everything that one normally associates with a Catholic institution of higher learning. The key differences for D'Costa concern ecclesiology. Post-liberal means a robust attention to and relationship between how the academic and ecclesial are interconnected. His guiding questions: How are Catholic universities and Catholic theologians accountable to the local bishop and the Magisterium of the Catholic Church? A further question regards the issue of public funding for church-related universities in the United States, where virtually all universities receive some form of state and federal aid.

Summarizing the main points concerning the "nature and objectives" of a Catholic university, D'Costa emphasizes four. The Catholic university must work towards a "higher synthesis of knowledge," with theology squarely at the center of this enterprise. No clear model of what this integration might be is given by *Ex corde* on D'Costa's reading. Nevertheless, such an integration must take place. Second, there must be a promotion of "the dialogue between faith and reason," presuming harmony rather than conflict between revelation and theology, on the one hand, and the range of the sciences, on the other. Third, all research and ends of knowledge have moral implications. These implications must situate the human good over pragmatic, economical, or other kinds of social ends. Fourth, D'Costa reads passage 19 of *Ex corde*, which holds that there should be a "theological perspective" underpinning all research and a strong relationship of engagement between theological inquiry and its priorities with all university disciplines and knowledge.[71] This last point demonstrates clear agreement with Buckley on the need for theology to be some type of architectonic.

To D'Costa's credit, he provides a balanced overview of the thorny canonical, juridical, and legal issues that have proved contentious for American Catholic educators. He also unpacks key issues from the American bishops' document *Ex Corde Ecclesiae: Application to the United States*. Some of those issues include the requirement of greater and majority Catholic hiring, professions of faith, the responsibilities of faculty and staff to maintain the Catholic character of the university, and, of course, the canonical requirement that teachers of theological disciplines have a *mandatum* to teach. He acknowledges the evolving context and ambiguity of such norms within the diversity of Catholic institutions and competing interpretations of canon law and American civil law. In both his analysis of how different commentators interpret the norms of *Ex corde* and its *Application,* D'Costa evenly lays out two models of interpretation, a "maximal" and a "minimal."[72] D'Costa admits that the terms "maximal and minimal models" are "loose" and, within his analysis, they are not connected to specific institutions.[73] The following features are common to both. Some episcopal oversight is necessary for the Catholic institution, and without it, the Catholic character would be defective. Next, who is employed at different levels of the institution matters for ecclesial identity. Both models "agree that maintaining a Catholic character in staff is a legitimate enterprise, requisite for the intellectual character of the institution, not just for pastoral duties."[74] Finally, both models agree on some form of ecclesial authorization for teachers of theology, but the meaning of *mandatum* remains unclear, and the mode envisioned for implementing it, inconsistent.

One way to understand what D'Costa means by "maximal" and "minimal" paradigms would be to view any given Catholic university or college within Richard Janet's helpful taxonomy of American Catholic higher education. Janet supplies three: canonical, creedal, and cultural. A "canonical Catholic college would define its Catholicity largely through its relationship with the institutional church and its conformity with the precepts and canons of that church." One example of "canonical" would be Catholic University of America, founded and run by the American bishops with a special juridical relationship to Rome.[75] For Janet, a key feature of canonical institutions is their "complete submission to local or universal church authorities as a primary means of guaranteeing their Catholic identity."[76] A creedal college or university "would define its Catholicity through the campus community's adherence to the tenets of the defining creeds of the Catholic faith." Creedal institutions define themselves strictly according to the guidelines of *Ex corde ecclesiae* (not to imply that canonical ones do not, but their charter would be aligned with *Sapientia Christiana*, promulgated in 1979). For such institutions, Catholic doctrine dominates and defines "the mission, curriculum, and campus life" of their varied curricula. Examples include Benedictine College, The Franciscan University of Steubenville, Christendom College, and Aquinas College.[77] The final model, the cultural, covers the vast majority of Catholic institutions of higher education in the United States. Janet states:

> *They define their Catholicity not primarily in terms of obedience to institutional church authority or adherence to the creeds but by a commitment to the ideals and values inspired by the Catholic faith... Rather than insisting on a level of community religious practice, "cultural" Catholic colleges interpret the academic mission of Catholic higher education in terms of a more or less serious engagement with the Catholic intellectual tradition and the themes and points of emphases inherent in that tradition.*[78]

Janet's taxonomy would seem to align well with D'Costa's distinction between "maximal" and "minimal" models, since what the varying degrees of "minimal" share is an emphasis on "subsidiarity," while the "maximal" models seek greater church oversight.[79] As D'Costa interprets *Ex corde ecclesiae*, it becomes clear he takes it as the normative document for the post-liberal proposal. There is a serious concern with authority, institutional relationships between local ordinaries and universities, local ordinaries with theologians teaching with a *mandatum* (whatever the term means— and D'Costa does not provide a clear sense other than that it specifies and strengthens a clear ecclesial bond), and a strong concern for a holistic and general loyalty to Catholic teaching. Quoting *Ex corde*, he notes, "*institutional* fidelity" means "a recognition of and adherence to the teaching authority of the Church in matters of faith and morals."[80] Though D'Costa does not "adjudicate between these two views," he clearly favors the more maximal, canonical, and creedal institutions as having a better chance of withstanding the currents of secularization. Nonetheless, both models could fail if neither "is driven by a vision of what constitutes a Catholic university."[81]

It is troubling that D'Costa would hold that the vast majority of American Catholic colleges and universities, which are more cultural than creedal or canonical, are no longer viable contexts for the teaching and enterprise of Catholic theology. This conclusion is all the more ironic given that D'Costa's own work, if counted as good and reflective theology, emerges from the secular University of Bristol.

D'Costa's vision of a post-liberal Christian university is far more restrictive than that of Buckley or Farley. Indeed, one of the major assumptions for D'Costa's analysis concerns a negative judgment about the possibility of theological understanding without certain essential ecclesial features, such as liturgy and prayer. The absence of more self-identifying Catholic features that nourish a certain view of theological understanding is precisely why, in his view, a new environment is needed for teaching and practice of theology. Buckley and Farley can be justly critical about the negative consequences of secularization, but they have a more expansive position concerning the operation of grace within human intelligence as such. They do not call for a new form of Christian institution or require devotional practices to do good theology. Instead, Buckley and Farley attend constructively to new ways in which the religious and the academic can be related. It is to these points of contrast that I now turn.

Prayer, Epistemology, and Catholic Theology

Just as the modern university proves to be an impossible location for Catholic theology due to its driving principles of rationalism and secularization, so no Catholic theology can be studied or taught in a post-liberal Catholic university without the epistemological requirement of specifically ecclesial prayer, worship, and the pursuit of holiness.[82] D'Costa maintains that "the notion of prayerful theology is structurally absent from the academy and is required in the revival of theology. Without prayer, worshipping the triune God will remain an increasingly marginalized concern and not the heart of theological endeavor."[83] It is at this point in D'Costa's argument that we begin to see clearly how seriously he demands that theology and religious practice mutually implicate and condition *theological study as such*. Now, I suspect that few thinkers within the past and present Christian tradition—Catholic, Protestant, and Orthodox—would register a strong dissent from this claim on its face.[84] His point enjoys the weight of tradition and centuries of church affirmation. How can one really know and study an object, engage in discourse about it with others, when one has little knowledge or formative vocabulary or living experience with it mediated through "tradition" (what D'Costa speaks of as "cohabitating with one's beloved")?[85] For this reason, such "sectarian habits" are *methodologically* necessary in the study and teaching of theology. Again, he claims "theology, if it is to be done with full intellectual rigor, *cannot be done* outside the context of a love affair with God and God's community, the Church."[86] There is some kind of implicit recognition about this point within theological circles. It is commonplace for contemporary theologians, for instance, to call attention to the historical split between spirituality and theology and judge it negatively.

Here it might be easy to misinterpret D'Costa's intentions. He is not reducing Catholic theology to some elevated or postmodern form of catechetical enterprise, despite his call for a tradition-specific university he characterizes as "desirably sectarian." Certainly, his argument should not be read reductively such that theology's focus is overly narrow, attending only to the believer and her church. He has wonderfully insightful chapters devoted to renewing a theological religious studies and constructive proposals for integrating theology with cosmology and physics.[87] His theology should not be misread, therefore, as naïvely inward-looking or Neo-Barthian. His argument, however, rests on a critical presupposition that challenges both Buckley's and Farley's proposals to the core.

D'Costa's argument is not simply or narrowly about how theology is to be conducted but about the nature of a post-liberal Catholic university

as such. Teachers and students of theology at different levels are included within the assumptions and the consequences of his ideas. The major
difference and possibility, then, turns on the issue of faith and shared
discourse for theology to serve as an architectonic wisdom within the university, either in Buckley's generalized form or in Farley's more specific
model of theological hermeneutics. The problem for Buckley's generalized
vision, in D'Costa's view, is his reading of theological language and discourse as somehow "accessible" to those without explicit faith that is generated, nurtured, and sustained by religious practices. How can students
or teachers grasp what a believer understands, since faith is a gift that
only reaches maturity through narrative construction, communal language,
and a traditionally mediated religious identity that holds worship as pre-
condition and as *telos*? After all, such criteria must be vitally operative in
D'Costa's reading of *Ex corde ecclesiae*. Ironically, *Ex corde* nowhere specifies that only Catholics can profit from or exclusively *understand* theological discourse.[88] Moreover, such a point is precisely one consequence of
D'Costa's argument. He might try to evade this issue by submitting to the
judgment of Vatican II that there are "rays of light and truth" within "modernity and other cultures," but his entire point rests not upon content but
upon *methodology*.[89] In terms of procedure, can non-Catholic undergraduate students understand theological discourse and profit from it? If theology
is to play the role of an architectonic wisdom, Buckley's position holds out
the possibility of some kind of universal rationality in which all students
and teachers participate. One can see this in Buckley's affirmation of Jesuit
humanism and his paradigm of Christ as uniting—not opposing—the divine
and the human.[90] Such presuppositions are denied by D'Costa. He views
any humanistic strain as merely another symptom of degenerate rationalist
modernity. We find this position in his discussion of sectarianism. Describing the polarized positions of James Gustafson and Stanley Hauerwas over
the issue of Gustafson's charge that Hauerwas is "sectarian," D'Costa says
the following in Hauerwas's defense.

> *The charge of sectarianism when theologically related to the question
> of the autonomy of the created order, serves to show the assimilation of
> the accusers to a form of rationalist modernity. [Richard] McCormick...
> and Gustafson in his project presume to read creation neutrally,
> and then relate this reading to one that fulfils the natural reading
> supernaturally in the gospel, or for Gustafson in rational theism. The*

reason why I have spent some time on this issue is critically to focus on the problematic assumption of a neutral, and therefore universally shared, sense of the order of creation. My main argument in this chapter and book calls into question the assumption that any neutral reading of creation such as this is epistemologically possible, and in this respect Gustafson and McCormick rely on presuppositions that can be criticized theologically.[91]

Would Michael Buckley's proposal for theology as an architectonic wisdom be met with the same criticism D'Costa levels at Gustafson and McCormick? An indication of this comes from Buckley's Thomistic understanding that the desire for truth (universal) precedes the object of faith (particular). Interpreting Aquinas, Buckley writes:

> [T]he formal object of faith is the primary, i.e., the absolute truth. Christian faith for Aquinas is not a blind leap into the dark: it is not opposed to cognoscitive rigor, nor does it constitute a voluntaristic sacrificium intellectus. "One would not believe if she or he did not see that these things should be believed."... The content of faith and the source of faith are conditioned by this absolute or primary commitment—an uncompromising, nonnegotiable commitment to the truth: "Nothing can fall under faith except so far as it stands under the first truth." In this way, faith does not contradict intellectual activity, but "brings the intellect to completion." Only this commitment to truth can make authentic faith possible: both the commitment of God to its revelation and the surrender of a human being to its absolute primacy.[92]

What Buckley calls, in Rahnerian terms, an "openness to the real," intellectually precedes the narrative, the liturgy, the prayer, and the community for the students of a Catholic university. This assumption can be read as human reason becoming a propaedeutic to faith in the way Aquinas speaks of a theology proper to philosophy as well as *sacra doctrina*.[93] That is why faith and truth are so closely related, but also why students can study and teach theology without the type of religious commitment and explicit religious formation that D'Costa insists they possess. Creation is not neutral for thinkers like Buckley and Farley: Creation is providentially good and ordered toward God, despite the effects of sin. It is interesting to note, however, that there is no such indication of a denial of some form of universal rationality or love of truth that precludes students belonging to other religious traditions (or none) from understanding theological discourse in *Ex corde*. For Buckley and for D'Costa, a universal rationality becomes either fundamental or deeply problematic. Indeed, it would seem that the entire promise or problem of theology in a Catholic university turns on how one decides and *defines* the prior issue of reason, truth, and faith.[94]

Conclusion

To sum up, this essay has shown that theology as "architectonic" entails the formative mind of the student, disciplining and refining their own modes of interpretation related to tradition, truth, and faith. The architectonic is not a course or even a sequence or courses. It is not a "capstone" or an honors seminar. It is not found in a series of guest lectures by distinguished theology professors. Theology, in this interpretation, is not restricted to a specialty field or a disciplinary department. If theology is going to be a pervasive disposition or habit of mind or mode of interpretation, it must be nurtured and operative across the curriculum and present at every level of a student's education, from freshmen to senior year. In many ways, the closest analogues are the related skills of reading and writing. It seems impossible to progress from one year or from one course to another without a student being required to write and read. Such conditions should also apply, to some degree, to theology as an architectonic. Theology as "architectonic" cannot be the burden of one person, one department, or even one school within the university. It must be the shared responsibility of the learning community that *is* the university. There must moreover be a collective willingness on the part of the faculty to realize it. Architectonic does not, then, denote a positioning of a body of knowledge into a hierarchical, historical, and professionally enforced order within the different university departments. Rather, it means cultivating and bringing to bear a hermeneutical, perspectival emphasis into conversations with vital questions, topics, and purposes of science, business, art, literature, and psychology that touch on the human condition.

By surveying the different proposals of Buckley, Farley, and D'Costa, I have tried to reveal the integrative possibilities of and challenges to theology as an "architectonic" wisdom within the Catholic university. Buckley presumes that the current situation of Catholic higher education can serve as a useful and fruitful location for theology as an architectonic wisdom. With some greater specification and attention to the genre of theology as a personal sapiential *habitus*, Farley agrees. The advantage of Farley's constructive vision is that he shows how architectonic need not be thought of exclusively as an occasional gathering of faculty and students or more abstract theological arts better suited to graduate study, as Buckley's proposal seems to champion. As I have only suggested, theology as an "architectonic" can be done and promoted within the framework of theological and academic discourse as a whole. Farley's vision is flexible and adaptive to different institutional locations that would make a difference in the study and teaching of theology. The challenge to both Buckley and Farley comes from D'Costa. D'Costa's powerful argument not only abandons existing institutions as too assimilated to modern assumptions for the doing and teaching of theology but also rejects the assumption of shared discourse since this presupposes a flawed universal rationality or dubious humanism. There is much at stake in the enterprise of Catholic theology and its place in the Catholic university. If this survey has shown anything, it is that the real practical problems and deeper philosophical assumptions must be confronted seriously and engaged in through a much wider conversation than occurs today.

The Jesuits and
the School of Salamanca:
How the Dominicans Formed
the Society of Jesus

JOHN MONTAG S.J., INSTITUTE OF JESUIT SOURCES,
ST. LOUIS, MISSOURI

WE BEGIN WHERE ALL GOOD stories begin: in the middle of things. More specifically, we begin in the midst of the academic year 1527, decisive in the teaching of theology and philosophy in Spain, and ultimately throughout Catholic Christendom. And a very Spanish year it was: The Spanish Emperor had just released the King of France from prison, and while his armies invented modern warfare in the sack of Rome, he took the Pope prisoner; Cortez completed his conquest of Mexico, and sent back to Europe tomatoes and chocolate. In England, Henry sought a divorce from his Spanish wife, while the first few copies of Tyndale's New Testament came ashore. More central to this story, however, are events that bring us to Salamanca and its university, poised at that moment to take on the mantle of authority and prestige that Paris had long enjoyed. In the midst of a deep and growing suspicion of Erasmus and his influence, coupled with the violent expulsion of the *illuminati* and the dangerous wandering spiritualists of the day, Salamanca saw the arrival of a vagabond student of philosophy and theology, Íñigo de Loyola, who within a few years would found the Society of Jesus. Just as fatefully, it witnessed the arrival from Paris of Francisco de Vitoria, a young Dominican professor who brought a new way to teach theology, one that would profoundly transform the course of Catholic thought.

This essay stands very much in line with many of Michael Buckley's own interests in historical origins and the development of ideas. Especially with regard to the Jesuits and their influence, Buckley has sought to trace innovations and intellectual transformations to their origins in traditions and the institutions of the Church. In what follows, I want to focus not on Jesuit innovations within higher education, but rather on their precursors—

on the seldom-considered background to enormous changes in theological and philosophical education that came to the fore only a century later, as if out of nowhere. Salamanca was a sort of cauldron of religious politics and pedagogical brilliance, and by the end of this glimpse into that boiling concoction, I hope to suggest, if only obliquely, how Galileo and Descartes, Hobbes and even Kant owe much to what happened there. More explicitly, I want to show how both religious and university politics shaped what was to come in the way we think of philosophy, theology, and their relationship to one another. As the title makes plain, the Jesuits owe much to their one-time rivals, the Order of Preachers, who by their pedagogy gave such insight to their Jesuit students about the sheer instrumentality of the university for the sake of their mission.

The Spanish Context

Our narrative cannot ignore the need for a sense of Spain in the late fifteenth century, because that context dictates the character of the University of Salamanca later on. By 1475, the so-called "Catholic Monarchs," Isabela and Fernando, had established their claims within the old kingdoms of Iberia, and they began a more ambitious plan of administrative consolidation that can only be regarded as modern. Their plans were in full swing by 1478, when Isabela re-established the Inquisition in Spain, not as the local tribunal of ecclesiastical concerns it had been, but as an instrument of the state, answerable finally to the Crown rather than to Rome or the bishops. Through such political and bureaucratic maneuvers, the Monarchs promoted the myth of Spanish unity that had grown over the centuries of the *Reconquista*. They did so for the sake of an increasingly totalitarian control, and in entrusting the new Inquisition to the control of the Dominican order, they fomented a subsidiary myth of strict Spanish orthodoxy in matters of the faith. By the time of her death in 1504, Isabela had won so many concessions from the Pope that she personally controlled the appointments of every bishop in America, and these concessions extended to all appointments in Spain itself by 1523. Gallicanism never saw such success.

The Dominicans, for their part, were most trusted of all, and their entanglements with the structures of the state served both parties: the powerful religious order helped in aligning the Church with the Crown's project of consolidation, so that being orthodox and being Spanish both came under the Crown's auspices. By the same token, although the bishops had the task of preserving orthodoxy, the Dominicans held a growing power and authority as its arbiters within the bureaucracy of the Inquisition and especially in the universities.

"The Dominican Project"

This brings us to the issue of "Thomism" as an ideological expression of this authority. "Thomists" had first appeared in 1304 in northern Spain; the term was an epithet to reproach the Dominicans for preferring Thomas to Scripture.[1] But pre-modern Thomists in Spain read Thomas piecemeal,[2] and failed to recognize (as Vitoria would in the sixteenth century) that the most profound value of the *Summa* was in its vision as a whole—the way it could provide a theological rationale for the whole of university education as formation of the individual.

Unlike that of Paris, the theology faculty of Salamanca began in the fourteenth century under the auspices of the mendicant orders, and due to a relative scarcity of secular clergy during the fifteenth century, it soon became little more than the training faculty for the mendicants in residence.[3] Dominicans usually held the Prime chair from the beginning, while Franciscans held that of Vespers.[4] This division would appear to confirm the two-school image of medieval theology—the Aristotelian-Thomists versus the Platonic-Augustinians—but such was never really the case before the modern era. With the internal Franciscan reforms and the particular difficulties of their Spanish provinces in the fifteenth century, the Augustinians and Franciscans retired from university teaching for the most part, leaving it to the Dominicans and the few seculars.[5] The last secular to hold the chair of Prime, Pedro Martínez de Osma, was denounced to the Archbishop of Toledo in 1476—probably by the Dominicans[6]—and finally condemned by the brand-new Inquisition in 1479 for allegedly questionable doctrine. He represents an important transition, from a stable and unproblematic period of rather static pedagogy to a more contentious and searching period. The following generations of Spanish theologians would first seek new grounds and a broader comprehension for theological enquiry, while continuously measuring their efforts against often ideological assertions of "orthodoxy". This new impetus accompanied the radical reforms of the religious orders in the consolidated kingdoms of Spain, as well as the foundation of many humanist institutions throughout the peninsula that placed theological study at the heart of their existence.[7] Thus, with the condemnation of Martínez de Osma and the appropriation of "Thomism" by the Dominicans, began the ascendancy of theology within the university, and of the Thomists within theology. From 1479 until 1606, the Dominicans never lost the key chair of the Hour of Prime.[8]

The First School of Salamanca

The Dominican ascent within the theology faculty at Salamanca reached its peak around the mid-sixteenth century and continued for more than a hundred years, throughout the glory of the Spanish *siglo de oro* and of the University of Salamanca itself.[9] The so-called first "School of Salamanca" succeeds the initial period of Dominican hegemony in the faculty of theology after 1479, at the very moment that Isabela and Fernando united their kingdoms of Castile and Aragon. With each opening in the faculty, a Paris-trained, dynamic young Dominican became available and often won election. In those chairs that they didn't win, the Dominicans eventually pressured the Augustinian and secular professors into conformity with Thomistic teaching. In most cases, however, the non-Dominicans did not regard Thomas as an imposition on their teaching. Thomas soon became the patrimony of all at Salamanca, Dominican or otherwise, much the way Scripture and Peter were patrimony of all. This was especially the case after mid-century, when first the Jesuits and then other new and reformed orders chose Thomas as their master, creating a common focus for the different religious orders. Thomists triumphed in the official institutionalization of the *Summa* as the core text in the statutes of 1561, which dictated (against all precedent) that Prime and Vespers share in a three-year course of lectures with the lesser Thomas chair. Formerly, Peter's *Sentences* had served for direct commentary in both public chairs; the various *Summae* and *Sentence*-commentaries of the great masters had been reserved for the lesser chairs associated with the theology pertaining more explicitly to particular religious orders.[10] Now the practice was reversed: after a rather cosmetic effort to conform the *quaestiones* for discussion to Peter's text, an in-depth, systematic survey of Thomas's *Summa* would follow in the public chairs. In addition, it became the common practice in those other university-wide chairs (Duns Scotus and Durandus[11]) to cite the relevant *quaestiones* in the appropriate commentary, and then simply to lecture on Thomas as well.[12]

This remarkable situation came about as a result of that event of 1527 alluded to earlier, namely, the arrival of Francisco de Vitoria as the new Prime Professor of Theology. Vitoria sowed two important seeds of contention: he became the first to reject the Master of the *Sentences*, to break with all precedent and practice outside the walls of his cloister a way of teaching he had learned under his professors at the Dominican convent of St. Jacques in Paris. He also promoted the illegal practice of reading his lectures as dictation. By all accounts, Vitoria was a brilliant teacher; he engaged the humanist atmosphere of his day with alacrity, and brought into his lectures the events of the world. His lectures on the Indies, for example, took advantage of the fiercely indignant correspondence with his American confreres over the unjust treatment of native peoples, and thus marked the beginning of the development of a modern theory of human rights. His successors, Domingo de Soto and Melchior Cano, carried on in this open, generous form of theological enquiry through mid-century, always in conformity with the humanistic vision of *Christianitas*, or Christian formation, embodied in their characteristically Dominican reading of Thomas's *Summa*.

The greatest impetus for the general acceptance of Thomas was not so much a consensus about his orthodoxy. Thomas was simply a new common ground for theological discussion and inquiry—in effect, a new "authority"—and at the same time a much greater *religious* pedagogue than the Lombard. That is to say: his teaching provided for a clearer and more explicit sense of the aim and means of developing a Christian life, under vows or otherwise, within the context of the university. Salamanca generally took its orientation from the practical intentions of its powerful and wealthy student body who, for the most part, had gainful employment within civil or ecclesiastical government as their objective. The Augustinian or even "Christian" end of the universities, imagined by the Parisians after Hugh of St. Victor, had long been wholly stifled by this utilitarian end.[13] As long as education was a piecemeal training in employable disciplines such as civil or canon law, rather than a training toward one's ultimate *salus*, theology would find only a marginal place in the university, and Thomas only a marginal place in theological instruction. Hence, the move toward "Thomism" at Salamanca countered the same sort of professionalism and lack of coherence that the twelfth-century humanists had decried at Paris, and could itself be seen as having a deeply humanistic inspiration under Vitoria. It constituted a Dominican plan of evangelization within the structure of the university, and like all true evangelization, it subverted much of what the university had become. Nevertheless, it gave rise to a problematic contradiction: on the one hand, Thomas became universal; on the other, only Dominicans were apt to read him well.

Cano's Loci

The next key step in consolidating the Dominican university project came under Vitoria's successor, Melchior Cano. Cano too had a searching and humanistic attitude toward theology; unlike most of his contemporaries, he wrote a polished and elegant Latin prose. Cano began his great work, *De locis theologicis*, in 1540 but would leave it unfinished upon his death twenty years later. He succeeded Vitoria in his chair in 1546, while his Dominican confrere and successor, Domingo de Soto, held the Vespers chair. Cano intended his ten "theological places" to be a necessary reform in scholastic theology. In fact, it is a reappropriation of the "territory" of Peter Lombard's *Sentences* in terms of Vitoria's own humanistic textual criticism in his lectures on Thomas's doctrine.[14] Whereas the Lombard merely collected rhetorical "common places" or *loci* from Scripture and patristic sources, Cano, following the earlier humanist Rudolph Agricola, postulated his *loci* as the "domiciles" of authority, the place from which one refutes or approves a given thesis.[15] Cano's maneuver finally puts an end to the open dialectical "space" provided by the Lombard's compilation, by defining and systematizing the "places" or authorities in theology in terms of a hierarchy.[16] The work fulfills what Vitoria began, and is a brilliant and influential beginning to systematic theology, worthy of much discussion. For the Dominicans at Salamanca, it articulated not only the proper hierarchy of authoritative "theological places," but the theoretical rationale of their own authoritative teaching as a new scholastic "place," supplanting the earlier place not defined or delimited by religious identity.

This has important implications. Given the Dominican power and dominance at Salamanca, and their substitution of the rather under-determined text of Peter with the religiously highly determined text of Thomas, where were the grounds for any other religious order to have a voice in Salamanca? In other words, if Thomas's was the foundational text for training in theology, as everyone by now tacitly admitted, and if the Dominicans were the only authoritative expounders on Thomas, as they wanted to claim, what would keep the Jesuits, Carmelites, Augustinians, and Franciscans who studied in Salamanca from being forced to become quasi-Dominicans? Religious training belonged in the religious houses, but Salamanca faced the danger of becoming, in some sense, entirely a Dominican house of studies.

The Second School of Salamanca

As a result of the contradiction introduced with Thomas under Dominican oversight, the open and dynamic pedagogy of the First School was doomed, and lasted only until the time of the important restructuring of the University's statutes in 1561.[17] The death of Cano and the conclusion of the Council of Trent generally mark the beginning of what came to be called the Second School of Salamanca. The San Esteban priory's authority by now had no rival in all of Spain, or indeed, in the Catholic world: Eight of its members had attended the deliberations at Trent, including Cano, who served as the Emperor's ambassador and *peritus*. When the Dominican Juan Mancio de Corpus Christi returned from Trent, and in 1564 took up the chair of Prime as Cano's successor, he and the rest of the community may have expected their hegemony to continue. Cano's *De locis theologicis*, the crowning achievement of the first school, was published posthumously in 1563. But Mancio and his brethren were deeply shocked when an Augustinian friar won the chair of Vespers in 1565,[18] a chair they had held in tandem with Prime since Soto began his career with Vitoria nearly forty years earlier. A noticeable shift had taken place, not only in the theology faculty at Salamanca, but all over Spain: the shift from a politics of *"mano abierta"* to *"mano dura."*[19] A hard-line defense of "orthodoxy" followed on the profound shifts in education going on in Europe, many of which sifted into Spanish faculties, despite much vigilance. Peter Ramus's usurpation of teaching by "method," for example (i.e., his reductive binary schematics of knowledge, by which he sought to eliminate rhetoric and Aristotle from the curriculum, and to replace professors with textbooks[20]), had found its way even to Salamanca.[21] A tale told of Juan Mancio (one of Suárez's professors) illustrates the atmosphere. In 1575, the Spanish Ramist, Sánchez de las Brozas, confronted Mancio during a lecture on Aristotle, saying that Aristotle did not understand what he was saying in his definition of rhetoric. Mancio is said to have reacted, "that is heresy, because St. Thomas is founded on Aristotle, and our faith on St. Thomas. Hence, to reprove Aristotle is to speak ill of the faith."[22] Suárez and the Jesuits rejected not Thomas, but this attitude toward Thomas, beginning from around this time.

The Jesuit Project

Having mentioned the Jesuits, it is time to pick up on that other event that occurred in Salamanca in 1527, namely, the arrival of the vagabond future founder of the Society of Jesus, Iñigo de Loyola—or Ignatius, as he came to call himself around that time. Ignatius was a Basque of minor nobility who turned to religious life after a long recovery from a traumatic injury received while defending Pamplona from the French several years before. He had spent the intervening time learning to pray and living as a wanderer and beggar before realizing that to do what he really desired, he needed an education. After a short stint at the illustrious new University of Alcalá, where he spent most of his time caring for the sick, he decided to make his way to Salamanca. There is little point in dwelling on his stay there, since he spent much of his short time being harassed and imprisoned by the Dominicans under the auspices of the Inquisition. That same year, 1527, he left for Paris, where he gathered his first lasting companions. Before taking their degrees, they took religious vows together as a company. By 1540, the new order had been approved by the Pope, and it soon began to grow dramatically.

Michel de Certeau points to the "ambition to totalize" throughout the latter part of the sixteenth century, and the Jesuits certainly shared in this spirit.[23] This ambition characterizes the rise of the Jesuit university "system," governed hierarchically and internationally as an integral element of the Society's own structure. This structure, in turn, arose out of a similarly totalizing plan that became formative of the Jesuit order inasmuch as it expressed the order's foundational charisms. The "totalizing plan" has its roots in the *Spiritual Exercises* and the Society's *Constitutions*, but concretely, it was the result of fifty years of consultation and collaborative reflection during the last half of the century. The educational expression of this plan, published finally in 1599, is known as the *Ratio Studiorum*, and it served as the guide for hundreds of Jesuit schools throughout the world, until the Society's suppression in 1773. Two aspects of this code of study are relevant, specifically regarding theology. First, despite Cano's vitriolic, almost insane hatred for the Jesuits, his structural division between what came to be known as "positive" and "scholastic" theology very much characterizes the Jesuit approach. Second, according to the directives of Ignatius, the Society promoted Thomas explicitly as the master of theology, while at the same time cautioning Jesuits against slavishly adhering to those opinions of his that ran contrary to teachings generally held by the Society—teachings such as the Immaculate Conception.

Given their adaptive approach, the Jesuits led the way in devising an answer to the dilemma mentioned earlier, namely, how to come to terms with Dominican hegemony while remaining true to Thomas. Their answer accomplished three ends. It helped strengthen the place of Thomas in the curriculum, while it also opened a space for a Jesuit construal of philosophy, theology, and higher education in general, thus precipitating more clearly their own religious identity. At the same time, it ultimately undermined the faculty of theology and the University itself. In short, they fought fire with fire, establishing their own reading of Thomas in support of their own religious identity, and imitating the Dominicans by opening their own house of religious formation to the University. Setting aside this formative "Jesuit reading" of Thomas, to which many scholars such as Suárez, Molina, and Bellarmine contributed, I want to turn to the background again, to the university politics in the midst of which the theological and philosophical controversies took place.

Jesuits at Salamanca

In a University Faculty meeting in January 1570, the local Jesuit superior asked that the Society be integrated into the University in the way of the other religious orders, but under two conditions: that its members not be obliged to vote in the elections for professorships, nor to seek professorships in the University. From 1548 until 1570, there had been no need for the Jesuit house to apply for such membership, for during this time, the Society had no professors of its own who could teach in-house. Jesuit students attended all their lectures in the University as if they were seculars. After 1570, enough young professors (including Francisco Suárez) had finished studies that the Jesuits, like the other orders, could train their own members in their Salamanca house. In order to qualify their students for degrees at the University, religious houses that engaged in any teaching of their own had to be officially integrated into the University. Thus, in accord with the stipulated exemptions, the Jesuit house was integrated like any other, and things proceeded more or less smoothly for several years. During the academic year 1586-87, however, problems began that were to last for seventeen years.

The conflict centered on the Jesuit practice of reading theology lectures in-house, while keeping them open to anyone who would benefit, according to the approach stipulated in the Jesuit *Constitutions*.[24] The "open doors" practice conflicted with the interests (and statutes) of the University, first because the lectures were given during regular University hours, thus taking students from the University professors, and second because such lectures were beyond the control of the University faculty. The Jesuits and the University, in the person of the Dominicans of San Esteban, soon were at an impasse. The University syndicate denounced the practice on December 4, 1586 before the faculty, which appointed a commission to examine an apostolic letter from Pius V and ratified by Gregory XIII, which the Jesuits claimed granted them privileges to read theology. The letter under consideration was *Cum litterarum*, in which Pius was quite explicit in granting the privileges he did. It reads in part as follows:

> By our apostolic authority and by means of these present documents, we decree and declare that the professors of this same Society [of Jesus], teaching as they do humane letters, the liberal arts, theology, or any discipline whatever in their colleges, even in places where there are abundant universities, can freely and licitly give their lectures, even public ones (provided they do not conflict with a university's lectures during a two-hour space in the morning and a one-hour space in the evening). Moreover, we decree and declare that it shall be permitted to students of whatever sort to attend such lectures, and other scholastic exercises as well, and that whatever students in them will have attended lectures in philosophy or theology can be accepted in their proper grade in any university whatever. Furthermore, we decree that such esteem be accorded the courses these students have attended in these colleges that they be looked upon as if the students have earned the grade of "sufficient"—not less but equal and without any difference whatever than if they had studied in the aforementioned universities themselves. They can and should be admitted to any grade whatever, both baccalaureate and licentiate, master's or doctor's; should these degrees be attained, we grant a special licentiate and faculty, namely that our stern prohibition, under penalty of major excommunication, lies upon rectors and any other officials in any university whatever, and others, to be held to observing this our decree, by penalties to be inflicted at our discretion, lest under whatever pretense they dare and presume to hinder or disturb the rectors and scholars whom we have described above.[25]

To this the University responded that the Jesuits, like all the other orders, had privileges to read only to their own religious.[26] Pius's intentions seem quite explicit; nonetheless, in the context of Salamanca at the height of its powers, even a papal injunction was less than decisive. One possible basis for the University's resistance was that the Jesuits had been integrated into the University a full year (February 1570) before the Apostolic Letter was issued (March 1571). The terms under which they came into the University should determine their activity, in the view of the University authorities. Indeed, the Jesuits had not acted even according to the terms Pius stipulates; in giving their lectures during the hours proper to the university's curriculum, they gave legitimate cause for complaint. Nonetheless, the letter appears to grant an extraordinary privilege to the Jesuits, one contrary to the entire tradition of the medieval *studium*: under papal sanction, they held a *licentia ubique docendi* without having to submit to any authoritative academic guild—that is, any university faculty. Thomas Aquinas himself had appeared at Paris under a similar sanction, but this Jesuit license was unprecedented in the breadth of its scope.

Dominican Strategies and Jesuit Tactics

De Certeau again provides helpful notions, worthy of a short excursion here, for understanding the events that followed this initial conflict. He distinguishes "strategies and tactics",[27] which we can differentiate by recognizing the networks and circumstances in which they operate, and how their employers profit from such circumstances. "We are concerned with battles or games between the strong and the weak, and with the 'actions' which remain possible for the latter."[28] With regard to the theology faculty at Salamanca from 1570 to 1625, "the strong and the weak" correspond to the Dominicans and Jesuits, respectively. Their "battles" took place on two fronts: the struggles over the appropriation of Thomas Aquinas, and over the control of teaching within the theology faculty itself. By "strategy" is meant the manipulation of relationships by any person or institution; it claims a *place* as its own, distinct from its environment, as a base from which to manage its targets or threats.[29]

Important effects accompany this strategic appropriation of place. As de Certeau explains, "the 'proper' is *a triumph of place over time*," allowing the capitalization of advantages and a kind of autonomy with respect to circumstances. It also makes possible a "panoptic practice" by which one can survey what is foreign (and future) and thus control it.[30] By contrast, "a tactic is a calculated action determined by the absence of a proper locus.... The space of a tactic is the space of the other. Thus it must play on and with a terrain imposed on it and organized by the law of a foreign power.... [I]t is a maneuver... within enemy territory."[31]

The validity of a tactic depends not on the place, but on the time it gains for its employer. "Strategies pin their hopes on the resistance that the *establishment of a place* offers to the erosion of time; tactics on a clever *utilization of time*, of the opportunities it presents and also of the play that it introduces into the foundations of power."[32] Tactics create time where no space is given; they allow movement, adjustment, and recovery when consolidation is impossible. These militaristic images probably overstate the difficulties between religious orders in Salamanca, but they nonetheless point up the tactical nature of the Jesuits' early approach, before they gained approval at court: They simply bided their time, poaching on a foreign territory over the next seventeen years.

Nevertheless, we must recognize as well the Jesuits' own strategies—their ongoing efforts to capitalize language (such as that of St. Thomas) and social relations—towards an autonomous identity. Between 1540 and 1600, the first generations of Jesuits were intent on the project of creating a new religious order. A great part of that effort went toward the establishment during this period of several hundred colleges in Europe and in Spanish and Portuguese domains around the world. Many Dominicans (such as Cano) regarded this as a *rival* identity, and sought to destroy it; others (such as Cano's successor, Domingo de Báñes) struggled against it only insofar as it encroached on their own "place," as it most dramatically did at Salamanca.

The Lawsuit at Salamanca

And so we return to the suit filed before the Royal Council against the Society of Jesus in 1586. This ongoing litigation became the most significant context for the battle between Dominican strategies and Jesuit tactics. Two "open-door" theology lectures given within the Jesuit college during University teaching hours precipitated the controversy. The Dominicans complained that if the Jesuits wanted to teach theology to externs, they should compete for chairs within the University like everyone else.

Otherwise, they should close their doors and teach only their own religious, as was the practice in all the other houses. The Dominicans feared that if left unchecked, the practice would extend to other communities, and that eventually the public classes would become drastically depopulated, since already 150 students attended the Jesuit lectures.[33]

The Jesuits defended themselves by appealing to their *Constitutions* and the terms under which they had been formally integrated into the University in 1570. They taught externs because Ignatius had intended that they freely teach any who could profit from it. Indeed, they quite scandalously ignored many established boundaries between religious and laity. They refused to present themselves for elections because their rule prohibited any seeking of offices. Behind all this, the Jesuits played on a serious ambiguity that dated to the very foundations of the medieval relationship between religious orders and universities. Insofar as religious houses taught the material of the philosophy and theology faculties, they were, in effect, separate "universities" in the original sense of the word:[34] the particular guild which gathered itself into a teaching-and-learning organ.[35] What had always integrated religious houses to the *studium* at large was the intermingling of students as well as professors within all the schools, religious houses, and colleges collectively. Here, the Jesuits capitalized on the asymmetry of the situation: they held no official professorship within the University, but integrated nonetheless—not by attending University lectures, but by teaching extern students.

A sentence finally came down in January 1591, against the Jesuits, who promptly appealed to the King.[36] Thus the case dragged on, until a compromise was suggested. The Jesuits would be given two classrooms in the Lesser Schools, across the plaza from the main academic building, in which to lecture outside the normal hours. One class would be on Scripture and "positive theology," the other in "scholastic theology." The compromise had an attraction for the University, in that it would give them some control over the hour, the place, and the courses taught (although not their content). Another appealing aspect was that the Jesuits were willing to teach without seeking any remuneration from the University—again, as according to their *Constitutions*.

That this suggestion was even entertained by the University indicated how the Jesuits' tactics of delay and refusal had wearied at least some of the authorities, including the rector. Unfortunately for them, several others had

more stamina, and refused to consider any such compromise. If this concession were made, they declared, the Dominicans would promptly abandon
the chairs they possessed and would refuse to take them up again. In the
words of their prior, they would

> *retire to their house, and the University would remain in God's hands,*
> *having tossed out its eldest son who had most truly served it, since it*
> *was apparent that they [the Dominicans] were no longer necessary.*
> *And they would close themselves up in their house, and if they wished*
> *to read they would read when they wanted, and allow in those to*
> *whom they wished to read, and from there they would watch who*
> *read and what was read in the University of Salamanca.*[37]

This was no tantrum or idle threat. The Dominicans would do exactly what
the Society of Jesus was doing: reserve its teaching to its own house, with
doors open. In effect, the Dominicans were trying to call attention to the
ambiguity that the Jesuits were exploiting with impunity, and to force a
decision against them. If the Jesuits were able to set themselves up as a
university apart, so could the Dominicans—and to "God's hands" with the
University. Meanwhile, they would continue to "watch," ever vigilant for
the sake of orthodoxy. Yet from another perspective, this was a strategy to
protect their "place," their hegemony within the faculty.

The main difficulty with the compromise proposal was not that it gave
special treatment to the Jesuits, but that it obviated the system of public
competition and accountability among the elected professors. The rector in
effect was foisting two pseudo-professors on the faculty and on the University, professors who did not have to compete for their chairs and were in
principle "infallible"—beyond University control.

In their response, the Dominicans made clear that the real issue was ideological. They invoked Thomas and Augustine as the banners of orthodoxy
held high by the Dominicans of San Esteban, and they saw the Jesuits as
deliberately rejecting this orthodoxy in opting out of the system. Jesuits
could not be trusted, because they could not be controlled. Although the
Dominican response vaunted the egalitarian election of professors within
the University, it ignored their own domination of the system itself.

To shorten a fascinating, intricate, and overly long story, decisions went
back and forth, and the Dominicans eventually carried through with their
threat, if only temporarily; but in the end, the sentence came down in favor

of the compromise for the Jesuits, who had simply outlasted the opposition. They had succeeded in gaining a "place" for their order, on their own terms rather than those of the Dominicans, which meant that they could interpret St. Thomas from that "place." This, however, opened the gates to all sorts of "place-seeking". Within the next thirty years, various additional professorships were appointed by the crown to assuage divergent parties in the University, until by the middle of the seventeenth century Salamanca had visibly entered a decline from which it would never recover.

Conclusion

I want to conclude with a review of three elements in the shifting context of the sixteenth century. Medieval theology, religious life, and the university left the crucible (cauldron?) of the sixteenth century alloyed in a new way, yet as something we can still recognize today in many universities and in the practice of theology, if perhaps not so clearly in religious life. Although theology's place within the contemporary U.S. university has often become precarious and domesticated to other fields such as religious studies, one can still recognize a Thomistic ideal at work in many institutions.[38] With the recovery of St. Thomas's thought at Salamanca, the relationship between religious orders and the university changed dramatically. Theology soon sought renewal by properly reintegrating Scripture and the texts of the tradition into school teaching.

But given the new attitudes toward teaching and authority, the new Thomistic "common ground" quickly became a theological battleground. From now on, there would be Jesuit Thomism and Dominican Thomism, although there could never have been comparable "Lombardisms" in the Middle Ages. Insofar as the Lombard's compilation of texts served as a "commonplace book," a resource from which to draw on authorities and build arguments, it did not provide polemics or grounds for contention among interpreters. Peter Lombard never appears as a figure of contention, but as a purveyor of authorities. With St. Thomas, the Dominicans first, and then the wider Church, find a surer guide in theological training and understanding. Placing Thomas where the *Sentences* had long been in the curriculum provided for a restructuring of theological inquiry as such, within the university. First the Dominicans, and then the Jesuits, asserted theology's role as the unifying guide to university formation. These different expressions of Thomistic theology may have been, to some extent or other, ideologized according to religious ideals, or otherwise. Nevertheless, by each grasping hold of their Thomistic ideals, both orders incorporated the university as such more deeply into their own training and identity.

But the Jesuits, having carved out an identity on the Thomistic battleground, eventually went a logical step further in converting the institution itself from merely a *context* for its mission and identity in the Church (as it had been for medieval mendicants) into the very *means* toward that mission and its own identity. Jesuit formation and training took place within the university context—within the walls of the Jesuit community, for the most part. In a similar way, so did Dominican training. But, while the Dominicans held sway over the University of Salamanca, they could hardly abide interpretations of St. Thomas that ran contrary, or parallel, to their own reading. For their own part, the Jesuits used St. Thomas for their own formative purposes; they needed to have "space" for their own reading, which they contrived to get after many years of struggle with the Dominicans. In the meantime, they learned, from the Dominicans themselves, the extent to which the university could be "instrumentalized" or made to serve their own mission, according to their Constitutions, for the help of souls. In subsequent centuries, Jesuit secondary and higher education would become the very hallmark of their identity, and one of the greatest missionary endeavors of the Church. Were it not for the fundamentally Dominican insight that St. Thomas's teaching provides the best rationale for university learning, the Jesuits would never have been able to institutionalize their evangelical mission in the form of the university.

Part Four

NEW DIRECTIONS IN SYSTEMATIC THEOLOGY

The Eternal Plan of Divine Providence and the God Who Dialogues: The Contribution of John H. Wright, S.J.[1]

RICHARD W. MILLER; CREIGHTON UNIVERSITY

"WHAT DO YOU HAVE THAT you have not received?" (1 Cor. 4:7)[2] As St. Augustine looked back, at the end of his life, on the major shift in his thinking on the question of grace, he identified this passage from Paul as the key testimony.[3] It convinced him that grace is absolutely gratuitous. While Western Christianity has accepted Augustine's insistence on the absolute gratuity of grace in the conversion of the Christian, it has not reached wide agreement on a way to theologically articulate the sovereign operation of God and the capacity of free creatures for genuine choice. Indeed, one could read much of the history of Western theology on this question as echoing Augustine's experience: "I worked hard in defense of the free choice of the human will, but the grace of God conquered."[4]

A great deal is at stake, however, in the relinquishment of the created will's capacity for free choice. If human beings do not have free choice, then they cannot respond to God's call to conversion and friendship, as revealed in the biblical tradition and in Christian faith and practice, and enter into an interpersonal relationship with God. Furthermore, if human beings do not have free choice, then God must be responsible for their moral evil and savagery.

The inability of theologians to hold together the sovereignty of God and the free choice of the human person has led many contemporary theologians to de-emphasize or even reject God's sovereignty. Anne Carr in her survey of contemporary theological literature summarizes the horizon in which a great number of theologians understand the doctrine of providence: "God is understood not so much as sovereign king and hierarchical lord but as cooperative participant and respectful friend in the process and struggle of individual lives and of human history."[5] The process tradition in contemporary philosophical theology is the most ardent proponent of this view, and the school of thought most opposed to the so-called classical view represented by Augustine. Although process theology raises an important question about the adequacy of the classical view for articulating a theology of God that is true to the dialogical relationship between God and creatures that lies at the heart of Christianity, its own constructive response to this issue seriously compromises God's perfection.

This paper will address the perennial problem of reconciling the sovereign operation of God and the capacity of free creatures for genuine choice in the context of the doctrine of providence. The question for this inquiry is: How is one to construct a theology of providence that preserves the dialogical character of God's activity with respect to free creatures as revealed in scripture?

In responding to this question, I will draw upon the work of John H. Wright, S.J. Wright's work represents a major breakthrough in treating this question. Through his analysis of the whole of scripture and his creative appropriation of Thomas Aquinas's thought, Wright successfully addresses the concern of classical theology to preserve the divine perfection and contemporary theologies' insistence that any doctrine of God has to hold onto God's care for and involvement with creatures. Wright preserves the divine perfection, such that all the power, perfection, and goodness of the creature are a gift from God, and thus the creature adds no new perfection to God. He also holds onto human free choice and the dialogical relationship between God and creatures that is the centerpiece of Christianity. While Wright provides a major breakthrough on this question that informs all of one's theology, his contribution to this perennial problem has not yet been widely appreciated by theologians and has sometimes been subjected to contrary interpretations.[6]

Wright's constructive theology of providence is grounded in his two-volume work *Divine Providence in the Bible: Meeting the Living and True God* that identifies a pattern of divine and human interaction throughout the Old and New Testaments.[7] He gave a brief preview of his biblical research in an article entitled "The Eternal Plan of Divine Providence."[8] In this article, he argues that to preserve God's perfection, one does not need to understand the eternal plan of providence as a plan in which God determines in advance everything that will be realized in the created order. If one assumes this, then (as the debate between Luis de Molina and Domingo Bañes in the 16th century demonstrates) the central question becomes: Does God know what a person would freely choose to do in any possible set of circumstances (free conditioned futures) before any actual divine decree (i.e., antecedent to

God's knowing what God will actually will to communicate[9])? If this is the central question of providence, then theology must choose between Bañes or Molina because "the positions are finally contradictory and hence allow no third position."[10] Neither position, however, is satisfactory because both of them end up in contradiction.[11] Wright concludes in this article that "a divine knowledge of individual conditioned free futures is not required in order to establish an acceptable doctrine of providence; but a divine knowledge of actual free choices clearly is required."[12] His subsequent article entitled "Divine Knowledge and Human Freedom: The God Who Dialogues" responds to this precise problem through developing an understanding of the structure of God's causative knowledge of the actual choices of free creatures.[13]

In responding to the question of this paper, I will relate Wright's insights from his later article on the God who dialogues to his earlier article on the eternal plan of providence and his scriptural analysis in his *Divine Providence in the Bible: Meeting the Living and True God*, including the second volume on the New Testament. I will expound, clarify, and bring together in a synthesis the central threads in Wright's thought in order to articulate a coherent theology of divine providence that preserves the dialogical character of God's activity, as revealed in scripture, with respect to free creatures. As such, this essay seeks to offer a creative completion of Wright's thought.

The Perfection of God and the Notion of a Plan of Providence

If the purpose of God's activity outside the inner life of the Trinity is to share God's self in union with free creatures, then how is God going to realize this purpose? When we speak about how God intends to accomplish God's creative and redemptive purpose, we speak of God's having a plan. If God as omniscient cannot receive knowledge from another, then it appears that all the details that God intends to realize in the created order must be known prior to the realization of this plan through God's will and power. Similarly, if God as omnipotent cannot be passive to the effects of another, then it appears that God must execute the plan without God's power being in any way resisted. At first blush, God's omniscience and omnipotence seem to require that the eternal plan of providence be "an exact, efficacious, immutable divine determination of all events that will occur or not occur, made prior to taking account of any actions of created beings."[14] The perfection and sovereignty of God seem to require that God determines in advance everything that will be realized in the created order, including the free choices of creatures. This makes genuine created free choice impossible. The so-called classical tradition of Christian theology in its insistence on God's perfection and thus God's sovereignty continuously ran into this problem.

The various strands of contemporary theology that are akin to process theology respond to this impasse by rejecting classical theology's understanding of the immutability of God. The eternal plan of providence does not figure in the process tradition, which in wanting to emphasize God's relation to and involvement with the world sees God as becoming with the world. The founder of process thought, Alfred North Whitehead, understands God as "lacking the fullness of actuality and as being devoid of consciousness."[15] In addition, God's free creative act is described as being "untrammeled by reference to any particular course of things."[16] The problem for the classical view of providence and the process view of God's relation to the world and human activity is that neither view "corresponds with the God who reveals Himself to us in the Hebrew and Christian Scriptures, the God who dialogues."[17]

Recovering a Biblical Theology of Divine Providence

In responding to the classical view of providence and contemporary views inspired by process thought, John Wright recovers a biblical understanding of God's providence. In his examination of the whole of scripture, Wright discovers amidst the great diversity of biblical texts and stories an identifiable pattern of interaction between God and creation that is repeated over and over. This pattern of divine-human interaction is typified by three moments: (1) God's absolute, free divine initiative in creation and redemption; (2) human beings' free response, in obedience and faith or sin and unbelief; (3) God's response to the human response, in a judgment of blessing or condemnation.[18] Integral to this pattern of divine-human interaction are four themes that run through the whole of scripture and that are crucial to a proper understanding of the eternal plan of providence: the omnipotence and infallibility of the divine government, the frustration of God's plan in the face of free human resistance, the adaptability that characterizes God's dealings with human beings, and the collective and communal quality of God's purpose and the means for attaining God's purpose.

In his work *Divine Providence in the Bible,* Wright shows how these themes run through the scriptures, from the very earliest tradition of the Pentateuch through the New Testament. Here I will give just a few examples from the Old and New Testament that indicate the presence of these themes in scripture.[19]

While the first theme of the omnipotence and infallibility of the divine government abounds in scripture from the earliest tradition of the Pentateuch, one text that is often cited by theologians of the so-called classical view of providence comes from Second Isaiah (Is 55:6-13) where it is revealed that God's purposes shall be accomplished and God's gifts shall not return to God empty. In the classical view of divine providence, the omnipotence and infallibility of God was commonly held. What was not, however, adequately recognized was the last three aspects of providence found in scripture: namely, the frustration of God's intention in individual instances, the adaptability of God in response to free creatures, and the collective and communal quality of God's purpose.

While scripture clearly reveals that God is Lord of history, it also discloses that God's plan can be frustrated. In First Isaiah (5:1-4) God complains that the vineyard only produces wild grapes even though God has done everything possible for it to produce good grapes.[20] In Ezekiel (24:11-14), God wearies God's self in an attempt to purify God's people. They, however, remain obstinate so God will punish them.[21] In the New Testament the theme of God's frustration is also apparent. In Matthew (23:37), Christ grieves that his repeated attempts to gather the people of Jerusalem around him have been frustrated.

The third crucial theme for a proper understanding of divine providence is "the adaptability that characterizes God's dealings with human beings."[22] The Yahwist source in Genesis 3 "attempts to tell how human history became a history of sin,"[23] but also "shows God's radical response of mercy to this sinfulness by situating the call of Abraham in Genesis 12 against the dark background of primeval wickedness, especially the universal pride of the story of the Tower of Babel."[24] The election of Israel can be understood as God's response to the plight of human beings.[25] In Jeremiah (18:1-11), the adaptability of God is revealed in Jeremiah's image of the potter who can "remake a vessel that has been spoiled."[26]

God adapts God's actions depending on whether those God intended to punish repent for their unfaithfulness, and those God intended to bless become disobedient. While the image of a potter would seem to lend itself to the idea that God gets whatever God wants because the potter can mold the clay as he pleases, the image actually is used to show "a readiness in God to do one thing or another, depending on how men conduct themselves toward Him."[27] This theme of God's adaptability in dealing with human beings also pervades the New Testament. In the example, cited above, from Matthew 23:37 of the people of Jerusalem frustrating Christ's intention to gather them around him "as a hen gathers her brood under her wings," Christ's action is conditioned by their choice; for Christ warns them that Jerusalem will be destroyed because they have refused to hear him. The idea that God adapts God's actions in response to human actions and the interior dispositions of human beings is apparent also in Jesus' teaching that God forgives those who forgive their neighbors (Mt 6:14-15; Mk 11:25).

The final biblical theme that will be particularly significant for a proper understanding of divine providence is the collective or communal quality "both in the end aimed at by God's dominion of the world and in the means ordered to this end."[28] Although there was development in the biblical understanding of God's final purpose for God's creatures, the communal, collective, and social character of the end of God's activity (i.e., the wellbeing of the people of God) remained primary from the beginning of the Old Testament through the New Testament. The kingdom is not "an inevitable but incidental consequence of having many individuals attain salvation";[29] rather, "the constitution of the kingdom is primary."[30] Since the early Church, when Christian writers (e.g., Justin Martyr, Irenaeus of Lyon, Clement of Alexandria, Origen, and Augustine) treated God's final salvific purpose in the context of predestination, they focused on the salvation of the individual person.[31] Augustine's interpretation of Paul's teaching on predestination in Romans 8–9 that came out of the Pelagian controversy has been particularly influential in Western theology. This has led to Paul's teaching on predestination being understood in terms of the salvation of the individual person, which has led to a neglect of the biblical idea of the primacy of the communal or collective character of salvation. Predestination in Paul, however, "does not have the later connotation of distinct individuals eternally marked out for everlasting salvation. Its object is the community of Christians, the Church, which as a body will unfailingly be glorified in heaven."[32]

Not only is the purpose or end of God's creative and redemptive activity understood in collective and communal terms, but so also are the means for attaining God's purpose understood in collective or communal terms. In the Old Testament, Israel as a nation is understood as the chosen people of God, and as such they are the "bearers of God's purpose."[33] Israel was born and sustained by the unfailing power and mercy of God to benefit the Jewish people, and through them all others. They are "to be the faithful remnant, carrying forward God's purpose among the nations."[34] Here the whole theology of the remnant becomes significant:

> *The remnant of Israel, whether numerically few or many, is the group who remain faithful to God and in whom the divine promises and purposes are being fulfilled. The remnant is indeed God's work; for other nations may be destroyed without a trace, but Israel, by God's power, will never be without some who keep alive the destiny committed to them.*[35]

In the New Testament "it is the Church, the Body of Christ, the new Israel that is the divinely guaranteed means for achieving the end of God's merciful design."[36] And it is by being incorporated into the community of believers that "one gains fellowship with God and with God's Son Jesus Christ."[37] Charity or agapic love is so important for God's purpose because it is the primary habit and activity "that leads to the fulfillment of God's purposes; for charity both links individuals to the end and unites them to one another in a single community of fellowship in the Holy Spirit."[38] In this view, "the individual is not lost sight of nor swallowed up in an impersonal collectivity; but the emphasis is on his integration into a community of love and life, not upon his individual glorification, with this community as a secondary thing."[39]

In summary, the omnipotence and infallibility of the divine government, the frustration of God's loving initiative in the face of free human resistance, the adaptability that characterizes God's dealings with human beings, and the collective and communal quality of God's purpose are evidenced throughout scripture. These themes, which must be incorporated into any theology of providence that is true to the biblical witness, reveal a real dialogue between Creator and creature.

A Constructive Theology of Divine Providence

The divine and human dialogue is characterized both by initiative and response. The divine initiative is unconditioned and free, while God's response
is conditioned by the free choice of the human being as the other partner in
the dialogue. The so-called immutable God of classical theism can exercise
absolute initiative but seems incapable of responding to the human being.
The "temporal, growing, relative God"[40] of process theism is capable of
response but cannot exercise absolute initiative. With a clearer view of both
the scriptural account of the dialogical character of God's dealings with
human beings and the failure of classical and process-oriented theologies to
articulate a theology that is true to the scriptural testimony, we have a better
sense of the meaning and significance of our original question: How is one
to construct a theology of providence that is true to these scriptural themes
and to the dialogical nature of God's activity with respect to free creatures
as revealed in scripture?

While this theology of providence is not a reconstruction and reinterpretation of Aquinas' thought, it is influenced by St. Thomas, especially his
view that God is the pure subsisting act of existence. As such, God does not
depend on another for God's existence, goodness, life, and activity. Thus all
that is and all that can be are grounded in the pure actuality of God.

God can create beings other than God because God's being can be
shared or communicated. There is then "an aspect of possibility in the
absolute necessity of God, not with regard to Himself but with regard to
the creatures, a possibility rooted in active potency."[41] God in knowing
God's self knows[42] the ways in which God's being can be communicated
(i.e., divine goodness).[43] The limited ways or modes in which God's being can be shared are traditionally referred to as the "possibles." In this
vein, Wright maintains, "as God in the immediacy of total self-presence
grasps God's own being as communicable, He grasps the full range of all
possible events, situations, things and activities."[44] The possibles or "the
divine ideas in the general sense," as Wright refers to them,[45] should not
be understood as somehow "ready-made in God's essence," but they find
their formally distinct intelligibility through the activity of the divine mind
contemplating the divine goodness as communicable.[46] While the divine
ideas in a general sense find their ultimate foundation in the divine goodness as communicable, they are manifested through the divine intellect

contemplating the divine goodness as communicable. And the divine ideas in a general sense are the ground for maintaining God's freedom of choice. God in knowing God's self and in rejoicing in God's self knows that God's being can be shared with others. God wills to bring into being creatures so that they can share or participate in God's being and life. God acts out of love and perfect freedom, not out of inner need and necessity. The "idea of a possible universe, with all the ways it has of sharing in God's being and life and goodness, provides the sufficient but noncompelling reason for God's causative action. This general idea, then, is possible final and exemplary causality."[47]

In God's choice to share God's perfection in a particular way, the divine will is joined to the idea of a possible universe in the divine intellect and gives to this idea an inclination or order to an external effect.[48] This intelligible order that eternally exists in the divine intellect that the divine will has freely chosen is what we mean by the eternal plan of providence. Wright distinguishes three aspects of this plan that can be analyzed in terms of their intelligible though not temporal priority: the divine purpose, the antecedent plan, and the consequent plan of providence.

Prior to examining these three aspects of the intelligible order that exists in the divine intellect, it is crucial to recognize that the ultimate context for this whole discussion is God's love: God's intention to share God's self in the most intimate of friendships with creatures. God's will and God's power are not absolute; rather, there is an ordered relation between the divine will, the divine intellect, and the divine power. This ordered relation of the divine will to the divine intellect that determines the divine power to a definite effect is the structure of God's causative knowledge. While God's will or God's love is guided by what is truly possible which is manifested by the divine intellect contemplating the divine goodness, "the actual guidance of wisdom which is manifested in the world is that which divine love has chosen."[49] Love, then, "forms the ultimate context for understanding divine activity: love that is guided by wisdom and executed by power."[50]

It is critical to recognize that God's love is the ultimate context for this discussion because this examination of the three aspects of the eternal plan of providence can easily appear as impersonal. This is so first, because, for ease of presentation, throughout this discussion, the term "plan" (as the intelligible order itself in the divine mind) is used without always explicitly indicating that the plan is God's knowledge of what God has lovingly chosen to share with God's creatures. The term "plan" should not be understood as a blueprint in the manner of an architectural or engineering plan that God consults in his creative and redemptive activity. On the contrary, this abstract account of the intelligible order of ideas toward an end as it exists in the divine intellect is simply referring to the general outlines of God's exhaustive knowledge as God, out of God's infinite love, brings creatures into being and invites free creatures to share in God's life in the most intimate of friendships.

This abstract account, then, especially the general outlines of God's knowledge of what God makes objectively possible in this universe, far from giving us an abstraction or a distant God, is attempting to give intelligible grounds for the Christian belief that God is love and that the whole of God's activity bespeaks the interpersonal. If the objective intelligibility of the divine intellect contemplating and manifesting the divine goodness is not properly explicated, even in a schematic form, along with recognizing that the divine will must be understood in an ordered relation to the divine intellect contemplating the divine goodness, then the divine will inevitably slides toward a pre-rational absolute of power. If God's freedom is understood as absolute and not relative to the intelligibility of the divine being, God's activity could be completely arbitrary and God could in God's good pleasure do terrible things. Such a capricious God hardly resembles the God of love as revealed in scripture.

Three Aspects of the Eternal Plan of Divine Providence

The three aspects of the eternal plan of providence, in Wright's understanding of divine providence, are the divine purpose, the antecedent plan, and the consequent plan. To be adequate to the scriptural evidence, these three aspects of the eternal plan of providence will take into account the threefold dialogical pattern of divine human interaction (i.e., absolute and free divine initiative, human beings' free response, and God's response to the human response) along with the four biblical themes that are integral to this dialogical pattern (i.e., the infallibility of the divine government, the frustration of God's loving initiative in the face of free human resistance, the adaptability that characterizes God's dealings with human beings, and the collective and communal quality of God's purpose).

The Divine Purpose

The divine purpose concerns the ultimate purpose, or end, of God's creative and redemptive activity. It is the "special way in which He intends to embody the participation of God's uncreated goodness."[51] This intention cannot be spoken of as if God takes a risk in creating, and God's ultimate purpose could finally be frustrated. The scriptural insistence upon the omnipotence and infallibility of the divine government is grounded in the purpose that God intends to realize in the created order and God's exhaustive knowledge of the means (which is the antecedent/consequent plan of providence) for achieving that purpose.[52] As will become clearer, scripture's insistence upon the collective and communal quality of God's ultimate purpose will be the key to understanding the infallibility of the divine purpose, while allowing for the frustration of God's intention in individual instances. At this point, it is simply important to maintain that the divine purpose must be understood in collective and communal terms. God's ultimate purpose to be realized in creation is "a society of the supernaturally-elevated created persons united to one another and to the Holy Trinity in vision, love, and joy."[53] The divine purpose does not determine antecedently the precise number of individuals in the kingdom of God, but simply that such a society will exist. The divine purpose is "absolute, unfailing, prior to all vision of actual created activity and individual persons actually existing. This end of divine providence has then a certitude which derives ultimately from God alone, from God's love and wisdom and power.[54]

The Antecedent Plan of Divine Providence

The second aspect of the eternal plan of providence is the antecedent plan. The distinction between the divine purpose and the antecedent plan is simply the difference between the end and the means to the end. There is an objective difference between the end (the divine purpose) and the means to the end (the antecedent plan), "for the end is primary and what is ordered to the end secondary in willing."[55] Nevertheless, this does not mean that there is "a discursus in the mind of God, who in one and the same act wills both the end and the things that are ordered to the end."[56]

The central idea guiding this whole outline of the features of the antecedent plan, as God's knowledge of the means to achieve God's created purpose, is that God's knowledge is no way passive and dependent upon creatures. God is not determined from without, but God determines God's self from within through the choice of the divine will to order the divine goodness, as known by the divine intellect, to the realization of this particular created participation (i.e., the perfection of the universe) in God's uncreated goodness. It follows then that we cannot speak of something happening that catches God by surprise and requires "a hasty tidying-up of God's plans."[57] Rather, "the antecedent plan of God is totally comprehensive, embracing, and making objectively real all possibilities He wishes to be possible within the universe of creatures."[58] God does not simply foresee all the possible contingencies in the universe that God intends to bring into existence; but also precisely because the divine will chooses this idea of a possible universe in the divine intellect, God "determines all that will actually be possible in the world throughout the course of time."[59] While the whole range of limited ways in which the divine goodness can be shared are possible, which God knows in contemplating God's own goodness, it is only when the divine will is joined to the idea of a possible universe in the divine intellect that some of these possibles are made "truly possible within the created world."[60] In addition, not all of these limited possibilities that God makes truly possible in this created universe "will be realized as actual events or things."[61]

The intelligibility of created persons called to union with God involves freedom of choice. Freedom of choice requires possible courses of action. The antecedent plan opens up possibilities for created free choice and in doing so opens up possibilities for the interpersonal dialogue between God and free creatures. Since the intelligibility of created persons called to union with God also involves the possibility of sin, the divine plan for achieving the divine purpose of a society of created persons united to one another and to God will include the possibility of some of these created persons refusing salvation.[62] This divine permission of evil in the antecedent plan of God must be understood as God permitting the possibility of evil in the universe as a necessary consequence of the divine purpose of a universe of created persons united to God in the fullness of life and joy.

It is because God not only intends the salvation of all created persons (God's universal salvific will), but makes the salvation of all created persons truly possible, that God's universal salvific will is an aspect of the antecedent plan of providence. While the "means of salvation provided by the antecedent plan of God... are abundantly sufficient for the salvation of everyone,"[63] they are "antecedently infallibly effective for the salvation of some, but which ones in particular is not yet determined."[64] God wills the salvation of all creatures and makes the salvation of all creatures truly possible. Who will respond in loving acceptance to God's offer of salvation and who will refuse God's offer depends on creatures. While particular created persons can refuse God's call, this does not mean that God's purpose of realizing a society of the blessed united to God in love and friendship can ultimately be frustrated. The means for salvation can be frustrated in individual instances. They cannot be frustrated for the community as a whole. Rather, God knows prior to the free choices of creatures that the means established for the realization of a society of the blessed, which exclude no one, will be infallibly effective in the realization of that society.

Wright provides an analogy from the natural order, "which the supernatural order resembles and perfects,"[65] to illuminate the idea that there is an intelligibility in the group that is "not found in individuals isolated from one another and merely added together."[66] Excluding some unforeseen cataclysm that would destroy the world, we know with certitude that human beings will be in existence two hundred years from now. We know this "because we know that the means for guaranteeing the continued existence of the race are infallibly effective in the group, even though they may not be in each individual case."[67] Even though many people will choose not to have children, there is not the slightest possibility that all people will choose not to have children because the instincts of "sex, self-preservation, and parental care are so strong in human nature."[68] There are also examples from the natural order where we not only know with infallible certitude that something will be in existence in the future by examining the group as a whole, but we also know with a relatively high degree of accuracy how many instances will be realized in the future. Since most individuals in our society choose freely in choosing to marry, we are not able to know who will get married next year. We are, however, able to predict with notable accuracy the number of marriages that will be performed next year. The desire for companionship and the instincts of sex, self-preservation, and parental care condition human freedom such that although some people will not be motivated by these natural desires in their choices, these instincts and desires are so strong that many people will be motivated by these desires in making their choices. The intelligibility found in the whole group "is founded on the nature of human liberty as something not absolutely unconditioned and upon the forces acting everywhere to condition the exercise of this liberty."[69]

The infallibility of the antecedent plan of providence is analogous to the infallible knowledge human beings have in these examples.[70] Similar to our knowledge that in two hundred years the human race will be in existence or that a certain number (certain in the sense of falling within a predictable range) of people will get married next year because of the human instincts and desires for sex, self-preservation, and paternal care, God infallibly knows that while God's offer of salvation may be refused in individual instances, the light and attraction of God's grace offered to created persons in their freedom will be infallibly effective in the group as a whole. Hence, God knows antecedent to any created act of free choice that God's purpose of the realization of a society of the blessed in union with God will be infallibly effective.

God not only knows that the light and attraction of God's grace offered to the creature in her freedom will be effective infallibly in the group as a whole, but God knows all the possible ways in which it can be effective. Here we are simply speaking of God's comprehensive knowledge of how God's grace will be abundantly sufficient to make the salvation of all created persons truly possible. The whole thrust of this discussion of the antecedent plan of providence is to indicate that God's knowledge is not passive and dependent on another. We do this by stating in general terms the comprehensive nature of God's knowledge of what God makes actually possible not only in God's creative and redemptive initiative, but also in terms of God's response to the human response to the divine initiative. To stress that God's knowledge is so exhaustive that no action can catch it by surprise, we indicate that God knows—antecedent to the creature's choice and antecedent to God's response to the creature's choice—how God's response will lead to the establishment of a society of the blessed. Hence, "no matter what the free determination of the creature may be, God has antecedently determined what will be its result, how it will fit into the building up of the heavenly Jerusalem, what will be the divine and efficacious judgment upon the free creaturely response to the divine initiative."[71] This is the foundation of the idea that God is able to draw good out of evil.

It should be clear from this outline how this view is quite different from those accounts that understand the eternal plan of providence as "an exact, efficacious, immutable divine determination of all events that will occur or not occur, made prior to taking account of any actions of created beings."[72] The latter account holds onto the divine perfection by having God determine all events prior to the actions of free creatures. Wright's account, on the other hand, preserves the divine perfection while maintaining that the eternal plan of providence opens up possibilities within which God operates in inviting and drawing creatures toward the fullness of life in union with God.

The Consequent Plan of Divine Providence
A. The Structure of God's Causative Knowledge in Creation, Conservation, and Government

God in knowing God's self knows the ways in which God's goodness can be communicated. God in God's infinite goodness chooses to share God's being and life in a particular way. Through this choice the divine will is joined to the idea of a possible universe in the divine intellect and gives to this idea an inclination or order to an external effect. As we have seen, it is the union of the divine will with the divine intellect that makes this universe and all its possibilities actually possible by giving this possible universe an inclination or order to an external effect. This possible universe that eternally exists in the divine intellect that the divine will has freely chosen encompasses the divine purpose and the antecedent plan of providence as two aspects of the eternal plan of providence. The bringing into existence of this intelligible order, through the divine will ordering the divine power to actually share the divine goodness in this particular way, is the third aspect of the eternal plan of providence: namely, the consequent plan of providence. This ordered relation of the divine will to the divine intellect that determines the divine power to a definite effect is the structure of God's causative knowledge. God knows what exists as distinct from God's self by knowing, in complete self-presence, the perfection that God's power is communicating. Thus God knows what exists as distinct from God's self through communicating existence to it. This is God's causative knowledge, in which God knows things by causing them.[73]

This "infallibly efficacious determination of divine causality to produce a definite effect"[74] is sometimes called an eternal divine decree. Notice that the "divine decree is not simply the divine intention as proceeding from the divine will, but the union of this intention with the divine idea, with the divine goodness known as shareable in a distinct and definite way."[75] If a divine decree is understood simply as flowing from the divine will, then the ultimate context for God's activity would be God's power, not God's love. In addition, if God's power is not rooted in the intelligibility of God's being (by understanding the divine will as relative to the intelligibility of the divine being as known by the divine intellect), then God's activity could be capricious and God could in God's good pleasure do abhorrent things. Furthermore, it is only in the production of the creature through the divine power that there is a relation to the creature as cause to effect. This "relation constitutes a divine idea in the strict sense, the intelligible likeness of something which is produced by God and participates in this idea."[76]

i. Creation

In creation, the divine will regards only and immediately the idea of this possible universe. The divine will is joined to the idea of this universe in the divine intellect and the divine power communicates existence to this idea, and the created universe "begins to be in dependence on the actual causality of God."[77] A visual aid might help grasp the insight.

Creation:

Divine Intellect   *Divine Will*

God knows, in knowing
God's self, the range of possible ways God can share
God's goodness, which
includes a countless number
of possible world orders
that God could bring into
existence. Each number here
represents a possible world
order that God could create.   The divine will chooses
1 2 3 4 5 6 7 8 9 10 11   world 16 (our world)
12 13 14 15   among the range of pos-
16   sible worlds that God
                                                      knows are possible in
                                                      knowing God's self.

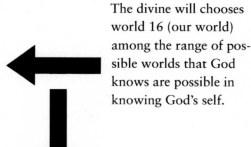

17 18 19 20 21 ....

Divine Power — following (not understood temporally, but in terms of a natural order of priority) the choice of the divine will, the divine power brings this universe (possible world order 16) into existence.

ii. Conservation

Conservation, unlike creation, is not an absolute beginning. God's conservation of the universe is not a new or different action from creation; for conservation is the continued communication of existence to the created order that God has brought into existence through creating. Creation differs from conservation because in creation the divine will is only and immediately ordered to the idea of a possible world order in the divine intellect. In conservation, on the other hand, God continues to communicate existence to already existing creatures, so the divine will is ordered to the divine intellect through the existing universe. In creation the existing creature "is in no way an ontological object of the divine will,"[78] because there is nothing yet in existence. In conservation, "the creature is truly and ontologically an object of God's will, not as an end but as ordered or directed to the end, which is the divine goodness itself."[79]

What does this last sentence precisely mean? Let us examine this statement first from the viewpoint of the creature and second in terms of the divine intention. The various perfections of an effect are immanent in its cause; for a cause cannot give what it does not have. This is particularly true when we examine creatures, who receive all their perfections from God. Creatures as limited participations in the Infinite Act of existence, which is what we mean by God, have *esse*. Because their perfection exists supereminently in God, creatures in their natural desire for their own perfection naturally desire God. Thus creatures in their very being are ordered toward God.[80] God, then, in truly regarding creatures regards creatures as related to God's self. This means that God in truly regarding creatures ultimately regards God's self.

Now let us examine this in terms of the divine intention. God is pure act. Every action is toward an end. In God, agent, action, and end are one. Thus God is necessarily oriented to God's self as the end of God's activity. The ground of God's freedom (and of created freedom) is God's necessary orientation toward God's self as the Infinite Good. It is this ordination toward the Infinite Good by a necessity of nature that is the condition of the possibility of God's free choice (and also created free choice). If God were not necessarily orientated toward God's self as end, then God would be necessarily oriented toward the finite. In this understanding, God would not have free choice and creation would emanate necessarily from God as a necessary aspect of the divine reality. This would eviscerate the divine perfection, because God would need creation in order to be God. God would be dependent upon creation. In order to preserve the divine perfection, we must say, with Thomas Aquinas, that God in one act (since its ultimate term is one) "wills both Himself to be and other things also; but Himself as end, other things as (ordered) to the end, inasmuch as it befits the divine goodness that other things participate in it."[81] While the divine intention truly regards creatures, "it ultimately actually regards the divine goodness itself."[82]

In creation the divine will is immediately joined to the divine intellect contemplating the divine goodness to be communicated. In conservation, because the creature already exists, the union of the divine will with the divine intellect is *through* the creature. Because the "divine will regards the divine goodness by regarding a creature... God wills God's goodness *through* the creature in its relatedness to Himself as end."[83] The creature enters into the intentional structure "through which God causes and knows its continued existence."[84] This is the key insight. When this insight is applied to the divine government, it allows Wright to reconcile the possibility of created free choice with God's causative knowledge.

An example and visual aid to support the example might help clarify the intentional structure of God's causative knowledge in conservation. Let us take the example of God sustaining a polar bear in existence. God in knowing God's self knows all the possible ways God's goodness can be communicated, including bears with only brown fur. In truly regarding the polar bear, however, the divine will does not choose to communicate the possible good of brown fur, but chooses to communicate the possible good of white fur. The possible good to be communicated is specified by the already existing polar bear such that the intentional union of the divine will and the divine intellect contemplating the divine goodness to be communicated is through the polar bear. The divine power communicates existence with all the various features of the polar bear, including white fur.

Conservation:

Divine Intellect

God in knowing God's self knows the possible ways God's goodness can be communicated. Among all these possible ways are bears in all their varieties.

Black and White fur, Brown fur Black fur, White fur Black fur with yellow markings, etc.

Divine Will

The choice the divine will makes between all the possible goods that can be communicated is specified by the creature—in this case, by the polar bear. Thus in sustaining the polar bear in existence, the divine will is ordered to the possible good to be communicated: namely, it is ordered to the possibility of white fur.

Divine Power—following (not understood temporally, but in terms of a natural order of priority) the choice of the divine will, the divine power communicates existence to the polar bear with its white fur.

Images can both illuminate and distort. To correct any possible distortions it must be noted that the creature should not be seen as a physical link between the divine will and the divine intellect, but as an intentional medium. For as is clear from the text accompanying the image, the creature in being truly regarded by the divine will simply specifies the possible good to be communicated as known by the divine intellect. The polar bear thus enters in the intentional structure through which the divine will chooses to communicate the divine goodness in a particular way. Furthermore, I have focused on one characteristic of the polar bear (i.e., its white fur) as an aid to grasping the central insight. This feature and all the features of the polar bear, however, do not exist in isolation; rather, they emerged as adaptations to its environment. All created things are interdependent. Thus if we widen our field of vision we can see that all creatures in every aspect of their being and nature, and as related to each other in the system of the universe down to the smallest particle, in being truly regarded by the divine will specify the possible goods to be communicated as known by the divine intellect. Consequently, actions of other creatures can limit the possible goods that can be communicated to a particular creature like the polar bear. Thus the dwindling of sea ice as a result of human activity (i.e., anthropogenic climate change) has made the polar bear an endangered species. If this continues, then God in truly regarding this world as an interdependent system of beings may not have the possibility of communicating existence to the polar bear.

An additional limitation of these images is that they are highly impersonal. It is important, when we turn to the divine government of free creatures, that the whole context of these images and this discussion be understood in terms of God's intention to share God's self with the creature in an incomprehensible intimacy.

iii. Divine Government and the Free Choice of the Creature

Creatures do not simply exist—they act according to their natures. Action is the natural outflowing of the act of existence (*agere sequitur esse*). As Etienne Gilson puts it, "Not: to be, then to act, but: to be is to act."[85] Birds do not simply exist, but they fly, gather food, and tend to their young. Human beings do not simply exist, but they think, love, build buildings, paint paintings, worship, etc.

Divine activity, then, is not limited to bringing creatures into existence (creation) and sustaining them in existence (conservation), but includes moving them to act according to their natures (divine government). Creation, conservation, and government are not new and different actions of God but different modes of God's communication of existence to the creature. Creation is different from conservation because creation concerns the bringing into existence of something, while conservation concerns the continued communication of existence to the existent being. Conservation is different from divine government because conservation "concerns a creature as receiving and continuing to exercise its own existence,"[86] while divine government as God moving the creature to act according to its nature "concerns a creature as giving or sharing what it is receiving."[87] In other words, God causes the creature to direct the perfection of existence, which it is receiving according to its limited form, to communication with another (and to itself, but in a different way).

The natural inclination of the creature to act comes from God. As Wright maintains:

This dynamism of the created agent, its inclination to communicate its actuality, is derived from the dynamism of the divine will which orders all things to participate in the goodness of God as end. This is not to say that this order or inclination is not also from the creature, from its own nature and power of acting; but created dynamism is not ultimate and always depends upon the self-sufficient dynamism of God's will.[88]

Not only do the power and inclination to act stem from God, but so also the perfection communicated (i.e., existence or actuality) comes from God. God's perfection, as the source of all that is (i.e., all existence and perfection), is preserved in this account because the creature in acting according to its nature adds no further perfection to the perfection of existence that it receives from God. The creature, in acting according to its nature, simply specifies the actuality that will be communicated through it to a patient (i.e., the thing acted upon). In other words, God causes the activity of creatures and the concomitant effect through these creatures. Thus to say that God causes the sun to shine does not mean that God shines;[89] rather, God "causes the created reality in and through the creature according to the nature of the creature."[90]

I will forego an examination of the intentional structure of God's causative knowledge in God's governing irrational creatures; rather, I will focus on the divine government of free creatures. Here the central question is: If God's knowledge is causative, then how can God know the free choices of creatures without destroying their free choice?

The central insight from examining God's causative knowledge in conservation is that the creature enters into the intentional structure of God's causative knowledge such that the union of the divine will with the divine intellect is *through* the creature. This insight holds true for the divine government of free creatures as God knows and causes the creatures' free choices. The second important insight that will be significant in examining God's causative knowledge of created free choices comes from the brief treatment of divine government in general. This insight is that the creature in acting adds no further perfection to the perfection of existence that it receives from God according to its nature, but simply specifies the actuality that will be communicated through it to a patient. With these insights in mind, let us turn to the structure of God's causative knowledge of created free choices.

The examination of God's causative knowledge of free choices will have two general steps: first, a description of a free choice from the point of view of the creature; second, a description of the free choice from the point of view of God's causative knowledge. Let us turn to an examination of the free choice from the point of view of the creature. Action requires a determinate end. If an agent were not necessarily oriented to some definite end, then it would be, at its root, indifferent. From an agent utterly indifferent to various ends, no action can result for there would be no reason for the agent to act.[91] In other words, if the creature were utterly indeterminate it would never act; for nothing can pass from potency to act except through the power of something already in act. The will of the creature, then, in order to act must always already be in act.

The created will can choose between finite goods because it is permanently actuated toward the Infinite Good, which contains in supereminent plentitude all the goodness of any good that a creature could desire.[92] Norris Clarke expresses the crucial point:

> *The permanent actualization of our will toward this good, preceding all particular acts of willing, contains virtually already within its power all particular acts of willing toward finite goods; for these add nothing higher to this primal actualization of our willing power which is always going on; they add only new limited participations or expressions of this primal transcendent fullness of willing the Good in itself, the Good of all goods. Hence this original, ever-present act of our will toward the Infinite is able to reduce itself to later particular and lesser acts with respect to all limited participations of this one necessary goal.*[93]

This permanent actualization of the created will toward the Infinite Good that is the condition of the possibility of free creatures' power of free choice is what Wright calls the will's active indifference prior to choice. It is this active orientation of the will toward the Infinite Good that makes the will indifferent to many finite goods and as such makes the will capable of choosing between finite goods.

The will also has a passive indifference prior to free choice because it is "able *to be moved* and intrinsically changed and developed"[94] by any one of a number of finite goods. All finite things as limited participations in the Infinite Good reflect the goodness of their source. In reflecting the goodness of their source, these finite goods exercise some pull on the will, but since none of them are the Good in itself, the lure of these possible finite goods does not determine the will. The will remains indifferent to them, and this is the will's passive indifference. Passive indifference includes not only the will's capacity to be moved by a particular good but the will's ability to be intrinsically changed in its choice of a particular good. I can be drawn to the beauty of a piece of jewelry even though I know that if I bought it I would not be able to pay for my children's education. In deciding to steal the jewelry, I am intrinsically changed by the choice; namely, I become a thief.

The active and passive indifference of the will is significant in this analysis for two reasons. First, the twofold indifference shows that the will is neither determined by God in its choice (indeed, God's causal activity allows for the creature to choose freely), nor is the will determined by the particular finite goods or circumstances because of the will's passive indifference; rather, the person under the influence of God's causal activity freely moves herself to some definite choice. Second, the recognition that the will is both active and passive aids in showing how the free creature in its choice adds no further perfection to the perfection of existence that it receives from God according to its nature, but simply communicates this perfection internally to itself (i.e., the subject does not simply choose this or that, but she becomes this particular person in her choice) and possibly also to another existent.

Now let us examine the free choice of the creature from the perspective of God's causative knowledge. The following elements are presented in a natural order of priority, although they are temporally simultaneous in the one existential event of created free choice.

First, God conserves the free creature's being and power of acting.

Second, "the divine will moves or applies the created agent to act, to choose freely among the various actions that are open to him.... This divine influence does not determine what the choice of the creature is to be, but only that *some* choice is to be."[95] The effect of the divine motion is the actualization of the free creature toward the Infinite Good. To say that the divine influence does not determine the choice of the creature, but only that some choice is to be, should not be understood as if the creature loses its freedom of exercise. In analyzing a particular choice between goods A, B, and C we say that the free creature can choose one of these (freedom of specification) or the creature can choose none of these (freedom of exercise). This is a valid distinction, when we are referring to a choice between a particular set of goods like A, B, or C. It is not valid, if we understand the freedom of exercise to mean that we are capable of not choosing at all. I am free not to choose one of those goods A, B, or C, but I am not free not to choose; for not choosing goods A, B, or C is itself a choice.

Third, the free creature chooses. In this choice the creature freely orders its permanent actualization toward the Infinite Good (active indifference) to a particular course of action. As we have seen, this choice of a definite course of action adds nothing higher to the primal actualization of the creature's willing power that is always going on.[96] Hence, free choice "implies per se no further or increased perfection in the agent's active power, but only the ordering of the perfection already possessed to communication."[97] As such, the creature's choice "requires no new causal influx of God in addition to that whereby He conserves the creature in being and applies it to act without determining its power of action to one."[98] In the act of free choice, viewed in terms of the determination to one of the creature's active indifference, the creature is not perfected because the creature in free choice is simply ordering the perfection she possesses toward communication.[99] The act of free choice as an ordering of the perfection to be communicated to a determined effect (active indifference) simultaneously determines the will (passive indifference) to one act. The creature specifies the perfection to be communicated and the particular good it will receive in its passive indifference.

Fourth, the choice the divine will makes between all the possible ways that the divine goodness can be communicated is specified by the created will moving itself (under the influence of the divine will) to one act. The intentional union of the divine will and the divine intellect manifesting and contemplating the divine goodness to be communicated is through the free creature freely determining itself under the influence of the divine motion.

Fifth, "the causality of God, the divine power, is actually extended to this free act whose specification is from the creature."[100] God knows and causes the creature's free choice.

Finally, "the existence of the free act is received in the creature from God; for what is proper to the first cause is the last thing to be realized in the effect."[101] We saw that the will's passive indifference includes the will's capacity to be moved by a particular good and the will's ability to be intrinsically changed in its choice of a particular good. Thus when the existence of the free act is received in the creature from God, the creature is intrinsically changed such that the creature becomes what she chooses (i.e., if I steal I become a thief; if I love agapically I become like God).

Let us take the example of someone choosing to play basketball, to simplify and illustrate the intentional structure of God's causative knowledge of a creature's free choice.

Divine Government and the Free Choice of the Creature:

Divine Intellect

God in knowing God's self knows the possible ways God can communicate God's goodness. Among these ways is a free creature acting in the following ways at any particular moment.

Watch TV
Read theology
Pray
Play basketball
Eat
Exercise

Divine Will

The choice the divine will makes between all the possible goods that can be communicated is specified by the created person's free choice (under the enabling yet non-determining influence of the divine will truly regarding the creature and its power of acting). Thus the choice of the person to play basketball specifies the good to be communicated by God.

Divine Power—following (not understood temporally, but in terms of a natural order of priority) the choice of the divine will, the divine power brings into existence the good specified by human choice: namely, the free human being playing basketball.

God knows the existing realities in the universe, including the free choices of creatures, not "by seeing them rooted in God's power,"[102] but by God knowing that God's power is ordered by God's will toward actually producing a particular good in the created universe. God's knowledge is causative, and God's causality is cognitive, such that the conditions for God to know some existing thing and the conditions for God to cause that thing are the same.[103] It is thus "finally contradictory to affirm that God can know some existing thing as existing apart from what is required for Him to cause that thing to exist."[104]

B. *The God Who Dialogues*

Non-rational creatures are determined in their actions in the antecedent plan of providence, but free creatures have possible courses of action open to them. These possible courses of action, as we have seen, were made possible in the antecedent plan of providence. The free determination of the creature within the antecedent plan of God is "what at once distinguishes and unites the antecedent and the consequent plans of God."[105] The consequent plan is that aspect of the antecedent plan which God actually executes in view of human free choices. God gives being "to those possibilities of the antecedent plan that correspond to the choices made by free creatures, and he orders the acts they have chosen to the end he intends."[106]

The consequent plan not only encompasses the free human response to the divine initiative, but also the divine response to the human response. The antecedent plan, as we have seen, makes possible the salvation of all persons, and thus it includes the whole of the divine initiative. Hence, "all the force, power, goodness, mercy, and gratuity that is to be found in the second or consequent plan of God is already virtually present in the antecedent plan of God."[107] The consequent plan of providence is a particular concretization of the antecedent plan, a concretization that is conditioned by the free choices of creatures.

In every free choice, the free creature is either accepting the influence of God in her life and thus is cooperating with the divine purpose, or the creature is obstructing or denying the influence of God in her life and is more or less departing from the divine purpose. God in intending to create persons called to union with God (divine purpose) makes possible (antecedent plan) and thus permits the possibility of sin because, as we have seen, the intelligibility of created persons called to union with God involves the possibility of sin and moral evil. When the free creature withdraws from the divine influence in her life, God in truly regarding the creature gives being (consequent plan) to the evil choice of the creature. No matter what the choice of the creature, God, in responding to the choice, orders it toward God's purpose of the establishment of the society of the blessed living in union with God.

This ordering is God's judgment. As an ordering toward the fulfillment of God's purpose, it is not simply a judgment on what the creature has done, but it is also an invitation to the creature to participate more fully in God's life through a call to repentance and further growth in the life of the Spirit. This judgment on every creaturely response to the divine initiative is the continuous judgment, whose full meaning is only revealed in the particular judgment upon the individual at her death and the general judgment of God upon all created things in the consummation of the universe.

Conclusion

God in knowing God's self knows God's goodness as capable of being given to others. God wills to bring creatures into being so that they can participate in God's being and life. God brings into existence creatures that both manifest God's goodness (all creatures) and can enter into the deepest friendship with God (rational and free creatures). Friendship involves reciprocity: a dialogue.

Salvation history is such a dialogue. It is a dialogue between God and free creatures. The pattern of this dialogue is revealed in scripture and is typified by three moments: God's absolute initiative, human free response to God's initiative, and God's response to the human response. Classical theology and strands of contemporary theology have focused on one aspect of this dialogue while overlooking others. Classical theology focused on the absolute divine initiative and God's sovereign operation without adequately showing how the human being could have genuine free choice if God is the source of all that is. As such, classical theology was not able to articulate adequately the possibility of the human response and the divine response to the human response in the divine/human dialogue. Strands of contemporary theology, especially process theology and its variants, responded to this problem in classical theology by diminishing God's sovereignty. This paper, in drawing upon the work of Wright, overcomes this impasse and reconciles the sovereign operation of God and the capacity of human beings for genuine choice. As such it holds together all moments of the divine and human dialogue.

A constructive response to the perennial problem of reconciling God's sovereign operation and human free choice in the context of the doctrine of providence must be grounded in a biblical theology of providence that is attentive to the whole of scripture. The classical view of providence focused too exclusively on the biblical theme of God as the Lord of history whose plan will be infallibly realized, without recognizing the other three themes that run through scripture: namely, the susceptibility of God's eternal plan to frustration in individual details, its adaptability, and the communal quality of God's purpose and the means to attaining God's purpose. Of these three themes, the understanding of God's purpose in communal or collective terms is the most significant, for it allows for the frustration of God's intention in individual instances and the consequent adaptability of God's plan so that God can make the disobedience and hardness of heart of creatures serve God's ultimate purpose. One simply cannot preserve genuine created choice, if one maintains that the infallibility of the divine government requires that God know infallibly, antecedent to the choices of free creatures, which individuals will constitute the community of the blessed living in eternal union with God. Such a view would require that God predetermine the choices of free creatures. This would attenuate any notion of the divine-human dialogue and any responsibility the creature has for her actions.

Contrary to a view of providence that predetermines the choices of free creatures, this paper, drawing upon Wright, develops an understanding of the eternal plan of providence which opens up possibilities for created free choice and thus opens up possibilities for the interpersonal dialogue between God and free creatures—a dialogue whose ultimate context is love, not power.

Both the sovereignty of God and the dialogical character of God's dealings with human beings can be maintained when one understands the eternal plan of providence in terms of three aspects—the divine purpose, the antecedent plan, and the consequent plan. The three aspects of the eternal plan of providence distinguish God's knowledge and determination of all that will be possible in this universe (antecedent plan) from his causative knowledge of those possibilities that will actually be realized in this universe as conditioned by the choices of free creatures and God's response to those choices (consequent plan), as God realizes God's purpose of a society of the blessed united with God in vision, love, and joy (divine purpose).

The sovereignty of God requires that the creature add no new perfection to God. Thus God is neither dependent upon the creature for God's knowledge of what is possible in the created universe, nor for God's knowledge of those possibilities that actually come into being in the universe. Antecedent to the free choices of creatures (antecedent plan), God exhaustively knows and even makes possible all the possible courses of action open to God's creatures. God also knows how the creature's choice, no matter what it may be, can fit into the establishment of the kingdom of heaven. God knows infallibly that God's purpose of a society of the blessed united to God will be realized because God knows how God will respond to the choices of free creatures. Moreover, God knows that God's response and the light of God's grace will be infallibly effective in the group as a whole, even though some individuals will choose to finally and definitely refuse God's universal invitation to eternal life.

The consequent plan are those possibilities of the antecedent plan that God actually realizes that correspond to the choices of free creatures and God's response to those choices as God realizes God's purpose. God cannot be understood as learning from creatures. Thus God's knowledge cannot be passive and caused. If it is not passive and caused, it must be understood as active and causative. The central insight to handle the thorny problem of how God's knowledge is causative, yet the creature remains free, comes from an examination of God's causative knowledge in conservation and divine government. This insight is that creatures enter into the intentional structure through which God knows and causes their existence in sustaining them in being (conservation) and moving them to act according to their natures (government), including rational creatures with their power to choose freely.

The divine influence on free creatures in their act of choice is a non-determining influence that enables the creature to choose freely. Divine causality and human freedom, then, must not be understood as opposed to each other; rather, it is precisely through the divine influence moving the human being to act according to its nature that the human being is capable of free choice and is thus capable of accepting God's call to friendship with God.

The human being in acting according to its nature adds no further perfection to the perfection of existence that it receives from God; rather, she simply specifies the actuality that is communicated through her to a patient. God "knows what *is*, because He knows what He has willed to *give* according to the disposition of the creature."[108] The creature gives God nothing.[109] Thus we can join our voice to St. Paul and St. Augustine—"What do you have that you have not received?"[110]

Trinity, Community,
and Social Transformation

Cara Anthony, University of St. Thomas, Minnesota

IN THE PAST SEVERAL DECADES, the West has seen a massive resurgence in theological studies on the Trinity. Many scholars mark the start of this trend with works by Karl Barth and Karl Rahner.[1] The most recent quarter century has been particularly fruitful: While in 1983 one writer observed that new works on the Trinity were "relatively rare,"[2] by 2001 another could say that "the affirmation of God as triune has emerged as the central or primary teaching, at least in the opinion of a sizable chorus of theologians."[3] Among these theologians, we have seen major systematic works on the Trinity from Catherine LaCugna, Robert Jenson, John Zizioulas, Leonardo Boff, Wolfhart Pannenberg, Elizabeth A. Johnson, and others; and trinitarian theology has become a more explicit foundation for related theological topics such as Christian spirituality, ethics, ecology, ecclesiology, and inter-religious dialogue.

Despite this rich scholarship, many Christians still find the doctrine of the Trinity puzzling and perhaps unnecessary. Christians may speak of their faith in God and Jesus, and occasionally in the Holy Spirit. But the claim that the one God exists in three persons often seems like a bad math problem. Many pastors take the Trinity as the subject of their preaching only on the Sunday after Pentecost. In my own conversations with Christians who are not pastors or academics, the topic of the Trinity seems to embarrass people who seem to secretly worry that their faith is nonsensical and untenable. At the Catholic university where I work, the students express confusion over trinitarian doctrine, and they generally see no connection between this doctrine and their lives. There remains a gap between trinitarian theology and the experience of most people who faithfully take their place in the pews each Sunday.

This gap in the practical theology of ordinary Christians does not necessarily reflect a lack of devotion or care. The problem is not with the good work of theologians or the good faith of Christians. In fact, it is probably not a strictly doctrinal problem at all, if one agrees with Nicholas Lash that "it is not... by way of the technical 'grammar' of the matter that most people are brought to some understanding of what the doctrine means."[4] But if doctrinal formulations are not the most common or best way to enter into some understanding of the Trinity, it is unclear that other kinds of discourse, prayer, or practice are doing the job either. The trinitarian character of ordinary Christian life is often subdued and perhaps distorted.

What do I mean by subdued? To illustrate, it is instructive to note how differently Christians respond to other core doctrines. One good example comes from Catholic theology of the Eucharist. American Catholic congregations have experienced an upsurge in Eucharistic devotion, especially since John Paul II's 2003 encyclical *Ecclesia de eucharistia*. Both perpetual adoration and public Eucharistic processions have flourished in the last decade; pastors frequently preach on the meaning of the Eucharist, and it is fairly easy to find Catholics who have a good basic grasp of Eucharistic teachings, participate frequently in the liturgy, and speak of Christ's real presence in the Eucharist with the warmth and authority of personal experience. None of this, to my knowledge, is true of the doctrine of the Trinity.

What do I mean by the trinitarian dimension of Christian life being distorted? Let us look again at the Eucharist, which in many Christian traditions is the preeminent way for believers to enter into the mystery of the Trinity. Rowan Williams reminds us of the trinitarian pattern of Eucharistic prayer in this way:

> *When we come together to pray at Holy Communion, we do so as baptized believers, people whose lives have been "soaked" in the life of Jesus by the coming into our lives of the Spirit. And so our prayer is, so to speak, dropped into his, absorbed into his. We stand before God the Father, clothed in the identity of Jesus by the gift of the Spirit. We prayerfully give into Jesus' hands the bread and wine, so that his prayer may be made over them. His prayer is that they should become his body and blood. What he prays for happens, because he is the perfect channel of the Holy Spirit's action. So the bread and wine are given back to us, transformed by the Spirit, to make us more deeply what we already are, to confirm the bond that God has created between himself and us.[5]*

Inextricably linked with the Eucharist's trinitarian pattern is its ecclesial form. In the act of reconciling us to himself, God also reconciles us to each other. Sharing together in God's trinitarian life, we simultaneously receive a share in each other's lives.

But even though the prayers, songs, and actions of the liturgy are designed to draw worshippers into the life of Christ with his Father in the Holy Spirit, the trinitarian character of the Eucharist can still be lost. As many Christian commentators have noted, the liturgy itself is shaped by an individualistic, privatized religious culture in the United States. Mark Searle argues that Roman Catholic liturgy all too often is a reflection of this culture rather than an antidote to it. He explains that the tradition of religious dissent in the United States led to a repudiation of the civic model of a single church that dominates public life. The legacy of this model is the separation of church and state. While this arrangement yields obvious benefits, Searle cites two unintended results. First, "religion is privatized for the individual," so "it devolves into a matter of personal preference." Second, privatization means that Christian churches "have no public role to play and no official standing. They are demoted to secondary institutions caring for the needs of private individuals."[6]

In this situation, liturgy becomes less "an action of Christ the priest and of His Body the church," and more a shared celebration meeting the private needs of individuals, whether it be "because we like it, or because it makes us feel good about ourselves, or because we enjoy praying and singing with others." Searle calls such liturgy "shared therapy" and not common worship.[7] Hans Urs von Balthasar said as much in regard to European churches, where "even the criterion of the 'vitality' of a worship service remains ambiguous; the question is always raised as to whether it brings about a living opening and conversion of the heart or the self-enjoyment of one's own vitality."[8]

The cultural challenges noted by Searle and Balthasar have deepened in recent decades: It is all too easy to let our culture's hyper-individualism shape Sunday liturgy. Our desire for autonomy, convenience, and choice means that we often travel long distances to a favorite church for one hour of worship a week, and thus see fellow churchgoers *only* in that one hour; or we choose from among several churches to worship at each Sunday, depending on our other weekend activities. Economic pressures also change the way we worship: our jobs force us to relocate frequently, or working on the weekend makes regular Sunday liturgy a burden. Consequently, we often come together for Eucharistic celebration with people of whom we have only slight knowledge and to whom we have only tenuous social connections. Under these conditions, the impulse to carry on a strictly private, interior dialogue with Jesus becomes stronger, and our cultural tendencies towards social isolation and private experience find their way ever more into our celebration of the Lord's Supper.

This situation is a scandal and a countersign to the trinitarian symbolism of the Eucharist. Lack of human fellowship warps our ability to share in the love of God. We recognize this even as we acknowledge that the love of Christ is prior to our love for each other, and that *God* initiates kinship between us through the gift of the Holy Spirit. As Rowan Williams affirms, "the relationships of communion within the Church and with the rest of creation are the working-out of the gift that is given when the Spirit takes us into the heart of Jesus' prayerful relation to the Father."[9]

Nevertheless, our sacramental life reaches beyond the liturgy, and we are meant to encounter God in our everyday relationships. For this reason, our collective failure to be really present to each other hampers our ability to respond to God's invitation into trinitarian life at the Eucharist. When we do not belong to each other, we lose a primary source for imagining God. When we cannot grasp the possibilities for communion in *human* life, it is no surprise that we draw a blank when we try to think about *God's* life. The absence of Christian community from large portions of our lives effectively stifles the Spirit (1 Thess 5:19).

The responsibility for embodying Trinitarian life cannot fall so exclusively on Sunday worship. We know that the Eucharist is the "source and summit" of Christian life, but this conviction requires us to attend to the ways trinitarian life flows out from this source. The pressures of daily life make it difficult to bring trinitarian community into the regular activities of the rest of the week. These pressures should not be viewed as merely personal struggles, but as systemic social problems that narrow the horizons of Christian faith. For the church to be fully immersed in the "interwoven knot of action and love"[10] that is God's life in Trinity, Christian formation must more intentionally extend into civic and social structures that support our everyday activities.

This proposal is daunting: Do we have the ability to create such social structures? Anxiety about world affairs, fear of terrorism, widespread economic suffering, dwindling resources, and the threat of ecological collapse all eat away at a sense of promise and prospect. Christians enjoy no immunity to these realities, which lead many to despair of political and social harmony. This despair can lead Christians to hope instead for a supernatural life that occurs above, or after, the here-and-now. In the meantime, we retreat into small pockets of safety and comfort in our homes and among family and friends.

But as important as domestic familial relationships are, we yearn for more, and Christian faith teaches that we are meant to have more. The belief that the human person is inherently social is affirmed by the insights of psychology and our own experiences: We thrive when our social connections are numerous and strong, and we suffer when they are few and weak. Our need for communal life is hardwired into our brains: The surest and most enduring path to happiness is to develop many good relationships with varying levels of intimacy—from the closest family ties to the friendly exchange at a town meeting.[11]

Most important for the present discussion is the network of relationships designated as *community*. This is a slippery term in current parlance; we seem to apply the term to any conglomeration of people with a shared interest, no matter how tenuous. One can speak of "the coffee-drinking community" or "the community of poodle owners," but such uses fail to capture the full meaning of community and its importance for Christian faith. We are inquiring about both civic and ecclesial community, especially in the North American context. Given this focus, it is appropriate to turn to one of the most trenchant social critics of the last half century, Wendell Berry.

Berry is the author of more than forty books of poetry, fiction, and essays. Together with his wife, Tanya, he raised two children and has farmed a hillside in his native Henry County, Kentucky for over forty years. His novels and short stories portray life in a fictional town called Port Royal, loosely based on his real hometown of Port William. His writings celebrate family, community, and respect for the land, and often sharply critique the social and economic forces that threaten these values. Berry has written, "My work has been motivated by a desire to make myself responsibly at home in this world and in my native and chosen place."[12] Although his work is not overtly theological and often criticizes Christian institutions, Berry professes Christian faith and is a regular member of the local Baptist church in Port William. His worldview is unmistakably Christian, and in particular his understanding of community is shaped by the Apostle Paul's image of the Body of Christ.

Berry defines community as a set of relationships *intermediate* between private individuals and public life. In his view, a public is a large and diverse people who form a political entity, but they do not necessarily share common values and may or may not know each other.[13] Public life has laws and procedures that allow strangers to share certain expectations and get along. Berry argues that public life today may be able to maintain a thin veneer of civility, but it fails to cultivate respect; its power lies in the rule of law, but it cannot form consciences or inculcate virtue. For these finer activities one must rely on communities, which are more intimate than public life, but much broader than private relationships.

Crucial to Berry's understanding of community is its rootedness in a particular place. He writes, "by community, I mean the commonwealth and common interests, commonly understood, of people living together in a place and wishing to continue to do so. To put it another way, community is a locally understood interdependence of local people, local culture, local economy, and local nature."[14] Community is not limited to the local, but its primary meaning comes from this physical connectedness of people to a place and to each other. Only in this situation can people forge "an understood mutuality of interests" that cements their shared identity.[15]

Berry draws on images from nature and the Bible to clarify the nature of community, saying, "a healthy community is like an ecosystem, and it includes—or makes itself harmoniously a part of—its local ecosystem. It is also like a household; it is the household of its place, and it includes the households of many families, human and nonhuman. And to extend Saint Paul's famous metaphor by only a little, a healthy community is like a body, for its members mutually support and serve one another."[16]

Berry's emphasis on the community as a *body* in a particular *place* immediately reminds us of some of the weaknesses of affluent Christian lifestyles. Large homes, long solo commutes to work, and hours spent on the Internet are common features of our lives. But these seemingly innocuous habits erode our sense of place and our connection to those we are supposedly closest to. Spaced far apart, we cannot support and serve each other because we don't even know each other. Berry brings our attention back to the *physical space* in which healthy communities thrive. A shared place is the basis for personal relationships between individuals, and in this place there accumulates a wealth of shared experiences that, over time, draw people closer together. Shared place can gradually build unity and a common identity, even when community members come from diverse backgrounds and hold different points of view.

Having a fixed place, a community develops its own way of functioning. It "lives and acts by the common virtues of trust, goodwill, forbearance, self-restraint, compassion, and forgiveness."[17] These virtues cannot be enforced by public law or litigation, nor can an individual practice them alone. Rather, the community as a whole instills standards of decent behavior in its members, "not by coercion or violence but by teaching the young and by preserving stories and songs that tell (among other things) what works and does not work in a given place."[18] Berry includes among the works of community "the care of the old, the care and education of children, family life, neighborly work, the handing down of memory, the care of the earth, respect for nature and the lives of wild creatures."[19] These fundamental cultural activities cannot be passed off onto an impersonal public bureaucracy, nor can they be single-handedly sustained by even the most heroic individuals. In order for our most profound values and worldviews to take root, individuals at the local level must *as a group* commit to each other and take responsibility for the care of their neighborhood.

One of the more appealing features of Berry's community is that it offers the chance to be known and included in a larger network of human relationships, while still recognizing and supporting individuality. He writes, "the health of a community depends absolutely on trust. A community knows itself and knows its place in a way that is impossible for a public (a nation, say, or a state). A community does not come together by a covenant, by a conscientious granting of trust. It exists by proximity, by neighborhood; it knows face to face, and it trusts as it knows."[20]

Perhaps surprisingly, a close-knit community can be more welcoming to outsiders than a less cohesive one. Personal knowledge and trust enables members to accept individuals who would otherwise be marginalized. Berry says the community "learns, in the course of time and experience, what and who can be trusted. It knows that some of its members are untrustworthy, and it can be tolerant, because to know in this matter is to be safe. A community member can be trusted to be untrustworthy and so can be included."[21] Supporting and serving each other is less risky when members know each other; for instance, I am more likely to volunteer for a project if I know whom to call on for support when I need it. Potential new members can also find a place more readily when the community has confidence in its own resilience and shared resources.

Berry's community is thus a supple and subtle organism, designed to nurture both freedom and responsibility without resorting to force of law. But this very suppleness also makes the community more fragile than the state. Berry explains, "a community cannot be made or preserved apart from the loyalty and affection of its members and the respect and goodwill of the people outside it."[22] The ambition of private individuals, abetted by large-scale political and economic exploitation, erodes the cohesion, loyalty, and respect that communities require. Under these conditions, communities lose the power to form their members.

Berry has dedicated his life to opposing the forces that harm rural agrarian communities. He observes ruefully that the idea of community "ranks with 'family,' 'our land' and 'our beloved country' as an icon of the public vocabulary; everybody is for it, and this means nothing. If individuals or groups have the temerity to oppose an actual item on the agenda of technological process because it will damage a community, the powers that be will think them guilty of Luddism, sedition, and perhaps insanity."[23] Berry recognizes that people must work for public policies that support and protect small local communities.

Berry's understanding of community helps us focus on a set of relationships *between* the private and the public that many find weak or absent in their lives. He addresses the desire to both belong to each other, yet retain individuality. The community Berry describes is large and multifaceted enough to support all of life's basic activities, yet small enough to afford individuals a voice in it without being co-opted by vast, impersonal forces. He illustrates well the principle of subsidiarity—there are many activities that the local community does best.

Berry's communal vision is inspired by ecclesial images. He recognizes the importance of a civic space that is not identical with Christianity, but within which people can thrive religiously, economically, and socially. His understanding of community enables Christians to evaluate different elements of "culture" or "the world," as distinct from the church. He criticizes harshly any organization or system that crushes local communities, but he does not therefore reject all secular culture or civic life. Churches have a place in the kind of community that Berry defends.

Berry helps us see how civic and ecclesial communities share some literal common ground. The economic and political policies that threaten local community also threaten the local church, and there is literally "room" for cooperation between the two, even as the institutional separation of church and state remains in place. Christians need to integrate their neighborhood life with church life in order for the church to live out its communal character. Christians can better enact love of God and neighbor when it extends beyond the Eucharistic table to the workplace, the market, and the school.

Berry's insights may also require us to rethink our habits of being "church" in an era when Catholic parishes are being consolidated and people are hunting for the best worship service. The large, popular church that draws in people from all over surely can contribute locally, but the attention of its members may be divided, and their loyalties may be invested elsewhere—or nowhere. And although a church with a strong local base will not attract every resident of the neighborhood, it can still hear the voices of the neighborhood because a significant number of them are in the pews.

Furthermore, Berry encourages Christians to think about community formation and preservation in not just disembodied spiritualized terms, but also in light of economic and political realities that dislocate us physically, socially, and spiritually. His emphasis on the bodily character of community life is an antidote to the escapist tendencies inherent in our far-flung "virtual communities."[24] (As one example, almost all my knowledge of my family members this year has come to me through Facebook.) The action of sharing physical goods in a particular place forces us to recognize that our own well-being is linked to the well-being of other community members and of the biotic community in which we live.

Some have called Berry's depictions of community romantic and unrealistic, but others have recognized that his vision of community is prophetic. Like any prophet, Berry names a brokenness so ingrained in our lives that we hardly know how to speak of it, yet he also offers a hopeful vision of a better life that energizes and "encourages his readers to think freshly about the world and their place in it."[25] Before we can work for community, we must be able to imagine it.

It is precisely this imaginative activity that is most difficult when we try to talk about the Trinity. Although our attempts to fathom the mystery of the Father, Son, and Holy Spirit always fall short, I believe that in his depictions of community, Berry helps us imagine a human analogy for Trinitarian life. The fact that God's life in Trinity is a mystery does not mean that it is an abstraction. On the contrary, this mystery is present to us in word and sacrament and in every act of self-giving love.

Inspired by Wendell Berry's vision, I would like to offer a few ideas for both personal and structural change that would help us imagine God's life of mutual self-gift in the process of living it ourselves. My suggestions for structural change begin from Berry's observations on the importance of belonging to a place, but also arise from issues that have long been important to me.

My first suggestion is that Christians should be far more interested than they currently are in public policies that dictate land use: transportation policy, zoning ordinances, city planning, and property taxes (especially on farms and other open lands). Our physical proximity to each other and to needed resources determines the shape of our ecclesial life. Both monastic communities and the Amish have taken this step of intentionally creating a *space* for ecclesial life; it is now necessary to follow their example, but in closer cooperation with non-Christian neighbors. Reconfiguring the places where we live and work would also reclaim hours from our overly hectic days: The average American spends an hour a day driving from place to place.

Developing local economies that are responsible to the human and biotic community of a given place would guide us away from escapist attitudes that permit us to squander resources, and would foster a more sacramental sensitivity to the life around us. Strong local economies would help us to embody the mutual trust and reliance that we aspire to in our ecclesial lives, and would bring incarnational depth to our worship.

We could also alter some of our personal habits to give them a more communal edge. Family life in many cases is already a source of strength, but its full potential remains untapped as long as we limit it to the small nuclear family. Despite legitimate concerns about overpopulation, we must acknowledge that large families are a bit like mangrove forests: They create their own ecologies, and among their intertwined members many others find a home. Large families need a lot of support, and they often attract friends who are rich in time or resources but hungry for belonging. Similarly, we can learn something from families who have a member with a disability. Their situation forces them to seek out support groups and band together with others for survival, but they often discover that the crisis opens new doors of friendship and cooperation that make life not only bearable but also a joy.

We also need to reclaim the charism of hospitality. Too often (and I include myself in this critique) we substitute entertaining for hospitality, and our attention shifts from persons to things like menu, lighting, and seating arrangements. With so much planning and effort involved, we are less inclined to open our homes generously to a wider array of people. In doing so, we cheat ourselves and others out of powerful and sometimes life-changing experiences.

A brief story about my own parents illustrates this point. Many years ago, my mother and father befriended a small family who lived less than a mile from them, but whose poverty placed them practically in another world. Sherry and Mary Ann were a mother and daughter who lived in a ramshackle farmhouse with a wood stove for heat, no hot water, chickens in the kitchen, and deep layers of dirt. Both women had epilepsy and mental disabilities, and Mary Jane had suffered repeated episodes of sexual violence at the hands of her grandfather and his friends. Mother and daughter were devoted to each other, and they enjoyed visiting with my mom in our kitchen, where they would drink tea, eat sweets, and laugh. At first they were too shy to stay for dinner, but gradually they got comfortable staying with us for visits that stretched into the evening.

Over the years my parents became intermediaries and advocates for Shirley and Mary Jane. They took the women grocery shopping. They noticed when Mary Jane's many medications got out of control, and communicated with her doctors. They took Shirley to visit Mary Jane, now in the hospital. When invited, they met with social workers who were coaxing the women toward more comfortable housing, and together with other friends helped the pair get settled in their new home. At one point, Mary Jane received a bad blood transfusion and her doctors expected her to die; Shirley requested that her daughter be baptized, and my mother became Mary Jane's godmother. (Mary Jane promptly recovered, and Shirley always credited the baptism for her daughter's miraculous cure.) All this could be challenging at times, but my parents found Mary Jane and Shirley to be delightful, funny, and openhearted people who constantly humbled them with acts of kindness and generosity—two people who might be assumed to have nothing to give.

My parents also shared tremendous suffering and grief with their friends: Mary Jane died young, of massive burns caused by an accident with a gas stove. Shirley had died a few months earlier from a host of medical problems. But even with all the disaster and loss that accompanied these two lives, my parents still speak of Shirley and Mary Jane with awe, gratitude, and joy. For my parents, a simple but radical custom of hospitality drew them out of themselves and straight into the heart of the paschal mystery. I also think it is no coincidence that my parents have lived in the same place for forty years.

Trinitarian faith and practice mutually condition and inform one another. If we take seriously the physical, sacramental character of Christian life, then we acknowledge that the grace of the triune God expresses itself in our ecclesial life together and, it is to be hoped, in all our comings and goings in the world. Yet when we recognize the embodied, communal character of trinitarian life together, we are forced to acknowledge that the way we live in the world also shapes the way we practice trinitarian faith. The community of the Church and the culture we live in are both enacted in our lives, perhaps with some degree of harmony but also with considerable tension between them. Hence we must consider the possibility that social policies and our personal habits can either weaken Christian faith in the triune God or strengthen it. This is not to doubt the power of God to break through our individual and collective blindness and to transform us despite sin. But Christian faith also demands the *cultivation* of holiness, which requires reflection, planning, and sacrifice. Wendell Berry and others offer us inspiring visions of what life together can be if we take these steps.

Incarnate Meaning
and Mimetic Desire:
Notes toward the Development
of a Theology of the Saints

RANDALL S. ROSENBERG, FONTBONNE UNIVERSITY

T HE RELATIONSHIP BETWEEN THEOLOGY AND models of holiness is an
important theme in the work of Michael Buckley. In *Denying and
Disclosing God*, Buckley argues for the restoration of religious experience to its legitimate place as a form of evidence and cognition.[1] How is
God disclosed to ordinary human life? How do we arrive at a meaningful and responsible awareness of this divine self-disclosure?[2] Drawing on
Rahner's categories, chapter five of *Denying and Disclosing God* explores
"both the categorical and transcendental experiences that are classically
'religious.'"[3] By categorical, Buckley means concrete historical events by
which one is drawn to the disclosure of holiness—events which create the
conditions for assent to the reality of God.[4] By transcendental, Buckley
means the permanent and comprehensive orientation of the human mind
to truth, goodness, beauty, and justice as conditions for the possibility of
recognizing the holy as revelatory.[5]

Buckley's work presents the challenge of discerning the role of the saints
in theological discourse. In fact, he finds it "extraordinary that so much
Christian formal theology for centuries has bracketed this actual witness,"
offering it very little intellectual weight.[6] Buckley asks, "is it not a lacuna
in the standard theology, even of our day, that theology neither has nor has
striven to forge the intellectual devices to probe in these concrete experiences the disclosure they offer of the reality of God and so render them
available for so universal a discipline?" He adds that it "would be a difficult
and complex task."[7]

The present inquiry offers an initial contribution to Buckley's challenge.
This essay first draws briefly on the work of Hans Urs von Balthasar, recognizing it as the most prominent contemporary Catholic theological attempt to bridge the gap between the saints and theological discourse. It also

acknowledges, however, that a comprehensive systematic theology of the saints has yet to be written. Second, and more substantively, this essay explores the integration of Bernard Lonergan's category of "incarnate meaning" with René Girard's theory of mimetic desire as a means of developing some terms on which to build a theology of the saints. Insights from Buckley will be employed throughout this analysis. It is important to note that this essay does not treat the complex history of the church's saintly tradition in its hagiographical and bureaucratic forms. It also does not venture into the multiple ways that saints have been venerated in the tradition—as intercessors, models of virtue, and patrons. Nor does it give attention to contemporary discourse about the role of saints among the world's religions. Rather, this inquiry focuses in a limited way, in the words of Patricia Sullivan, on the "symbolic reality of the saints and the religious meaning behind our response to them."[8]

The Saints and Theological Discourse

Lawrence Cunningham notes that with the rise of "academic or scholastic theology in the Middles Ages there was a tendency to separate the study of the saintly life from the serious study of theology."[9] Even today, "writings about saints are not generally the subject of serious intellectual inquiry unless the saints are revered as much for their scholarship as for their other 'saintly' qualities."[10] Cunningham acknowledges that Balthasar's conscious attempt to overcome this chasm through his focus on the saints—even going so far as to develop a "metaphysics of the saints"—represents the most prominent attempt to employ the saints as a theological resource in Catholic systematic theology.[11] Cunningham suggests that the "theological foundations of sainthood have received short shrift in the theological tradition partially, one suspects, because of the perceived notion that the saints are part of the 'popular' tradition of Catholicism rather than central to the Catholic doctrinal tradition."[12] He adds that a "satisfactory systematic theology of the saints has yet to be written but the raw materials for such a study are there."[13]

In light of our aim to develop the theological and not simply popular foundations of sainthood, we follow Cunningham's lead and turn briefly to Balthasar's pioneering attempt to overcome the chasm between spirituality and theology in our contemporary era. Balthasar argues that the rich particularity of the Christian vision is embodied dramatically in a diversity of human forms, most eminently in the saints. As he writes in *Love Alone Is Credible*: "Lovers are the ones who know most about God; the theologian must listen to them."[14] In his vast corpus, he theologically integrates the witness of holy people and texts not usually found at the center of a systematic theologian's reflection: Thérèse of Lisieux, John of the Cross, Gerard Manley Hopkins, Dante, just to name a few.

Similar to Buckley's query about the lack of reference to the saints in standard theology, Balthasar laments the modern divorce of theology and sanctity. He suggests that so much of the Church's theology is embedded in the period that spans from the Apostles to the Middle Ages, chiefly due to the fact that the "great theologians were also saints."[15] In this era, "life and doctrine, orthopraxy and orthodoxy were wedded; the one fertilized the other, and they brought forth much fruit."[16] In the modern era, "the saints have not been theologians and the theologians have tended to treat their opinions as a sort of by-product, classifying them" as spirituality or spiritual theology.[17] Furthermore, modern hagiographers have explored the lives of the saints from historical and psychological perspectives. Although Balthasar does not reject such analyses as such, he does propose a more theological reading of the saints. The theological task is to develop a kind of "supernatural phenomenology of their missions from above."[18] In other words, the challenge is to penetrate the execution of their missions, and, without depersonalizing their concrete story or reducing their witness to abstract concepts, discern the intelligible in the sensible. Here, Balthasar emphasizes that the intelligible is "something supernatural, the discernment of which presupposes faith or even a participation in the life of sanctity."[19]

From this dramatic-theological perspective, the saints are not merely models of virtue, nor are they reduced to patrons worthy of invocation. Rather, for Balthasar, they constitute a "new interpretation of revelation" and the consequent possibility of illuminating "the scarcely suspected treasures in the deposit of faith."[20] In other words, they have a specifically theological function. Even if certain saints were not learned theologians, "their sheer existence proves to be a theological manifestation," that is, a "living and essential expression of the Church's tradition."[21] Thus far we have laid the groundwork for this essay's inquiry. Drawing on the work of Cunningham, Buckley, and Balthasar, we have noted the contemporary challenge to integrate the concrete witness of the saints into theological discourse. With this challenge in mind, we now transition to a more explicit discussion of incarnate meaning and mimetic desire.

Lonergan and Girard

This integration of incarnate meaning and mimetic desire builds primarily on a Bernard Lonergan-René Girard conversation initiated several years ago.[22] It is not axiomatic, however, that Lonergan and Girard ought to be regarded as pioneers in this difficult and complex task. After all, Lonergan's thick retrievals of St. Augustine and St. Thomas Aquinas focus overwhelmingly on their scholarly contributions to theology and philosophy. Granted, he refers in many places to St. Ignatius Loyola, in whose spirituality Lonergan was formed as a Jesuit. But, in his corpus as a whole, one cannot find the kind of thick and sustained reflection on particular saints as constitutive sites of theological meaning that one can, for example, in Balthasar's use of Thérèse of Lisieux. In addition, Girard's corpus, although his later work is deeply attentive to biblical revelation, offers a more sustained analysis of literary authors—Proust, Dostoevsky, Shakespeare, Cervantes, Flaubert, among others—than it does of the lives and insights of the saints.

Lonergan and Girard, nevertheless, have an important contribution to make to the question of the development of a contemporary theology of the saints. As much as the saints pervade Balthasar's theology, what is needed is a set of categories to control and illuminate the kind of meaning that a concentration on the saints might provide. Can the integration, then, of Lonergan's category of incarnate meaning with René Girard's theory of mimetic desire contribute to the development of a theology of the saints? This essay argues that Lonergan's category of incarnate meaning and its manifestation in art offers a way of articulating the saints as symbolic worlds wherein we may dwell for theological and religious inspiration. Furthermore, Girard's emphasis on mimetic desire enables us to speak of saints not only as sites of incarnate meaning, but more specifically as incarnate models of desire for the Christian community. In this sense Girard's account of mimetic desire illuminates, extends, and complements Lonergan's account of incarnate meaning.

Lonergan on Incarnate Meaning

In *Method in Theology*, Lonergan states that meaning "is embodied or carried in human intersubjectivity, in art, in symbols, in language, and in the lives and deeds of persons."[23] Lonergan labels this latter kind of embodiment or carrier of meaning "incarnate meaning." At the beginning of his very modest section on incarnate meaning, Lonergan cites the phrase of one of his most beloved influences, John Henry Newman: *"Cor ad cor Loqui-tor"*—hearts speaks to heart. In *Grammar of Assent*, Newman writes, "The heart is commonly reached, not through reason but through the imagination, by means of direct impressions, by the testimony of facts and events, by history, by description. Persons influence us, voices melt us, looks subdue us, deeds inflame us."[24] In his body of work, Lonergan offers several definitions of the term "incarnate meaning." In *Method*, it is "the meaning of a person, of his way of life, of his words, or of his deeds."[25] With a slight variation to this definition, Lonergan writes elsewhere: "A person, either in his totality or in his characteristic moment, his most significant deed, his outstanding achievement or sacrifice, *is* a meaning. That meaning may be cherished, revered, adored, re-created, lived, or it may be loathed, abominated, contemned."[26] He recognizes that, while the meaning discovered might be limited to one person, more often it may be meaningful for a group or even "for a whole national, or social, or cultural, or religious tradition." This kind of meaning "may attach to group achievement, to a Thermophylae or Marathon, to the Christian martyrs, to a glorious revolution." According to Lonergan, incarnate meaning may also be "transposed to a character or characters in a story or play, to a Hamlet or Tartuffe or Don Juan."[27]

In his essay "Time and Meaning," Lonergan employs the example of John of the Cross to explain his understanding of incarnate meaning.[28] What is noteworthy about Lonergan's account here is his particularly theological interpretation of incarnate meaning. He explains this interpretation by distinguishing the respective ways in which mystics and metaphysicians encounter reality. To put it succinctly, whereas metaphysicians *think* of reality in its totality, mystics more comprehensively and holistically *experience* this reality. "John of the Cross," writes Lonergan, "is a manifestation, a symbolic manifestation, of that experience of reality in its totality."[29]

Lonergan's emphasis on John of the Cross as a paradigmatically theological example of incarnate meaning is quite fitting in the context of this book's reflection on the work of Buckley.[30] Not only has Buckley initiated hundreds of students into the mystical world of John of the Cross, but he has also employed the Spanish mystic as a specifically theological response to the respective critiques of Feuerbach and Freud, and their agreement that "what is believed in religion is a projection of the human, that the divine must be 'deconstructed' and disclosed as the human."[31] Buckley's analysis serves as an example of the way incarnate meaning can bear fruit in a theological setting. As Buckley envisions, the task of theology "should be less to refute Feuerbachian and Freudian analysis than to learn from them what they have to teach about the relentless remolding of the image of God by religious consciousness and to suggest alternative stages to the processes they elaborate of anthropological recognition and reduction."[32] The model for an alternative, according to Buckley, is St. John of the Cross. Apophatic theology, after all, is not primarily about "conclusions or statements" but rather "an experiential process and a development of faith that points beyond experience and concepts, a process through negation into the infinite mystery that is God, a reality that beggars language."[33] The dark nights of John of the Cross in their active and passive dimensions are "finally dialectical movements in which the human is purified from projection by a 'no' which is most radically a 'yes,' a 'no' that is generated by the initial 'yes.'" In sum, Freud, Feuerbach, and John of the Cross agree that "much projection lies at the heart of our relationship with and conceptualization of God."[34] For Freud and Feuerbach, the proper response is to deny the reality of God; for John of the Cross and other mystics of the apophatic tradition, such an affirmation of projection recognizes that "the evolution or personal development of faith must pass through the contradictions that are the desert and the cross."[35] With Buckley's illumination of Lonergan's category, we can argue that John of the Cross incarnates a theological meaning, namely, the incomprehensibility of God. To put it in dramatic terms, John of the Cross's theological insight is not rooted in epic utterances about God, but is shaped instead by his mystical encounters with God. The example of John of the Cross, in other words, embodies Buckley's own retrieval of a "specifically religious intellectuality" that does not "bracket or excise religious evidence and religious consciousness and the interpersonal that marks authentic religious life and experience."[36]

In light of this connection between incarnate meaning and John of the Cross, we now consider Lonergan's claim that incarnate meaning often combines many of the other carriers of meaning.[37] We will confine our exploration to artistic meaning because it offers further resources, in a parallel way to Buckley's theological use of John of the Cross, for envisioning the encounter with the incarnate meaning of a saint as a withdrawal into a symbolic world of dramatic holiness, offering contemplative insight into the holiness of God and the challenge of discipleship. I have examined

Lonergan's theory of art in more depth elsewhere.[38] Here I would simply highlight three features relevant for a theology of the saints.[39]

First, the artistic experience, for Lonergan, reveals our orientation to transcendent mystery. Lonergan writes, "But the fundamental meaning important to us in art is that, just as the pure desire to know heads on to the beatific vision, so too the break from the ready-made world heads on to God. Man is nature's priest, and nature is God's silent communing with man. The artistic movement simply breaks away from ordinary living and is, as it were, an opening, a moment of new potentiality."[40] Lonergan isolates two fundamental human experiences that naturally orient us to God: the unquenchable desire to know and the artistic break from the ready-made world into a world of transcendent possibility.

Second, for Lonergan, art constitutes a withdrawal into a symbolic world. He isolates art's connection to the complexity of human consciousness and articulates the kind of meaning that it communicates. It is not primarily the kind of meaning we would associate with scientific demonstration. Rather, Lonergan refers to the meaning apprehended in the artistic experience as "elemental" meaning. Elemental meaning is the transformation of one's world. It occurs when one slips out of the ready-made world of one's everyday living—such as one's functions in society, ordinary conversation, and the media. It is the opening up of a new horizon which presents something that is "other, different, novel, strange, remote, intimate—all the adjectives that are employed when one attempts to communicate the artistic experience."[41] Lonergan describes this slip out of the ready-made world as a "withdrawal for return." It is an invitation to participate, to explore a symbolic world. Art is a

withdrawal from practical living to explore possibilities of fuller living in a richer world. Just as the mathematician explores the possibilities of what physics can be, so the artist explores the possibilities of what life, ordinary living, can be. There is an artistic element in all consciousness, in all living. Our settled modes have become humdrum, and we may think of all our life simply in terms of utilitarian categories. But in fact the life we are living is a product of artistic creation. We ourselves are products of artistic creation in our concrete living, and art is an exploration of potentiality.[42]

In this artistic experience, we are "transported from the space in which we move to the space within the picture, from the time of sleeping and waking, working and resting, to the time of music, from the pressures and determinisms of home and office, of economics and politics to the powers depicted in dance...."[43] Lonergan proceeds to demonstrate this theory by illuminating the function of different types of art: the picture, the statue, architecture, music, poetry, narrative, drama, and the lyric. In doing so, Lonergan supports his central claim that art is the exploration of the potentialities of concrete living. Unlike the language of science whose words simply have meaning based on logical calculations, deductions, and propositions, literary language has resonance in our consciousness. This resonance relates to the very "genesis, structure, and molding of our consciousness" integral to our childhood formation and education.[44] Literary language, in short, reveals the multi-dimensional field of subjectivity as experienced, the world of human potential, exhibiting in a concrete manner the many ways in which human beings "apprehend their history, their destiny, and the meaning of their lives."[45]

Finally, art has a kind of sacramental character. Lonergan acknowledges that this withdrawal may be illusory; but he also suggests that it may be regarded as "more true and more real."[46] Just as our mysterious and unquenchable desire to know ultimately reveals our transcendent orientation within the intellectual pattern of experience, the artistic experience can reveal our orientation to the divine within the aesthetic and dramatic patterns. For Lonergan, then, good art has an ulterior significance. It presents "the beauty, the splendor, the glory, the majesty, the 'plus' that is in things and that drops out when you say that the moon is just earth and the clouds are just water."[47] Art has the capacity to direct our attention to the reality "that the world is a cipher, a revelation, an unveiling, the presence of one who is not seen, touched, grasped, put in genus, distinguished by difference, yet is *present*."[48] The sacramental possibility of art points to the tension between the visibility and invisibility operative in the revelation of transcendent mystery. As the patristic scholar Frances Young writes, a "contemplative insight" is required to witness the sacramental depths of reality: that "Scripture along with nature, the incarnation, baptism and eucharist has the quality of witness, revealing yet concealing the hidden reality to which it points, evoking the powerful presence of transcendent mystery."[49]

What then is the connection between artistic meaning and incarnate meaning? Similar to artistic meaning, an experience of the incarnate meaning of the saints—their way of life, their words, and their deeds—constitutes a withdrawal from the ready-made world into the symbolic world of dramatic holiness, and facilitates a return to daily living, enriched by contemplative insight into the holiness of God and the challenge of authentic discipleship. This kind of withdrawal mediates elemental meaning and enables us to explore the self-disclosure of God in everyday living. As a way of illuminating this "withdrawal for return," it is relevant to note Cunningham's reflections on the connection between Christian practice and music. The Bible is studied primarily as a text to be embodied, similar to the relationship between a musical score and a musicologist, namely, "to establish the authenticity of the text" at its deepest level, which is revealed in its performance.[50] "That meaning derives," writes Cunningham, "both from fidelity to the text and as the score is enhanced by the performance of the musician."[51] Recognizing that not all performances are equal, Cunningham adds that "there are those who give a passing nod to the demands of the gospel life, but it is quite something else when someone grasps the same message and performs at a profound level." The saint represents "a classical performer of the word of God."[52]

An Expansion of Incarnate Meaning: Girard's Mimetic Desire

We have explored Lonergan's category of incarnate meaning, and enriched it with Buckley's use of John of the Cross. With Lonergan's suggestion in mind, we also integrated incarnate meaning and artistic meaning, envisioning the saints as symbolic worlds wherein we may dwell for theological and religious inspiration. Turning now to the work of René Girard, we show how the French thinker's account of mimetic desire, in a complementary fashion, enables us to speak of saints not only as sites of incarnate meaning, but more specifically as incarnate models of desire for the Christian community. As Girard writes, "To say that our desires are imitative or mimetic is to root them neither in objects nor in ourselves, but in a third party, the *model* or *mediator*, whose desire we imitate in the hope of resembling him or her, in the hope that our two beings will be 'fused,' as some Dostoevskyan characters love to say."[53] Girard has written widely about the problematic nature of mimetic desire, especially its tendency toward conflict and violence.

In fact, if one were to read selectively from Girard's corpus, one might get the impression that mimetic desire itself is an evil to overcome. In *Things Hidden Since the Foundation of the World*, for example, Girard writes that "following Christ means giving up mimetic desire."[54]

In terms of developing some adequate and explanatory terms and relations on which to build a theology of the saints, a key insight that cannot be overlooked is that "desire itself is essentially mimetic, directed toward the object desired by the model."[55] In other words, mimetic desire is not by its nature violent. The mimetic quality of childhood desire is "universally recognized," according to Girard. In fact, Girard has argued that we should not renounce mimetic desire as such:

> But as to whether I am advocating "renunciation" of mimetic desire, yes and no. Not the renunciation of mimetic desire itself, because what Jesus advocates is mimetic desire. Imitate me, and imitate the Father through me, he says, so it's twice mimetic. Jesus seems to say that the only way to avoid violence is to imitate me, and imitate the Father. So the idea that mimetic desire itself is bad makes no sense. It is true, however, that occasionally I say "mimetic desire" when I really mean only the type of mimetic desire that generates mimetic rivalry and, in turn, is generated by it.[56]

In fact, the goodness of mimetic desire is not only "the basis of rivalry and murder but of heroism and devotion to others."[57] Girard's emphasis on heroism and devotion in relation to mimetic desire offers a fruitful avenue of investigation in the context of a theology of the saints. He writes, "Nothing is more mimetic than the desire of a child, and yet it is good. Jesus himself says it is good. Mimetic desire is also the desire for God."[58] Girard reinforces this distinction in his more recent work: "Mimetic desire is intrinsically good."[59] He adds that if desire were not mimetic, "we would not be open to what is human or what is divine."[60] Recall that for Lonergan, two experiences reveal the human orientation to transcendent mystery: the pure desire to know and the capacity to break from the ready-made world, the type of experience captured by the artist. For Girard, the fundamental experience of mimetic desire also discloses our human orientation to the divine.

Girard's exploration of mimetic desire is worked out under the formula of "interdividual psychology."[61] For the purposes of this essay, it is fitting to note Charles Hefling's suggestion for ways in which the work of Girard might complement Lonergan's. Whereas in *Insight*, Lonergan focuses on individual psychology and the patient/therapist relationship, Girard's use of "interdividual" emphasizes dramatic relationships that constitute everyday living. Hefling explores mimesis in a horizon that privileges the language of Lonergan's later *Method in Theology*. He writes, "In 'dramatic,' everyday, commonsense interaction with others, with the *dramatis personae* of my living, I can and do respond to the 'ontic' value of an other, to someone else as be-ing and as a being."[62] "The intersubjective presence of that other," Hefling writes, "evokes my innate drive for self-transcendence, that is, for fuller or more authentic being-myself."[63] The specifically Girardian insight here is that "*being-like* another involves wanting what he or she wants. For in this way, in and with admiration for someone, there is evoked a further feeling, or a differentiation of feeling, as a response, not to the 'ontic' value of the other, but more specifically to the value of what the other values."[64] As a complement to Hefling's suggestions, we have argued in this present essay that Lonergan's account of incarnate meaning belongs in this conversation about the drama of interpersonal relations. Incarnate meaning captures the personal and interpersonal concreteness of the human life-world. Depending on how it is construed, it also articulates how the lives and deeds of persons of the past might symbolically shape the dynamic situation of the present, a point that relates to the following key distinction offered by Girard.

In his further specification of mimetic desire and mimetic drama, Girard distinguishes between external and internal mediation. In *Desire, Deceit, and the Novel*, he speaks of external mediation "when the distance is sufficient to eliminate any contact between the two spheres of *possibilities* of which the mediator and the subject occupy the respective centers."[65] Internal mediation, on the other hand, relates to the situation where "this same distance is sufficiently reduced to allow these two spheres to penetrate each other more or less profoundly."[66] Whereas proximity of distance in internal mediation heightens the possibility for mimetic rivalry, in external mediation, rivalry with the mediator is impossible.[67] As Girard puts it, "The hero of external mediation proclaims aloud the true nature of his desire. He worships his model openly and declares himself his disciple."[68] We will return to this distinction below after citing some examples from the work of Buckley.

In his discussion of the categorical dimension of Christian religious experience, Buckley privileges concrete encounters with models of holiness that create the conditions for assent to the reality of God.[69] He offers the stories of Edith Stein and Raissa Maritain as examples of such categorical religious experiences. The noteworthy connection—a connection not explicitly pointed out in Buckley's own commentary—is the mimetic desire operative in both stories. That is, the respective conversions of Edith Stein and Raïssa Maritain were both "socially mediated."

As Buckley recounts, Edith Stein's acceptance of God "emerged from her ability to read personal and intersubjective experience."[70] In the summer of 1921, she by chance picked up the *Autobiography of Teresa of Avila*. After reading through the night she closed the book and reflected: "This is the truth." Buckley comments, "This is not the chance reading of a pious tale by a religious enthusiast. It is the disclosure of the divine within a very complex human history to one who was able to interpret it as such."[71] The relevant point is that mimetic desire was central to Stein's judgment. Stein's desire and recognition for God were mediated through Teresa's desire and recognition. As we stated earlier, for Girard, to say that our desires are imitative or mimetic is to root them neither in objects nor in ourselves, but in a third party, the *model* or *mediator*, whose desire we imitate in the hope of being like the model. Not only did Stein accept the truth of God mimetically, she also became a Carmelite like Teresa and was later canonized under her monastic name as St. Teresa Benedicta of the Cross.

The conversion story of Jacques and Raïssa Maritain, as recounted by Buckley, also has a deeply mimetic quality. In terms of social mediation, Léon Bloy was deeply influential on the Maritains. Instead of employing the "apologetic of demonstration," Bloy placed before them "the fact of sanctity. Simply, and because he loved them, because their experience was near his own—so much so that he could not read them without weeping—he brought us to know the saints and the mystics."[72] Buckley comments that Bloy "introduced this young couple not to argument and inference, but to narrative, to the lives and writings, i.e., to the experience and holiness, of the saints."[73]

Finally, the conversion of St. Ignatius Loyola, a saint to whom Buckley is deeply devoted, further illuminates this connection between mimetic desire and the lives of the saints. As recounted in Loyola's *Autobiography*, while he was recovering from injury his usual books of interest—"worldly books of fiction"—were unavailable and so he was given instead a life of Christ and a book of the lives of the saints.[74] Ignatius was prompted to think:

"What if I should do what St. Francis did, and what St. Dominic did?" He continues, "St. Dominic did this, therefore, I have to do it; St. Francis did this, therefore I have to do it." During this period of deep reading, Ignatius's desire for the life of God flourished.[75] Similar to the narratives above, Ignatius' desire for God was rooted in the third party, in this case Francis and Dominic; Ignatius desired the object of their desire.

Conclusion

In his teaching and writing, Buckley not only raises the question about the role of the saints in theological discourse—he also employs saints as religiously intellectual responses to the challenge of atheism. Inspired and illuminated by Buckley's intellectual contribution, this essay proceeded to explore Lonergan's category of incarnate meaning in relation to Girard's account of mimetic desire, in the context of a theology of the saints. Both incarnate meaning and mimetic desire recognize the primacy of the personal and the intersubjective in the human experience of meaning and truth. In light of our brief presentation of Balthasar's emphasis on dramatic models of holiness, Lonergan offered us a further differentiation, namely, that the kind of meaning mediated by a theological use of the saints might best be called incarnate meaning. In other words, an encounter with the meaning of the saints, of their way of life, words, and deeds, constitutes a withdrawal from the ready-made world into the symbolic world of dramatic holiness and likewise a return to daily living, enriched by contemplative insight into the holiness of God and the challenge of discipleship. Buckley's employment of John of the Cross in dialectical conversation with Feuerbach and Freud represented an example of the theological use of the incarnate meaning of the saints. Furthermore, in a complementary fashion, Girard's emphasis on mimetic desire helped us to envision the saints not only as sites of incarnate meaning, but more specifically as incarnate models of desire—a dynamic that resides at the root of our encounter with the saints. If it is plausible to affirm the deeply mimetic nature of human desire, then it is also fitting to envision saints as models or mediators, whose desire we imitate in the hope of resembling him or her. In this vein, we extended Buckley's examples of the categorical disclosures of truth—Edith Stein and Raïssa Maritain—and added St. Ignatius, and pointed out that mimetic desire was operative in all three narratives.

Exploring the relationship and possible tensions between the various theological approaches mentioned in this essay was purposefully set aside; it is, however, a necessary conversation for a larger project on the theology of the saints. In many ways, the central themes discussed in this essay—incarnate meaning and mimetic desire—belong, broadly speaking, in what Lonergan has called "foundations" and more specifically as general theological categories.[76] The base of general theological categories, according to Lonergan, is the concrete human subject and its dynamism toward self-transcendence. The basic nest of such terms and relations can be distinguished and described in a number of ways—most relevant to this inquiry is the specific pattern of experience in which the conscious operation is occurring and the different ways that meaning is embodied or carried in the human life-world.

Furthermore, it is worth recalling Buckley's recognition of the complex and difficult nature of probing the experience of personal disclosures of holiness for the intellectual discipline of systematic theology.[77] Part of the difficulty of the task is prompted by the fact that the aim of systematic theology in the strict sense of the term (as distinguished from foundations), as I have argued elsewhere, is the theoretical understanding of the mysteries, an understanding which ought to be articulated in a predominantly technical way as it answers questions that continue to arise anew in every age concerning the mysteries of faith affirmed in doctrines.[78] What place, then, if any, can a study of a saintly life have in the explanatory and technical discourse of systematic theology? For now, this question awaits further exploration. Undoubtedly, the invocation of both the depth of Buckley's scholarship and his inspiration as a teacher will continue to animate this ongoing conversation.

Vatican II and
a New Church Mission
to the World

THOMAS M. KELLY, PH.D., CREIGHTON UNIVERSITY

I N HIS BOOK *THE CATHOLIC University as Promise and Project: Reflections in a Jesuit Idiom*, Michael J. Buckley, S.J. asserts the following:

> *Within the Church, renewed realization is emerging that the suffering of the vast majority of humankind stands in judgment upon its life, upon the vitality of its proclamation of the gospel, and upon the authenticity with which this gospel is embodied in the practice of those who are educated within it and who confess it as the truth of their lives.*[1]

I would argue that this statement is both true and made possible because of three key changes which occurred through the Second Vatican Council (1962-65). The first change occurred in how the Catholic Church understood itself and its relationship to the world. The second change occurred through a shift in how the laity were understood and missioned. The third change occurred through a re-framing of the call to holiness as something open to all, lay and clergy alike, and as something necessary for the church to fulfill its new mission to the world. It is fitting that the quote above is in reference to the new humanism that Buckley explores in chapter six of his book and how, from that humanism, there arises a very important commitment for Catholic and Jesuit Universities to have a concern for justice. In some ways the three key changes which occurred at Vatican II are embodied by the concern for justice the University must have if it is to be both Catholic and Jesuit. These three changes also represent some core values that I received as a student of Buckley. The first is that theology has to do with the world and its reality, whether we are speaking about atheism, God, and the world of science or the meaning of Catholic education—all must engage the world in constructive and honest ways. This engagement will be done as well by lay people, and particularly by lay theologians—the majority of the students who were blessed by Buckley's wisdom in his final fifteen years at

Boston College. Finally, this unique engagement with the world to which lay theologians are called is not separate from the call to holiness and authenticity in our professional lives, our personal lives, or our social and political commitments, however varied they may be. As a lay theologian trained by Buckley, I am deeply grateful for the opportunity to study theology—an opportunity which came about as the result of Vatican II and its new humanistic engagement with the world.

Vatican II

On October 11, 1962 Pope John XXIII opened the Second Vatican Council to reinvigorate and redirect a church that had become increasingly distant from the modern world. Sixteen formal documents later, it would close under Pope Paul VI on December 8, 1965. More than 2,500 men took part in the opening session; they included a global representation of bishops, superiors of religious orders, theological consultants, and observers from various denominations of Christianity from around the world. This Council was significantly different from Vatican I (1868), which included around 750 men, mainly from Europe. John XXIII would emphasize a need for *aggiornamento*, which roughly translates as a "bringing up to date." Increasingly the church found itself in a world with pressing social, economic, and political challenges which it was incapable of addressing for the people whom it served. From the Council of Trent in 1545 until Vatican II in 1962, the church had increasingly collapsed in upon itself, condemning new developments in intellectual thought and resisting the modern age characterized by democracy and the diffusion of political and economic power (liberalism). Ecclesiologist Richard Gaillardetz notes:

> *A rather polemical and defensive account of the church would appear, an account that would stress its institutional features. Ecclesiology during this period gave little attention to the church's spiritual origins in the Trinitarian missions of Word and Spirit. Defense of the legitimacy of church office and ordained ministry led to an emphasis on the sacrament of holy orders over the sacraments of initiation. In the following centuries, this defensive posture was directed not just against the churches of the Reformation but against other external forces perceived as threats to the church's mission and very existence.*[2]

Vatican II was the opportunity taken by the Church to evaluate the massive changes in the world, including those technological, political, and developmental challenges which had been slowly emerging over time. It began a deep reflection on what it meant to be a church in and for this world. To that end, there were a variety of topics addressed at the Council, such as how the church perceived itself in relation to other religions. In *Nostra aetate*, the *Declaration on the Relation of the Church with Non-Christian Religions*, for example, the church acknowledged that the Holy Spirit is active even *outside* the Catholic Church.

While a full and comprehensive history of Vatican II is neither necessary nor possible here, there are two documents from Vatican II and one document written prior to Vatican II that deserve special attention. A careful consideration of themes in these three documents will indicate the radical change embraced by Vatican II. The first document, *Lumen gentium*, is the dogmatic constitution on the church which puts forth how the Vatican II Church understands itself in a new light. In order to fully appreciate the content of this, it is necessary to reference *Mystici corporus Christi* written by Pope Pius XII in 1943. This document outlines how the church understood itself prior to Vatican II. It will become evident that *Lumen gentium* represents a significant departure from its recent past, most notably *Mystici corporus Christi*. The second document from Vatican II necessary to consider is *Guadium et spes*, the *Pastoral Constitution on the Church in the Modern World*. In *Gaudiem et spes*, the church puts forth how it understands the world and its mission to it. This document, the final document of the Council, will signify a radical departure and movement beyond the "charity" model formerly embraced by the Catholic Church. Even today, 50 years after it was written, this departure has not been fully accepted by many, including some in the magisterium.

Lumen gentium and *Mystici corporus Christi*

An important consideration for understanding the significance of *Lumen gentium* is the fact that it offers a vision for the entire church, and not just the hierarchy.[3] For this reason, *Lumen gentium* will frame its understanding of the entire church in a way that is a significant departure from previous formulations. Three essential contributions from *Lumen gentium* need to be emphasized. First, the overall image used to understand the Church changed significantly. Previously the Church had understood itself as the "mystical body of Christ"—this would change in Vatican II to the church as the "people of God." This new image characterizes not only the laity, but the entire church, prior to any division of hierarchy and faithful. Second, how the role of the laity was framed changed significantly. Third, there is a new recognition of how all members of the Church—from layperson to Pope—have a call to holiness.

In June of 1943, Pope Pius XII authored an encyclical *Mystici corporus Christi*, the Mystical Body of Christ. Within it, Pius XII put forth his vision of how the church understood itself, its relation to its Founder, its own internal governance, and its relation to the world then mired in a massive world war. He began:

> *The doctrine of the Mystical Body of Christ, which is the Church, was first taught us by the Redeemer Himself. Illustrating as it does the great and inestimable privilege of our intimate union with so exalted a Head, this doctrine by its sublime dignity invites all those who are drawn by the Holy Spirit to study it, and gives them, in the truths of which it proposes to the mind, a strong incentive to the performance of such good works as are conformable to its teaching.*[4]

At various points in this document, Pius XII will go on to refer to the church as the "mystical body of Christ," the "spotless bride" of Christ or "bride" of Christ, and "Holy Mother Church."[5] Twenty-one years later, Vatican II will frame the church's self-understanding quite differently. This change was not only linguistic but substantive as well. How different is the image of the church as the "Mystical Body of Christ" in contrast to "The People of God?" Why is this important? The difference is significant, a difference that reaches deeply into what is meant by "church" and how we understand ourselves within it.

The first image, "The Mystical Body of Christ," used in the encyclical from 1943, presents a very high ecclesiology. A "high" ecclesiology will emphasize above all else the Church's relationship to God, its spiritual purity, its uniqueness, and its elevation. The mission to the world thus becomes secondary. This is not done indirectly, but quite bluntly. In effect, the church considers itself "Christ in the world," in a very literal sense and with all that implies. "Indeed, if we are to believe Gregory of Nyssa, the Church is often called simply 'Christ' by the Apostle; and you are familiar Venerable

Brethren, with that phrase of Augustine: 'Christ preaches Christ.'"[6] Similar to certain forms of medieval Christology (at least as seen in Anselm's work), there is a "higher" and "lower" aspect of this reality—and while the church will acknowledge its "lower" reality (the church in the world), it will always emphasize its spiritual connection to the divine as it does in the following passage. "Just as our composite mortal body, although it is a marvelous work of the Creator, falls far short of the eminent dignity of our soul, so the social structure of the Christian community, though it proclaims the wisdom of its divine Architect, still remains something inferior when compared to the spiritual gifts which give it beauty and life, and to the divine source whence they flow."[7] This understanding of the Church appears to be an extension of the Christology put forth by Anselm. Similar to that Christology, "The former theology of perfect society offered a static vision of the church unrelated to peoples and history, as an entity isolated and alone in the universe."[8] There is a (reluctantly) acknowledged "human" side, but this is always minimized. It never diminishes the divine as the overriding principle of its existence. "Of course, in practice there were always involvements, but they were seen as defects and proof of the frailty of human nature. The aim was a church unmarked by the world..."[9] The "earthly" remains "inferior" to "spiritual gifts," which are really what the Church is about—just as the body remains inferior to the soul and the world remains inferior to heaven. This dualism will have as its focus the "spiritual" life, which includes the sacraments that nourish it. God's grace moves *only* through the church, especially its hierarchy, and thus the church itself becomes a proper object of adoration.[10]

The Second Vatican Council will have another understanding of this community called the Roman Catholic Church. It will see the church both in its human and divine dimensions—and thus first consider it as a mystery. The term "mystery" here indicates that because it is oriented toward God, but in service to the Kingdom of God as it breaks in upon the world, it cannot be reduced finally to any concrete and crystal clear understanding. "Mystery" does not mean we know nothing about it or should be uncritical of its failures. And prior to any distinction between hierarchy and laity, the church will understand itself first as a totality. This totality is called the people of God. The order of chapters in *Lumen gentium* supports this interpretation of the document. In the *second* draft released on September 29, 1963, the structure of the document looked like this:

I.   The Mystery of the Church
II.   The Hierarchy
III.   The People of God and the Laity
IV.   Vocation of all to holiness; Religious

The *final* version of the document, released on November 21, 1964 would have a different structure:

I.   The Mystery of the Church
II.   The People of God
III.   The Church is hierarchical
IV.   The laity
V.   The universal call to holiness
VI.   Religious
VII.   The Pilgrim Church
VIII.   Our Lady[11]

It was no accident that the Council thought it important to consider first the church as a whole. The placement of these chapters reveals many important aspects of the document. One will note the inversion of numerals II and III as most important. To offer the hierarchy for consideration after the People of God is to say that the hierarchy is not above or beyond the people, but part of that people itself. To separate the laity for its own consideration from the People of God gives a certain weight and importance to them in and of themselves. Finally, to give the "universal call to holiness" its own section, rather than collapsing it into a category with "Religious," indicates that the call really is universal and not simply an extension of religious life.

Yves Congar, the most influential ecclesiologist at Vatican II, had termed former approaches to understanding the church as "hierarchology," a preoccupation with the hierarchy of the church as the only suitable object of ecclesial reflection.[12] This structure clearly moves beyond that to first consider the entire church as the people of God. Second, the church is considered primarily a network of people connected and motivated by the love of God exemplified in the life and ministry of Jesus of Nazareth. In this sense, the church manifests "Christ" to the world by imitating and concretely making real the love he lived, died, and resurrected within. Third, all of those baptized share equally in membership. There is no "two-tiered" system where those ordained are considered "higher" or holier than lay people. Thus, there is never justification for clericalism, the practice and attitude of putting ordained functionaries at the center of all decision-making and community life. A new model of leadership would emerge that encourages ordained ministers to draw forth and utilize the gifts and talents of all to improve the communal life and worship of a particular church.[13] Make no mistake, though: there is still an irreplaceable need for a hierarchy. Communities need leaders. What now characterizes this hierarchy is its posture of servant leadership. The hierarchy exists in order to serve people of God, and both together serve the Kingdom of God. Finally, there was a re-framing of the relationship of pope to bishop. If the former structure emphasized the pope as singular ruler over the college of bishops, the new understanding would emphasize the pope as first among equals, and collegial collaboration as the highest governing value.[14] All of these new developments in the self-understanding of the church point to a significant sea-change for ecclesiology. To get at just how different this was, let us look more closely at the new image for church suggested at Vatican II—the people of God.

People of God

What is at the root of the image "People of God," and how does this represent a new direction in the church's self-understanding? The term "people of God" emerges from the beginning of the Hebrew Scriptures. The Hebrew people become a people in and through the Exodus. Recall that prior to the Exodus, those in slavery to the pharaoh of Egypt were drawn from various groups of wandering peoples around the Mediterranean. When God breaks into human history, it is in response to the suffering of those enslaved peoples, as the Book of Exodus so clearly states: "I have witnessed the affliction of my people in Egypt. I have heard their cry of complaint against their slave drivers. I have come down to rescue them."(3:7). The result of this divine compassion is the liberation of what would become the people of God from slavery, a slavery that was *not* just physical, but political, social, and of course, spiritual. What emerges is a people who form a covenant with God, a covenant they will consistently break and yet one to which they will always try to remain faithful. Various figures will guide this people of God. First there is Moses, then the Judges followed by various kings including Saul, David, and Solomon. When the office of King repeatedly fails by turning away from the covenant, various prophets come forth to fill the void of religious leadership, until the time of Jesus. These people of God are a fickle people, constantly trying to live according to the covenant and constantly failing. They are always forgiven by God, even after a traumatic exile to another land. Ultimately, they stay in some relationship with God, but never measure up to what they or the prophets hope for. Throughout the Hebrew Scriptures this people is always exhorted to treat each other the way God treated them—with mercy, especially for those most vulnerable (as they were in Egypt). Additionally, they are warned repeatedly by a variety of prophets to never confuse cultic worship in the temple with the actual doing of God's will. God's will can only be done by helping concretely the widow and orphan—those most vulnerable in the patriarchal society of that day.[15]

> *This rooting of the church in Israel makes its concrete and historic nature more manifest. The people of Israel is set in the midst of peoples, with the characteristics of a people. The Bible continually stresses the relations between Israel and the other peoples of the earth. Being people of God does not mean that Israel ceases to be human—with all the values and all the sins of the peoples of the earth. The new people of God will be no less human and no less subject to the challenges of history, with its failures and victories, its virtues and vices, as shown by the prophets of the Old Testament. Indeed, prophets continually emerge within the new people as a reminder of the church's human character.*[16]

According to *Lumen gentium*, Christ institutes a new covenant with this people through the Last Supper and thus forms a new people of God from his closest followers who symbolically represent the new 12 tribes of Israel. The "People of God" is thus a theological understanding of a community introduced by Christ, not simply a sociological one. This messianic people also have Christ as their head, but it is not simply heaven that is their goal—it is something much more theologically rich. This difference in mission is critically important. "Its end is the kingdom of God, which has been begun by God Himself on earth, and which is to be further extended until it is brought to perfection by Him at the end of time, when Christ, our life, shall appear, and 'creation itself will be delivered from its slavery to corruption into the freedom of the glory of the sons of God'."[17] This community, this new people of God will be the instrument through which God brings about the Kingdom of God on earth—a Kingdom where the will of the God and the will of human beings unite to form a new social and spiritual reality.

In the past, teaching on the Kingdom of God taught one of two things. The Kingdom of God was spiritualized as "heaven," and thus the goal of all Christian life, but in the next world. Or, it taught that the church was the Kingdom of God on earth, in line with the thinking of *Mystici corporis Christi*. In *Lumen gentium*, the Church of Christ "subsists in" the Catholic Church, but aspects of it can be found outside the church as well. "This Church constituted and organized in the world as a society, *subsists* in the Catholic Church, which is governed by the successor of Peter and by the Bishops in communion with him, although many elements of sanctification and of truth are found outside of its visible structure."[18] The Catholic Church is no longer strictly identified with the Kingdom of God; rather it is in service to it. Such a small change in language represents a significant change in theology. It is no longer for the glory of the Church that one works, however close it may be to its founder, Christ. Rather, now the people of God work for the Kingdom of God, as the Lord's Prayer has always reminded us. In order for this to happen, the Church must to be in service to something beyond itself. In fact, it has to enter more deeply into a world it formerly viewed itself as being above. This service in the world and to the world is the new work of the Church, and according to *Lumen gentium*, especially of the laity.

The Role of the Laity

In 1859, John Henry Newman was roundly denounced for suggesting that the faithful, by which he meant especially the laity, ought to be consulted in matters of doctrine, and he was forced to resign the editorship of the journal in which he had published an article advancing the idea.[19] The highest ranking English-speaking member of the Roman curia at the time, Msgr. George Talbot, spoke for many church officials when he dismissed Newman's suggestion as absurd: "What is the province of the laity? To hunt, to shoot, to entertain. These matters they understand, but to meddle with ecclesiastical matters they have no right at all...."[20]

Prior to Vatican II, the church was broadly considered under two quite different aspects—the ordained and "the faithful." The ordained included bishops and priests. The faithful were everyone else who had not received holy orders. *Mystici corporis Christi* (1943) uses the term "laity" only once.

Indeed, let this be clearly understood, especially in our days, fathers and mothers of families, those who are godparents through Baptism, and in particular those members of the laity who collaborate with the ecclesiastical hierarchy in spreading the Kingdom of the Divine Redeemer occupy an honorable, if often a lowly, place in the Christian community, and even they under the impulse of God and with His help, can reach the heights of supreme holiness, which, Jesus Christ has promised, will never be wanting to the Church.[21]

This "honorable, if lowly" group of people within the church was cared for by the ordained class, something Pius XII took very seriously. "Through Holy Orders men are set aside and consecrated to God, to offer the Sacrifice of the Eucharistic Victim, to nourish the flock of the faithful with the Bread of Angels and the food of doctrine, to guide them in the way of God's commandments and counsels and to strengthen them with all other supernatural helps."[22] The purpose of the laity, on the other hand, was fairly narrow. "For the social needs of the Church Christ has provided in a particular way by the institution of two other Sacraments. Through Matrimony, in which the contracting parties are ministers of grace to each other, provision is made for the external and duly regulated increase of Christian society, and, what is of greater importance, for the correct religious education of the children, without which this Mystical Body would be in grave danger."[23] Consistent with Catholic teaching since the time of Thomas Aquinas (1225-1274), Pius XII outlines the role of sexuality as reproduction and the role of the laity to be discovered in marriage, which existed for reproduction and the proper education of children. This was essentially the role of the laity. Finally, the "faithful" were called to model charity in the world, especially to those most vulnerable. As Pius XII states so clearly, this charity was seen as a pious act which symbolically addressed Jesus himself.[24] In terms of engaging the complexity of the world, especially in the midst of perhaps the greatest world war to that point in history, the church would not encourage engagement. There is no call here for concrete acts to address injustice or overt acts of peacemaking. Rather, it would encourage a flight *away* from conflict and into personal spiritual improvement. This static view of history, with an elevated sense of the sacredness of the Church, would not see human reality as worthy of engagement.

But today that duty is more clear than ever, when a gigantic conflict has set almost the whole world on fire and leaves in its wake so much

death, so much misery, so much hardship; in the same way today, in
a special manner, it is the duty of all to fly from vice, the attraction
of the world, the unrestrained pleasures of the body, and also from
worldly frivolity and vanity which contribute nothing to the Christian
training of the soul nor to the gaining of Heaven.[25]

Vatican II will see the laity and its role in a very different manner. "Everything that has been said above concerning the People of God is intended
for the laity, religious and clergy alike. But there are certain things which
pertain in a special way to the laity, both men and women, by reason of
their condition and mission."[26] Initially *Lumen gentium* defines the laity
negatively, that is, they are defined initially in terms of what they are not:
"The term laity is here understood to mean all the faithful *except* those in
holy orders and those in the state of religious life specially approved by the
Church." Only secondarily are they given a positive definition: "These faithful are by baptism made one body with Christ and are constituted among
the People of God; they are in their own way made sharers in the priestly,
prophetical, and kingly functions of Christ; and they carry out for their
own part the mission of the whole Christian people in the Church and in
the world."[27]

Undoubtedly the theological understanding of the vocation of the laity
has developed significantly in the last century. The theology of what was
called Catholic Action and the groundbreaking work of scholars such as
Yves Congar and Henri de Lubac laid the foundation for Vatican II's *Apostolicam actuositatem*, the Decree on the Apostolate of the Laity. Vatican
II states, "Since the laity, in accordance with their state of life, live in the
midst of the world and its concerns, they are called by God to exercise their
apostolate in the world like leaven, with the ardor of the spirit of Christ."[28]
The Decree on the Apostolate of the Laity emphasizes that the focus of the
laity's activity is in the world as contrasted with the clergy's work, which is
within the ecclesiastical structure. In short, normally the layperson works in
the world and the ordained person works in the church. This is reinforced
in *Lumen gentium*. "But the laity, by their very vocation, seek the kingdom
of God by engaging in temporal affairs and by ordering them according to
the plan of God."[29]

Vatican II teaches that "the common priesthood of the faithful and the
ministerial or hierarchical priesthood, although they differ in essence and

not simply in degree, are nevertheless interrelated: Each in its own particular way shares in the one priesthood of Christ."[30] Here the document seems to be making the distinction between ordained and lay in two ways. The first is by function. Within the church, the ordained work. "Outside" the church in the world, lay people exercise their apostolate. The second way a distinction between lay and ordained is argued is indicated by the phrase "they differ in essence and not simply by degree." This is an argument from ontology. Ontology is the study of being—and it seems one's "being" is different if one is ordained, though exactly how it is or becomes different is never specified. Neither explanation from *Lumen gentium* regarding the distinction between lay and ordained is theologically viable today.

> *This theology is completely based on the distinction between sacred and profane as expressed in the texts of Gratian and his followers, though this distinction was the very thing that they were trying to overcome. Indeed, the text has very strange statements, showing that it is not in accord with Christian reality. First, it says that the clergy is expressly devoted to the sacred ministry, but it recognizes that 'they may sometimes be engaged in secular activities.' Actually, until the current vocation crisis, a large portion of priests did not happen 'sometimes': tens of thousands of priests did so. Almost all Jesuits were involved in teaching, and the same was true of many other religious order priests. They were teaching secular subjects, not religion, and they were not exceptional cases at all. So why exclude the profane from the life of priests? It says that the mission of religious is to practice the beatitudes, but Jesus did not reserve the practice of the beatitudes to religious. They are the rule for the entire people of God—including lay people.*[31]

Additionally, laypeople work throughout the church, in the church, and for the church in a myriad of ways. Second, we know that ontologically, or from our very being, all human beings are called by God and capable of sin, regardless of our function in the church.[32] What has significantly changed because of Vatican II is that now, the layperson is encouraged, even required, to work for the Kingdom of God here on earth.

Universal Call to Holiness

Recall that within the explicitly two-tiered system prior to Vatican II, the most important members of the church were the bishops. To use an ascending analogy, bishops were "higher" and thus closer to the "head" of the church, Christ. "Consequently, Bishops must be considered as the more illustrious members of the Universal Church, for they are united by a very special bond to the divine Head of the whole Body and so are rightly called 'principal parts of the members of the Lord.'"[33] This understanding of bishops was consistent with the focus on the hierarchy prior to Vatican II. According to Jose Comblin, a noted Latin American ecclesiologist, "The hierarchy has been so sacralized and placed above the church that it has almost lost its human character and become a superhuman mediation—almost on the level of Christ himself."[34] Now, a new call would come forth that called *all* people to holiness. Says *Lumen gentium*, "Therefore in the Church, everyone whether belonging to the hierarchy, or being cared for by it, is called to holiness, according to the saying of the Apostle: 'For this is the will of God, your sanctification.'"[35] This holiness is not some abstract sentiment or quality, but is manifest in the "perfection of charity," evident in part when "a more human manner of living is promoted in this earthly society."[36] Thus, how we live and interact concretely with those in our community is essential to holiness. Not only is this holiness tangible, but it imitates Christ and His own movement toward the poor. "These people follow the poor Christ, the humble and cross-bearing Christ in order to be worthy of being sharers in His glory. Every person must walk unhesitatingly according to his own personal gifts and duties in the path of living faith, which arouses hope and works through charity." Beginning with the bishops and then priests, ministers of lesser rank, and finally to lay people, the document will outline how it understands this call to holiness. Interestingly, the model for such holiness is the traditional piety and charity referenced in countless documents throughout church history. The final paragraph of this section even has the ring of pre-Vatican II dualism to it: "Let neither the use of the things of this world nor attachment to riches, which is against the spirit of evangelical poverty, hinder them in their quest for perfect love. Let them heed the admonition of the Apostle to those who use this world; let them not come to terms with this world; for this world, as we see it, is passing away."[37]

Contrary to the final sentence of this exhortation to holiness, another document at Vatican II would outline in much greater detail what is the actual role of the Church in this world. It will sound quite different from a call to charity, and it will come in the final document of the Council, *Gaudium et spes*, *The Pastoral Constitution on the Church in the Modern World*.

Gaudium et spes

Recall that prior to Vatican II, the Church understood its relation to the state officially as two separate *societas perfectas*. These two "perfect societies" were independent and self-sufficient. This was clearly described in Pope Leo XII's encyclical *Immortale dei*.[38] *Gaudium et spes* will embrace a view of the Christian faith which sees it as actively in service to the world: "Nor, on the contrary, are they any less wide of the mark who think that religion consists in acts of worship alone and in the discharge of certain moral obligations, and who imagine they can plunge themselves into earthly affairs in such a way as to imply that these are altogether divorced from the religious life. This split between the faith which many profess and their daily lives deserves to be counted among the more serious errors of our age."[39] Because of the recognition that we must work for the Kingdom of God here on earth, the Church will have much to say as it guides and encourages a particular approach to social reality. This is evident from its first, famous paragraph.

> *The joys and the hopes, the griefs and the anxieties of the people of this age, especially those who are poor or in any way afflicted, these are the joys and hopes, the griefs and anxieties of the followers of Christ. Indeed, nothing genuinely human fails to raise an echo in their hearts. For theirs is a community composed of human beings. United in Christ, they are led by the Holy Spirit in their journey to the Kingdom of their Father and they have welcomed the news of salvation which is meant for every person. That is why this community realizes that it is truly linked with mankind and its history by the deepest of bonds.*[40]

In one clear opening paragraph, the *societas perfectas* approach to church and state, the perception of the church as isolated and alone in the world, a static view of history and the dualism that had only focused on "the above," have all been effectively left behind. As the document says in its introduction, "Thus, the human race has passed from a rather static concept of reality to a more dynamic, evolutionary one. In consequence there has arisen a new series of problems, a series as numerous as can be, calling for efforts of analysis and synthesis."[41] Here is a human community, in continuity with its Divine Founder, which is deeply concerned with the world, and "especially those who are poor or in any way afflicted." This introduces what has become one of the most difficult aspects of the new Church mission to the world to live out—a preferential option for the poor.

The preferential option for the poor is an attempt to mirror God's interaction with humanity revealed in Scripture in the way we treat the most vulnerable human beings with compassion and mercy. First, it was to a people enslaved to whom he first revealed himself. Second, there was a deep concern for those most vulnerable in communities of the Hebrew people, whether widows, orphans or the poor. Finally, a Messiah came who was born poor, lived poor, and died poor, one whose ministry was directed toward marginalized people in His own society even while that ministry was open to everyone. In all these instances of God's action, God reaches out to those most in need while always loving everyone.

Perhaps an analogy would be helpful here. Imagine a member of your family is physically and/or mentally challenged. Would that person require more time, energy, and resources than others in the family? Most likely. Does this mean that by giving that person more, you love or value that person more than other members of the family? Not at all. The person needs more and so they are given more. For the Church to make this commitment from the beginning of this document means two things. First, the Church's action in the world is to be defined by its preferential option for the poor. This is so because, second, it now has a deeper awareness of the need for social change in pursuit of justice which ultimately serves the Kingdom of God. Justice, rather than only charity, will finally define the Church's mission to the world.

There are five overriding themes in *Gaudium et spes* that articulate the Church's mission to the world in new and bold ways. First, when the church looks at the modern world it affirms one thing quite strongly from the beginning of the document. There is a new focus on the category of the "person" as the meaning and fulfillment of created reality. This means that, of all the ways to analyze and understand the world, the default will always be how any given factor, issue, or system realizes or diminishes the dignity of the human person. This is critical to emphasize. When analyzing various systems of economic production and distribution, or various political or social processes, which one safeguards human dignity? The human person exists in the world, but is not able to achieve the same level of dignity everywhere.

The Church's role is to help human beings discover their destiny and dignity. To do this faithfully means to always affirm that God's will is the guarantor of both. According to *Gaudium es spes*, the "human person deserves to be preserved; human society deserves to be renewed. Hence the focal point of our total presentation will be man himself, whole and entire, body and soul, heart and conscience, mind and will."[42] Now the entire integrated person becomes the center of Church concern, not merely the disembodied "soul."

> *Though made of body and soul, the human is one. Through their bodily composition they gather to themselves the elements of the material world; thus they reach their crown through each human being, and through each human being raise their voice in free praise of the Creator. For this reason human beings are not allowed to despise their bodily life, rather they are obliged to regard their bodies as good and honorable since God has created them and will raise them up on the last day. Nevertheless, wounded by sin, human beings experience rebellious stirrings in their body. But the very dignity of humanity postulates that human beings glorify God in their body and forbid it to serve the evil inclinations of their heart.*[43]

One sees very clearly in only the first fifteen paragraphs of this remarkable document a complete shift from a static view of history. What follows is an inductive approach to how we understand the human being as body and soul, created in the image and likeness of God. And what, precisely, does it mean to be created in the image and likeness of God? Augustine and the Catholic tradition ever since have argued that God is best understood as Trinity. The analogy he uses is that God is the one who gives loves perfectly (the Father), the one who receives love perfectly (the Son), and the one who shares love perfectly (the Spirit). God is perfect, embodied, relational love—one God in three persons. To say that I am made in this image means that I am made to give, receive, and share love. Human dignity rests in the possibility of realizing this in life by first having adequate material realities available for its flourishing. While the human being will always do this imperfectly, it is only through the movements of love in relationships that a person will find any true sense of human fulfillment. This brings us to the second major theme in the document, the social nature of human beings.

The document affirms that in their inmost nature, human beings are social and can neither live nor attain their full potential by themselves. Thus the document moves from a claim concerning the inherent dignity of each individual person, to the necessity and goodness of living socially. *Gaudium et spes* clearly states that "God did not create human beings as solitary, for from the beginning 'male and female he created them' (Gen. 1:27). Their companionship produces the primary form of interpersonal communion. For by their innermost nature, human beings are social beings, and unless they relate to others they can neither live nor develop their potential."[44] Emerging from the central Christian doctrine that love of God is love of neighbor and love of neighbor is love God, there is an obligation to cultivate interpersonal relations. This is confirmed by the document: "To people growing daily more dependent on one another and to a world becoming more unified every day, this truth proves to be of paramount importance."[45] This is even truer in a world increasingly characterized by interdependence. Here the document anticipates the globalization that will develop very rapidly in the 1980s and 1990s. And this leads us to the third major theme of the encyclical, the criteria for how a truly human society cultivates increasingly complex relationships.

The social nature of human beings should be formed and managed with the *genuine* and *common* good of the human race foremost in mind. A deep concern for the well-being of all is necessary for the goodness and development of the individual. It is not an either/or but a both/and. For many North Americans, this is counter-intuitive. Part of our historical development has included the ethos that by pursuing our individual self-interest, the common good will somehow emerge (analogous to the invisible hand?).[46] *Gaudium et spes* arrives at a quite different position. By pursuing the common good our individual good emerges. From a Catholic perspective, society is not supposed to be a contractual partnership of essentially separate individuals, as it is often viewed and experienced within the United States. It is instead a partnership in the pursuit of goods that are best realized and fulfilled in common. For example, a basic level of health care among all members of a society is necessary for a community to genuinely and truly flourish. Health care facilities and the treatment they provide are not only commodities for those with substantial financial resources to buy and sell. The church's commitment to the common good as the most basic principle of social, economic, and political relationships challenges the self-interested orientation that is manifest in a radical free-market perspective, a perspective the Catholic Church has been very critical of in many of its documents. It is in this orientation that health care becomes a commodity like other consumer goods whose allocation is solely determined by who can afford to pay, rather than by right and necessity. These goods are meant to be shared and distributed in an even fashion, working toward the better health of all and contributing to the standard of health for the entire community. Your individual good emerges from a society that cares for its entire people.

Fourth, in order to facilitate the common good, the church deeply commits itself to the pursuit of justice by seeking more humane and just conditions of life and directing institutions to guaranteeing human dignity.[47] This is remarkably different from a mere commitment to charitable activity. Charity is always good, but never enough. There will always be the need to provide necessities for those who lack them—such as water, food, medicine, and housing. The Church has a long and impressive history of doing this. Working for justice, however, gets at the systemic roots of *why* there is so much need, and tries to change the social realities that create the need in the first place. Much has been made of Archbishop Dom Helder Camara's comment "When I give food to the poor, they call me a saint. When I ask why the poor have no food, they call me a Communist." His first statement epitomizes charity—addressing the symptoms that result from broken human systems. The second statement represents the initial phase of justice—seeing human reality as it is and asking, why? Here we have a critical moment when the Church understands its own mission in the world. Recall that for many centuries in Latin America, the church had given its blessing to the colonial enterprise and later resisted calls for independence from the very countries that had enslaved indigenous peoples. The Church, understandably, would alienate many of the poor and marginalized who comprised the majority of Latin America (and still do). Beginning with *Gaudium et spes*, and especially through later documents such as *Populorum progressio*, as well as by documents written by the Latin American Bishops, the Church would begin to alienate the wealthy. To understand how, we turn now to the fifth overall theme of this document.

Following the argument outlined above, the fifth and final theme should come as no surprise. All social, economic, and human development ought to be directed to the complete fulfillment of all citizens, with those wealthier individuals and nations opting to help those less developed individuals and nations. Beyond charitable endeavors, the obligation by wealthier individuals and nations to assist those in need has not been embraced by many of the wealthy in either the U.S. or Latin America. Vatican II points out the scandalous imbalance of social and economic resources as well as hinting at some of the consequences. "While an immense number of people still lack the absolute necessities of life, some, even in less advanced areas, live in luxury or squander wealth. Extravagance and wretchedness exist side by side. While a few enjoy very great power of choice, the majority are deprived of almost all possibility of acting on their own initiative and responsibility, and often subsist in living and working conditions unworthy of the human person."[48] Wealth and poverty are related. As a relational reality, those with riches can no longer understand themselves as unrelated, or not responsible for those in poverty. Unfortunately this scandal of inequality has both widened and deepened globally since 1965, and while we have seen some progress in development by poor nations, contemporary global economic inequality remains stark. The pursuit of justice with relation to economic forces goes well beyond the traditional categories of charity. Additionally, the church will speak to the reasons for such inequality.

> *To satisfy the demands of justice and equity, strenuous efforts must be made, without disregarding the rights of persons or the natural qualities of each country, to remove as quickly as possible the immense economic inequalities, which now exist and in many cases are growing and which are connected with individual and social discrimination.*[49]

It is clear from this document that the tradition of Catholic Social Thought, begun in 1891 with *Rerum novarum,* is finally penetrating the ecclesiology which for so long had resisted it. Prior to Vatican II, the social encyclicals seemed to be an unrelated corollary to the true business of the church in the world. This separation, or compartmentalization, is now over. *Gaudium et spes* reiterates the core principle of Catholic Social Thought and pledges *as a work of the Church* to articulate this vision more forcefully in the world: "God intended the earth with everything contained in it for the use of all human beings and peoples. Thus, under the leadership of justice and in the company of charity, created goods should be in abundance for all in like manner."[50]

Summary

Changes in how the Catholic Church understands its role in the world at the Second Vatican Council were nothing less than astonishing. The change includes a move from a Church that perceived itself as "above" the affairs of the world, and only grudgingly part of it, to a Church deeply in mission to the world as it cooperates with God's grace to welcome the Kingdom of God. Vatican II moved a Church heavily focused on its hierarchy and holiness to one which validates every member of the Church as called to a specific vocation by God. Finally, the Church embraces justice especially for the most vulnerable. It now seeks to address the causes of dehumanization as its main posture toward the world, a posture which will always include charity but never be limited to only charity.

As with any major shift in identity, these changes have been difficult for many members of the Church. It could be argued that the majority of North American Catholics have not accepted or internalized the profound changes articulated at Vatican II. There are many reasons for this, but much of the contemporary tension in the church centers on differing interpretations of or outright rejection of some of these changes.

Notes

Introduction

1. Simone Weil, *Waiting for God*, trans. Emma Craufurd (New York: Harper & Row, 1951), 74.

Chapter 1: Oracles, Dissent, and Conversation: Reflections on Catholic Teaching

1. Eamon Duffy, *Saints and Sinners: A History of the Popes*, 2nd ed. (New Haven and London: Yale University Press, 2002), 319–386.

2. "A Place for Dissent," *The Tablet*, 6 June 2009, 2.

3. Timothy Radcliffe, *Why Go to Church? The Drama of the Eucharist* (London: Continuum, 2008), 54.

4. Radcliffe, *Why Go to Church?* 61.

5. Nicholas Lash, *The Beginning and the End of 'Religion'* (Cambridge: Cambridge University Press, 1996), 21.

6. Augustine, *On Christian Teaching*, trans. R. P. H. Green (Oxford: Oxford University Press, 1997), 8.

7. See Nicholas Lash, "Road-signs: Reflections on the Christian Doctrine of God," *Faith, Word and Culture*, ed. Liam Bergin (Dublin: The Columba Press, 2004), 98–115.

8. Ring Lardner, *The Young Immigrants* (Indianapolis: Bobbs Merrill, 1920).

9. See Nicholas Lash, "Authors, Authority and Authorization," in *Authority in the Roman Catholic Church: Theory and Practice*, ed. Bernard Hoose (Aldershot: Ashgate, 2002), 59–71.

10. "*Autre chose est agréer une doctrine, autre chose obéir à un ordre.*" Yves Congar, "*Sur la Trilogie 'Prophète-Roi-Prêtre,'*" *Revue des Sciences Philosophiques et Théologiques*, 67 (1983), 97–116; at 109.

11. Lash, "Authors, Authority and Authorization," 61, quoting Robert Ombres, "What Future for the Laity?" *Governance and Authority in the Roman Catholic Church: Beginning a Conversation*, ed. N. Timms and K. Wilson (London: SPCK, 2000), 98.

12. See Congar, "*Sur la Trilogie,*" 98.

13. See John Henry Newman, *The Via Media of the Anglican Church*, Vol. I (London: Longmans, Green, 1877), xv–xciv.

14. See Congar, "*Sur la Trilogie,*" 7.

15. Lash, "Authors, Authority and Authorization," 61.

16. See *L'Ecclésiologie au XIXe Siècle*, *Unam Sanctam* 34 (Paris: Les Editions du Cerf, 1960), 329–349. The essays in this collection first appeared, earlier the same year, as numbers 2, 3, and 4 of the *Revue des Sciences Religieuses*.

17. Congar's essay *"Sur la Trilogie"* reviews L. Schick, *Das Dreifache Amt Christi und der Kirche* (*Europäische Hochschulschriften, Reihe XXIII Theologie. Bd 171*), published in Frankfurt by Peter Lang in 1982. See Bertulf van Leeuwen's essay on *"La Participation à la Fonction Prophétique du Christ,"* in *L'Eglise de Vatican II, Unam Sanctam* 51, ed. Guilherme Baraúna, French edition directed by Congar (Paris: Les Editions du Cerf, 1966), 425–455.

18. He speaks of Newman "apportioning" the offices "among different classes (theologians, devout laity, and popes)": Avery Dulles, "The Threefold Office in Newman's Ecclesiology," *Newman after a Hundred Years*, ed. Ian Ker and Alan Hill (Oxford: Clarendon Press, 1990), 375–399 at 397.

19. Dulles, "The Threefold Office," 397.

20. Robert Murray, "Authority and the Spirit in the New Testament," *Authority in a Changing Church* (London: Sheed and Ward, 1968), 12–38, at 19.

21. *"C'est le peuple, c'est l'Eglise, qui est prophétique, sacerdotal et royal" ("Sur la Trilogie")*, 106.

22. Newman, *Via Media*, xl.

23. *"Auctoritas gubernandi, facultas docendi, potestas miracula faciendi ad confirmationem doctrinae"* (*Commentary on 1 Corinthians*, cited by Congar, "Sur la trilogie," 107).

24. Newman, *Via Media*, xl.

25. Newman, *Via Media*, xli.

26. Gary Macy, *The Hidden History of Women's Ordination* (Oxford: Oxford University Press, 2008), 7.

27. Quoted from Margaret Mary Littlehales, *Mary Ward: Pilgrim and Mystic* (Tunbridge Wells: Burns and Oates, 1998), 254.

28. I am grateful to Dr. Gemma Simmonds, C.J., for obtaining the text of the Bull for me, and for supplying these details of the order's history.

29. Quoted from Bill Broderick, "Examining the Validity of Anglican Orders," *National Catholic Reporter*, 13 August 1999.

30. From the website of the Holy See. < http://www.vatican.va/roman_curia/pontifical_councils/chrstuni/card-kasper-docs/rc_pc_chrstuni_doc_20060605_kasper-bishops_en.html> (11 January 2011)

31. See Nicholas Lash, "Churches, proper and otherwise," *The Tablet*, 21 July 2007, 13–14.

32. *The Tablet*, 23 April 1966, quoted from *Pope and Pill*, edited by Leo Pyle (London: Darton, Longman and Todd, 1968), 83.

33. *The Times*, 3 August 1968, quoted from *Pope and Pill*, 84.

34. *The Times*, 3 August 1968, quoted from *Pope and Pill*, 84.

35. Article 15 of the recent encyclical, *Caritas in veritate*, endorsing *Humanae vitae*, refers the reader to the address which, on 10 May 2008, Benedict XVI delivered to an International Congress held at the Lateran University commemorating the 40th anniversary of the publication of the encyclical. "The Document," says the Pope, "very soon became a sign of contradiction. Drafted to treat a difficult situation, it constitutes a significant show of courage in reasserting the continuity of the

Church's doctrine and tradition" < http://www.vatican.va/holy_father/benedict_xvi/speeches/2008/may/documents/hf_ben-xvi_spe_20080510_humanae-vitae_en.html > (11 January 2011). Paul VI might have displayed even greater courage had he accepted the report of the Pontifical Commission.

36. Robert Murray, "Vatican II and the Bible," *The Downside Review* (January, 2003), 14–25; at 24. This was a special issue on "Abbot Butler and the Council," celebrating the centenary of Christopher Butler's birth.

37. Francis A. Sullivan, *Magisterium: Teaching Authority in the Catholic Church* (Dublin: Gill and Macmillan, 1983), 24, 29.

38. Ladislas Örsy, *The Church: Learning and Teaching* (Dublin: Dominican Publications, 1987), 63. The book begins: "I am grateful for the help I have received from Michael Buckley." This chapter, on "Teaching Authority," and the following, on "Assent and Dissent," are revised and enlarged versions of materials published in *Theological Studies* earlier that year. Later in the book, he makes clear that rejecting the terminology of two "magisteria" does not obliterate the distinction: "The difference between the *cathedra pastoralis* (the authority of the bishop is rooted in his sacramental office), and the *cathedra magistralis* (the authority of the teacher is as good as his reasons) remains intact" (p. 148).

39. Article 115. See Nicholas Lash, "Teaching in Crisis," *Understanding Veritatis Splendor*, edited by John Wilkins (London: SPCK, 1994), 27–34.

40. Gregory Baum, "Can the Church change her position on birth control?" *Contraception and Holiness, The Catholic Predicament*, a Symposium introduced by Archbishop Thomas D. Roberts (London: Fontana, 1965), 260–286; at 264, my emphasis.

41. Duffy, *Saints and Sinners*, pp. 358, 359, 370.

42. Giuseppe Alberigo, "The Announcement of the Council," *History of Vatican II. Vol. I*, ed. Giuseppe Alberigo (Maryknoll: Orbis, 1995), 1–54; at 37.

43. Joseph A. Komonchak, "The Struggle for the Council during the Preparation of Vatican II (1960–1962)," *The History of Vatican II, Vol. I*, 167–356; at 179.

44. Komonchak, "The Struggle for the Council," 179.

45. Alberigo, "Conclusion. Preparing for what kind of Council?" *The History of Vatican II, Vol. I*, 501–508; at 503.

46. Duffy, *Saints and Sinners*, 372.

47. See Nicholas Lash, *Theology on Dover Beach* (London: Darton, Longman and Todd, 1979), 107.

48. When, a few years ago, the Jesuits held a General Chapter, Timothy Radcliffe, then Master of the Dominicans, wrote a letter of warm congratulation to his opposite number, the Jesuit General, Hans-Pieter Kolvenbach. He added a postscript: "P.S. We were right about grace!"

49. John Henry Newman, *Letters and Diaries of John Henry Newman. Vol. XXIV*, ed. C. S. Dessain and Thomas Gornall (Oxford: Oxford University Press, 1973), 355.

50. Lord Acton, *CUL Add MSS 4989.3*. See Nicholas Lash, *Newman on Development* (London: Sheed and Ward, 1975), 136.

51. See Sullivan, *Magisterium*, 174–178.

52. Örsy, *The Church*, 101.

53. Sullivan, *Magisterium*, 209.

54. Pope John Paul II, "Address at Meeting with the Bishops of the United States of America," 16 September, 1987, <http://www.vatican.va/holy_father/john_paul_ii/speeches/1987/september/documents/hf_jp-ii_spe_19870916_vescovi-stati-uniti_en.html> (12 January 2011).

55. Örsy, *The Church*, 90–93.

56. See Frank Sullivan on "obedience of the judgement," *Magisterium*, 162–166.

57. Congar: see note 10 above.

58. Francis A. Sullivan, "The teaching authority of episcopal conferences," *Theological Studies*, 63 (September, 2002), 472–493; at 472.

59. Notwithstanding the fact that, twenty years earlier, he had taken the opposite view. See Joseph Ratzinger, "The Pastoral Implications of Episcopal Collegiality," *Concilium: Dogma, I* (1965), 30; discussed by John Mahoney in "On the Other Hand ..." *New Blackfriars* (June, 1985), 288–298. That number of *New Blackfriars* was a special issue in which Eamon Duffy, John Mahoney, Fergus Kerr and I discussed the book-length interview, *Rapporto sulla fede*, which the Cardinal gave in 1984 to Vittorio Messori.

60. Sullivan, "The teaching authority of episcopal conferences," 477.

61. A former member of the International Theological Commission, cited by Robert Mickens, "Letter from Rome," *The Tablet,* 1 August 2009, 34. Cf. John Thornhill, "The Church and the Churches," *The Tablet*, 23 November 1985, 1242. I am most grateful to Robert Mickens for help in locating some of the material in this section.

For the record, it is worth noting that, when the Synod did meet, its Final Report made clear that its members "were not ready to agree that episcopal conferences 'have no *mandatum docendi*' .... Rather, they saw the teaching authority and theological basis of episcopal conferences as open questions" (Sullivan, "The teaching authority," 478–9).

Finally, at an international Symposium in Salamanca, in 1988, the participants were asked "whether episcopal conferences as such exercise an authentic magisterium with regard to the faithful of their territory" (Sullivan, ibid., p. 480). Each of the five language groups agreed, independently, that they did. A few days later, the Congregation for Bishops issued a document, purporting to be the official fruit of the study of the question requested by the 1985 Synod, and entitled "Theological and Juridical Status of Episcopal Conferences," which, in effect, simply reiterated Cardinal Ratzinger's personal position (see Sullivan, ibid., p. 481).

62. Herbert McCabe, "Manuals and Rule Books," *Understanding Veritatis splendor*, 61–68; at 62.

63. McCabe, "Manuals and Rule Books," 63.

64. *Veritatis splendor*, no. 113.

65. Not, I think (for reasons that would require another paper to spell out) "assent." See Frank Sullivan's discussion of Christopher Butler on "dissent" and "assent" in *Magisterium*, 158–162.

66. "Note from the Secretariat of State Concerning the Four Prelates of the Society of St. Pius X," English at < http://www.vatican.va/roman_curia/secretariat_state/2009/documents/rc_seg-st_20090204_note-decree-cbishops_en.html >; Italian at < http://www.vatican.va/roman_curia/secretariat_state/2009/documents/rc_seg-st_20090204_note-decree-cbishops_it.html> (12 January 2011).

67. See note 3 above.

68. See Michael J. Buckley, *The Catholic University as Promise and Project* (Washington, D. C.: Georgetown University Press, 2007), 24–25.

69. This motto, probably first coined by a 16th-century German Lutheran, was quoted by John XXIII in his first encyclical, *Ad Petri cathedram*.

Chapter 2: *Widening the Dialectic: Secularity and Christianity in Conversation*

1. Michael Buckley, *At the Origins of Modern Atheism* (New Haven: Yale University Press, 1987), 16. Subsequent parenthetical citations refer to *At the Origins*.

2. James Force writes that in *At the Origins*, "Michael Buckley has gone for broke [... The book] will undoubtedly be taken as an indispensable new focus for future discussions about the relation of reason to religious apologetics in the early modern period and about method in the history of ideas." ("The Origins of Modern Atheism," *Journal of the History of Ideas* 50, no. 1 (1989): 153); John Milbank states, "Buckley, however, offers his own reading as a substitute for this oft-told tale of emancipation from religious tutelage: modern atheism is rather the unintended creation of a confused and contradictory theological apologetic which arose in the 17th and 18th centuries." He later adds that the book "is a splendid, bold endeavour" ("Review," *Modern Theology* 8, no. 1 (1992): 90, 92). Indeed, even Charles Taylor gets in the act when he writes that his narrative in *A Secular Age* means to complement to the work done by, among others, Buckley. [*A Secular Age* (Cambridge, MA: Belknap Press of Harvard University Press, 2007). 295; Taylor elsewhere praises Buckley's "penetrating book" and describes its thesis as a "striking fact" (ibid, 225, 328)].

3. Force, "The Origins of Modern Atheism," 153, 154.

4. Force, "The Origins of Modern Atheism," 158, 159.

5. David Wilson, "Review," *The Journal of Religion* 71, no. 2 (1991): 441.

6. Paul Casner, "Review," *Restoration Quarterly* 32:3 (1990): 191.

7. John Milbank, "Review," 90.

8. Milbank, "Review," 90, 92.

9. Buckley, *Denying and Disclosing God: The Ambiguous Progress of Modern Atheism* (New Haven: Yale University Press, 2004), xii.

10. Buckley, *Denying and Disclosing God*, 25–47; see Alan Kors, *Atheism in France, 1650–1729*, vol. 1, *The Orthodox Sources of Disbelief* (Princeton: Princeton

University Press, 1990); James Turner, *Without God, Without Creed: The Origins of Unbelief in America* (Baltimore: The Johns Hopkins University Press, 1985).

11. *Denying and Disclosing God*, 29.

12. *Denying and Disclosing God*, 28.

13. *At the Origins*, 362–63.

14. This section leans heavily on two works: *"Dialektik"* [multiple authors] in *Historisches Wörterbuch der Philosophie*, eds. Joachim Ritter and Karlfried Gründer (Basel: Schwabe Verlag, 1971), 2:163–226; Roland Hall, "Dialectic," in *Encyclopedia of Philosophy. 2nd Edition*, ed. Donald M Borchert (Detroit: Thomson Gale, 2006), 3: 52–56.

15. *Republic* 534b; *Cratylus* 390c.

16. *"Dialektik,"* 172; see *Topics* VIII (162a); Plato similarly associates eristic with the counter-productive tactics of the Sophists (*Sophist* 231e).

17. *"Dialektik,"* 173–74; Cicero, *de finibus bonorum et malum*, II, 18. The translation is taken from Harris Rackham's Loeb edition (Cambridge, Mass: Harvard University Press, 1961), 98–99.

18. Buckley, *At the Origins*, 6.

19. Buckley, *At the Origins*, 340.

20. Frederick Beiser, *Hegel* (New York: Routledge, 2005), 160; see also Hall, "Dialectic," 55 and Buckley, *Denying and Disclosing God*, 122, for the same emphasis.

21. The definitive scholarly treatment of this topic comes from the enjoyably polemic article by Gustav E. Mueller, "The Hegel Legend of Thesis-Antithesis-Synthesis," *Journal of the History of Ideas* 19, no. 3 (1958): 411–14, who traces the misunderstanding to Heinrich Moritz Chalybäus's lectures on Hegel, which the young Karl Marx read and repeated (ibid, 413–14); see also Hall, "Dialectic," 54; Beiser, *Hegel*, 161. Buckley himself is aware of this misapplication (*Denying and Disclosing God*, 122).

22. Buckley, *Denying and Disclosing God*, 29.

23. Buckley, *Denying and Disclosing God*, 122.

24. Buckley, *Denying and Disclosing God*, 122.

25. Charles Taylor describes the difference in interpretation as follows: "As I have indicated, this debate tends to become polarized between 'boosters' and 'knockers,' who either condemn or affirm modernity en bloc, thus missing what is really at stake here, which is how to rescue admirable ideals from sliding into demeaning modes of realization." See "A Catholic Modernity?" in *A Catholic Modernity? Charles Taylor's Marianist Award Lecture*, ed. James L Heft (Oxford: Oxford University Press, 1999), 36. He uses the same language of "boosters" and "knockers" in *The Ethics of Authenticity* (Cambridge: Harvard University Press, 1991), 11. Taylor returns to this theme in the "Epilogue" to *A Secular Age*, where he argues, not surprisingly, that his own account, while compatible with Milbank's (among others') story of modernity as "intellectual deviation," is able to explain the rise of modern secularism more comprehensively (*A Secular Age*, 773–76). See also, *A Secular Age*, 637: "Some think that the whole move to secular humanism was just a mistake, which needs to be undone. We need to return to an earlier view of things. Others, in which I place

myself, think that [...] there is some truth in the self-narrative of the Enlightenment: this gain was in fact unlikely to come about without some breach with established religion."

26. See in particular Peter Gay, *The Enlightenment: An Interpretation: The Rise of Modern Paganism* (New York: Alfred A. Knopf, 1966); *The Enlightenment: An Interpretation: The Science of Freedom* (New York: Alfred A. Knopf, 1969); Harvey Gallagher Cox, *The Secular City: Secularization and Urbanization in Theological Perspective* (New York: Macmillan, 1965).

27. Jonathan I. Israel, *Enlightenment Contested: Philosophy, Modernity, and the Emancipation of Man 1670–1752* (Oxford: Oxford University Press, 2006), 10.

28. Israel, *Enlightenment Contested*, 10.

29. Israel, *Enlightenment Contested*, 870; the reference is to Williams, *Truth and Truthfulness* (Princeton: Princeton University Press, 2002), 254.

30. John Milbank, "Knowledge: The Theological critique of philosophy in Hamann and Jacobi," in *Radical Orthodoxy: A New Theology*, eds. Milbank, Catherine Pickstock and Graham Ward (London: Routledge, 1999), 23–24.

31. Milbank, "Knowledge," 32.

32. David Bentley Hart, "Christ and Nothing," *First Things* 136 (October 2003): 55.

33. In a way, the project here overlaps in significant ways with Randy Rosenberg's. See, "The Catholic Imagination and Modernity: William Cavanaugh's Theopolitical Imagination and Charles Taylor's Modern Social Imagination," *Heythrop Journal* 48 (2007): 911–31. Rosenberg uses the framework suggested by Lonergan, where one can read difference as complementary, genetic, or dialectical. Within this framework, Buckley's approach would be genetic, not dialectical. For this distinction see Rosenberg, ibid, 912; For Lonergan, *Method in Theology* (Toronto: University of Toronto Press, 1971), at 236; and the essay "Sacralization and Secularization" in *Philosophical and Theological Papers: 1965–1980* (Toronto: University of Toronto Press, 2004), 259–81.

34. For Taylor see Ruth Abbey, *Charles Taylor* (Princeton: Princeton University Press, 2000). Abbey also maintains a website with a bibliography of work on Taylor: <http://nd.edu/%7Erabbey1/> (14 Jan. 2011); For Girard see Michael Kirwan, *Discovering Girard* (Cambridge, MA: Cowley Publications, 2005); Richard J. Golsan, *René Girard and Myth: An Introduction* (New York: Routledge, 1993). Although now dated, Golsan's book includes one of the most extensive Girard bibliographies in print (ibid, 181–237).

35. Taylor, *A Secular Age*, 146–58; *Modern Social Imaginaries* (Durham, NC: Duke University Press, 2004), 49–67. Subsequent citations of *A Secular Age* will be parenthetical.

36. Taylor, *A Secular Age*, 792n. See Jaspers, *Vom Ursprung und Ziel der Geschichte* (Zürich: Artemis, 1949). Taylor also makes explicit his debt to Robert Bellah in regard to pre-Axial religion. See Bellah's essay, "Religious Evolution," in his *Beyond Belief: Essays on Religion in a Post-Traditional World* (New York: Harper & Row, 1970), 20–50, esp. 25–32.

37. Taylor, *Modern Social Imaginaries* (Durham, NC: Duke University Press, 2004), 54.

38. Taylor does not adopt Jaspers wholesale (*A Secular Age*, 792 n. 9). What matters is not so much the age, but the break between the two religious systems. For Taylor's qualifications, see ibid, 438–45.

39. James Alison, *Undergoing God: Dispatches from the Scene of a Break-in* (New York: Continuum: 2006), 16.

40. René Girard, *Violence and the Sacred*, trans. Patrick Gregory (Baltimore: The Johns Hopkins University Press, 1977).

41. René Girard, *Evolution and Conversion: Dialogues on the Origins of Culture* (New York: Continuum, 2007), 67.

42. For Girard on Rousseau, see *Evolution and Conversion*, 187–88.

43. On Göbekli Tepe, see the *Newsweek* article from February 19, 2010: <www.newsweek.com/2010/02/18/history-in-the-remaking.html> (14 Jan. 2011).

44. Girard, *Evolution and Conversion*, 72.

45. René Girard, *I See Satan Fall Like Lightning*, trans. James Williams (Maryknoll, New York: Orbis, 2001), 93.

46. Girard, *Violence and the Sacred*, 259.

47. René Girard, *The Scapegoat*, trans. Yvonne Freccero (Baltimore: The Johns Hopkins University Press, 1986), 112–15. Girard writes, "Caiaphas is the perfect sacrificer who puts victims to death to save those who live. By reminding us of this John emphasizes that every real cultural *decision* has a sacrificial character (*decidere*, remember, is to cut the victim's throat) that refers back to an unrevealed effect of the scapegoat, the sacred type of representation of persecution" (ibid, 114).

48. Charles Taylor, *Sources of the Self: The Making of the Modern Identity* (Cambridge, Mass: Harvard University Press, 1989), 129.

49. Taylor, *Sources of the Self*, 230.

50. Taylor, *Sources of the Self*, 231.

51. For his treatment of the Christian reform efforts in *A Secular Age* see ch. 2, "The Rise of the Disciplinary Society," 90–145.

52. Taylor writes of the Franciscan emphasis on *haecceitas*: "Though it couldn't be clear at the time, we with hindsight can recognize this as a major turning point in the history of Western civilization, an important step towards that primacy of the individual which defines our culture" (*A Secular Age*, 94).

53. This spirit of "making all things new" forms the central organizing theme of a delightful and under-appreciated book: George Herring, *Introduction to the History of Christianity* (New York: NYU Press, 2006).

54. See also Taylor, "A Catholic Modernity?" 30.

55. In this respect Girard's account departs from the more inclusive Axial approach of Taylor.

56. Girard, *The Scapegoat*, 117.

57. One gets a sense of this from his choice of titles. *A Secular Age* speaks for itself. Some form of "modern" finds its way into almost all of his works: the subtitle

of *Sources* reads: *The Making of* Modern *Identity*. His Marian address, "A Catholic Modernity," his second book on Hegel: *Hegel and* Modern *Society*, his precursor to *A Secular Age*: *Modern Social Imaginaries*, even his truncated *Sources*: *The Ethics of Authenticity*, was originally titled: *The* Modern *Malaise emphases mine*.

58. In *Sources of the Self* Taylor considers the subtraction theory in order to explain the loss in belief, "But what is questionable is the thesis that they [scientific rationality and industrialization] are sufficient conditions of the loss of religious belief. [...] If religious faith were like some particulate illusory belief, whose erroneous nature was only masked by a certain set of practices, then it would collapse with the passing of these and their supersession by others; as perhaps certain particular beliefs about magical connections have. This then is the assumption which often underpins the institutional account" (402–3).

59. Taylor, "A Catholic Modernity?" in *A Catholic Modernity? Charles Taylor's Marianist Award Lecture*, ed. James L Heft (Oxford: Oxford University Press, 1999), 26.

60. See Taylor, *inter alia*, *A Secular Age*, 816 n. 6; he cites Weber, *The Protestant Ethic and the Spirit of Capitalism*, trans. Talcott Parsons (New York: Scribner, 1958) and Marcel Gauchet, *Le désenchantement du monde* (Paris: Gallimard, 1985).

61. Taylor, "A Catholic Modernity?" 31.

62. Taylor, *Sources of the Self*, 319, emphasis mine.

63. It should be noted that Taylor's take on modernity is more pejorative in the final, twentieth chapter of *A Secular Age*, "Conversions." Although it is not clear whether he speaks from his own voice, or for Ivan Illich, Taylor declares, "Corrupted Christianity gives rise to the modern" (ibid, 740; see also 741).

64. Taylor, "A Catholic Modernity," 13–37 at 16. It seems that Taylor's "necessary condition" is meant in the same way as Buckley's "necessary" evolving pattern (see n. 24 above).

65. This concession comes in response to a point raised by Gianni Vattimo about Girard. See Girard, *Evolution and Conversion*, 234, 262 n. 1.

66. See René Girard, "The Modern Concern for Victims," in *I See Satan Fall Like Lightning*, trans. James Williams (Maryknoll, New York: Orbis, 2001), 161–69, at 161.

67. Girard, *Evolution and Conversion*, 246.

68. Girard, *Evolution and Conversion*, 258; see also Girard and Gianni Vattimo, *Christianity, Truth, and Weakening Faith: A Dialogue*, ed. Pierpaolo Antonello, trans. William McCuaig (New York: Columbia University Press, 2010): "Christianity deprives us of the mechanism that formed the basis of the archaic social and religious order, ushering in a new phase in the history of mankind that we may legitimately call 'modern.' All the conquests of modernity begin there, as far as I am concerned, from the acquisition of awareness within Christianity." (ibid, 26).

69. Girard, *Evolution and Conversion*, 239.

70. Girard, *Battling to the End: Conversations with Benoît Chantre*, trans. Mary Baker. (East Lansing, Mich: Michigan State University, 2010), 198.

71. Similar to Girard, Buckley shows how modern science and Christianity are intertwined. Buckley writes, "How ironic it is to read in popular histories of the 'antagonisms of religion and the rising science.' That was precisely what the problem was not! These sciences did not oppose religious convictions, they supported them. Indeed, they subsumed theology, and theologians accepted with relief and gratitude this assumption of religious foundations by Cartesian first philosophy and Newtonian mechanics" (*At the Origins*, 347).

72. Girard, *The Scapegoat*, 204.

73. Girard, *The Scapegoat*, 204.

74. Buckley, *Denying and Disclosing God*, xv. Subsequent parenthetical pagination refers to this text.

75. Taylor defines the immanent frame as a set of preconditions or unchallenged framework, a "sensed context in which we develop our beliefs." In the case of modernity, it is an immanent order made possible by such factors as disenchantment (*A Secular Age*, 539–93, esp. 549).

76. Taylor, *A Secular Age*, 744.

77. Girard, *I See Satan Fall like Lightning*, 173.

78. Girard, *Battling to the End*, x.

79. Girard, *I See Satan Fall Like Lightning*, 178, 179.

80. Girard, *Evolution and Conversion*, 257.

81. In private conversations around 2008, Buckley told me that he was reading Taylor and that he had never spent any time with Girard, although he was familiar with but unsympathetic to his theory.

82. Girard, *Battling to the End*, xvi.

Chapter 3: What's Reason Got to Do with It? Examining Contemporary Theologies of Religious Pluralism

1. Michael J. Buckley, S.J. *Denying and Disclosing God: The Ambiguous Progress of Modern Atheism* (New Haven: Yale University Press, 2004) 138.

2. *Denying and Disclosing God*, 138.

3. *Denying and Disclosing God*, 138. Cf. Friedrich von Hügel, *The Mystical Element of Religion as Studied in Saint Catherine of Genoa and Her Friends* (London: J.M. Dent & Co., 1909), 50–82.

4. Gavin D'Costa, *The Depth of Riches: A Trinitarian Theology of Religious Ends* (Grand Rapids: Wm B Eerdmans, 2001), 3.

5. Francis Clooney, *Theology after Vedanta: An Experiment in Comparative Theology* (Albany: State University of New York Press, 1993), 193–94 and James Fredericks, *Faith among Faiths: Christian Theology and Non-Christian Religions* (New York: Paulist, 1999), 167.

6. A few years ago, Gavin D'Costa, Terrence Tilley, and Perry Schmidt-Leukel offered *Modern Theology* readers a lucid disputation on a serious contemporary theological issue: whether other religions serve as a preparation for salvation

(D'Costa), are salvific in principle (Tilley), or are different but equally valid paths to salvation (Schmidt-Leukel). [*Modern Theology*: 22 (2006) 51–63; 23 (2007) 435–468; and 24 (2008) 271–297.] This exchange began as a textual disagreement about *Dominus Iesus*. The three theologians read the document differently: D'Costa accents the document's exclusivism, Tilley stresses its inclusivism, and Schmidt-Leukel argues that both tendencies are present in the document and are fundamentally inconsistent with each other. Each theologian's decision about how to read *DI* also affects how he relates it to the famous line from *Nostra aetate*: "The Catholic Church rejects nothing that is *true* and *holy* in these religions." [*The Declaration on the Relation of the Church to Non-Christian Religions (Nostra aetate)* (1965) para.2. Italics mine.]

7. S. Mark Heim's provocative 2001 Trinitarian study *The Depth of Riches: A Trinitarian Theology of Religious Ends*, Gavin D'Costa's 2000 book *The Meeting of Religions and the Trinity*, and Terrence Tilley's 2007 *Religious Diversity and the American Experience* are but a few samples.

8. D'Costa, *The Meeting of Religions and the Trinity* (Maryknoll: Orbis Books, 2000), 5.

9. D'Costa, *The Meeting of Religions and the Trinity*, 8.

10. D'Costa, *The Meeting of Religions and the Trinity*, 8.

11. D'Costa, *The Meeting of Religions and the Trinity*, 8. Already in 1993 D'Costa suggests that the only way to negotiate conflicting truth claims is through tradition-specific starting points. But these suggestions do not get developed until the year 2000 with his *Meeting of Religions*. See his "Whose Objectivity? Which Neutrality? The Doomed Quest for a Neutral Vantage Point from which to Judge Religions," *Religious Studies* 29 (1993) 79–95.

12. D'Costa, *The Meeting of Religions and the Trinity*, 23.

13. D'Costa, *The Meeting of Religions and the Trinity*, 23.

14. D'Costa, *The Meeting of Religions and the Trinity*, 24.

15. D'Costa, "Christ, Revelation and the World Religions: A Critical Appreciation of Keith Ward's Comparative Global Theology," in *Comparative Theology: Essays for Keith Ward*, T. W. Bartel, ed. (Pilgrim Press, 2003) 38.

16. D'Costa, *The Meeting of Religions and the Trinity*, 23.

17. D'Costa, *The Meeting of Religions and the Trinity*, 23.

18. D'Costa is explicit in his support of what he deems the "Yale School" hermeneutical strategy and the performance of a text. He refers here to the work of Hans Frei, George Lindbeck, and Gerard Loughlin [cf. "The Resurrection, the Holy Spirit and World Religion" in *Resurrection Reconsidered*, ed. Gavin D'Costa (Oxford: Oneworld Publications, 1996) n. 5, 165].

19. D'Costa, "Whose Objectivity, Which Neutrality? The Doomed Quest for a Neutral Vantage Point from which to Judge Religions," *Religious Studies* 29 (1993) 79.

20. D'Costa, "Christ, the Trinity and Religious Plurality" in *Christian Unique-ness Reconsidered: The Myth of a Pluralistic Theology of Religions*, ed. Gavin D'Costa (Maryknoll: Orbis Books, 1990) 19.

21. D'Costa, *The Meeting of Religions and the Trinity*, 28.

22. D'Costa, *The Meeting of Religions and the Trinity*, 38.

23. In an earlier article, D'Costa had already argued against Keith Ward and Harold Netland that despite several commonalities in formal structure, and maybe commonalities in values in theory and practice, "at a fundamental level there are substantial ontological differences [between religions] that cannot be dissolved." D'Costa, "Whose Objectivity, Which Neutrality?" 94.

24. D'Costa, *Dialogue and Alliance*, 5; "A Christian Reflection on Some Prob-lems with Discerning 'God' in the World Religions" (1991) 15.

25. D'Costa, "Postmodernity and Religious Plurality: Is a Common Ethic Pos-sible or Desirable," *The Blackwell Companion to Postmodern Theology* (Oxford: Blackwell Publishers, 2001) 141. Following MacIntyre, D'Costa recognizes that in-ternal critiques often exist, such that complex levels of intra-traditioned debates emerge. He provides contemporary examples of outcaste Hindus and women Chris-tian philosophers and theologians.

26. D'Costa, *Dialogue and Alliance* 5 (1991) 16.

27. D'Costa, *The Blackwell Companion to Postmodern Theology*, 143. D'Costa points the reader to Milbank's article, "The End of Dialogue," in *Christian Unique-ness Reconsidered*, 174–191.

28. D'Costa, *The Meeting of Religions*, 46.

29. Cf. D'Costa, "Christ, Revelation and the World Religions," 37–38.

30. Terrence Tilley, *The Wisdom of Religious Commitment* (Washington, D.C.: Georgetown University Press, 1995) 12, 26.

31. In his 1995 work, along with his graduate students from Florida State Uni-versity, Tilley surveys the territory of contemporary postmodern theologies and then constructs a test case in the final chapter: how do they deal with the problem of re-ligious diversity? They find that the positions considered fall into two basic patterns, one that minimizes the difference of religious traditions (Habermas, Griffin, Altizer, Taylor, and Wyschogrod) and the other that accepts an irreducibility of particularist positions (Tracy, Gutiérrez, Welch, and McClendon). The authors side in the end with the second group, as it recognizes the otherness of religious difference and the otherness of God. This collection, however, offers an introductory summary of postmodern theologies, while glossing quickly over serious theoretical issues that lie at the root of the theological disagreements analyzed.

32. Tilley, *Story Theology* (Collegeville: Liturgical Press, 1990) 14.

33. Tilley, *Story Theology*, 177.

34. Tilley, *Story Theology*, 177–178.

35. Tilley, *Story Theology*, 183. In concluding this chapter on the truth of stories, Tilley points out that "no single story will be likely to meet the unanimous consent of humanity… to call it true" (p. 211). But this was not listed among the criteria that make a story true. If it were, it would ensure that *no story* be judged as true. One is

hard-pressed to know what to make of this desire for unanimous consent (see William J. Cahoy's review in *Worship* 66 (1992) 283).

36. Tilley, *Story Theology*, 216.

37. Tilley, *Story Theology*, 175.

38. In a later work Tilley provides the following clarification: "...the role-specific responsibilities of theologians are significantly different from the responsibilities of religious 'believers.' In brief, theologians are charged to discover (including using the tools of philosophers and cultural critics), and argue for transforming when necessary and proclaim when appropriate (adding rhetoricians' tools) the convictions of the faith community. Believers have to live in and live out the faith tradition and in doing so to witness to and to proclaim the faith. As such, they are not responsible for investigating, analyzing, or transforming the tradition—unless they take the role of theologians, for example, in existential challenges to their faith." Terrence Tilley, *History, Theology and Faith: Dissolving the Modern Problematic* (New York: Orbis Books, 2004) 90.

39. See John Haught's review in *Theological Studies* 47 (1986) 187.

40. Tilley, *The Wisdom of Religious Commitment*, 9. Tilley translates Aristotle's *phronesis* as "wisdom" or "practical wisdom" (see *The Wisdom of Religious Commitments*, 27, n. 4).

41. Tilley, *The Wisdom of Religious Commitments*, 9, 14.

42. Terrence Tilley, "In Favor of a 'Practical Theory of Religion': Montaigne and Pascal," *Theology Without Foundations: Religious Practice and the Future of Theological Truth*, eds Stanley Hauerwas, Nancey Murphy, Mark Nation (Nashville, TN: Abingdon Press, 1994) 52. A different version of this essay comprises chapter one of *The Wisdom of Religious Commitment*.

43. Tilley, "In Favor of a 'Practical Theory of Religion,'" 71.

44. Tilley, *The Wisdom of Religious Commitments*, 152.

45. Tilley, *The Wisdom of Religious Commitments*, 155.

46. Tilley, *The Wisdom of Religious Commitments*, 157.

47. Tilley, *The Wisdom of Religious Commitments*, 159.

48. These criticisms were documented in a symposium on *The Wisdom of Religious Commitments* published in *Philosophy and Theology* 10 (1997) 65–99. Participating in the symposium were John K. Downey, Patricia A. Johnson, and Anthony J. Godzieba.

49. Gavin D'Costa, "A Response to my Critics," *Philosophy and Theology*, 94.

50. "Anthony Godzieba, "God and Self in Terrence Tilley's *The Wisdom of Religious Commitment*," *Philosophy and Theology* 10 (1997) 79.

51. Anthony Godzieba, "God and Self in Terrence Tilley's *The Wisdom of Religious Commitment*," 83.

52. D'Costa, "A Response to my Critics," *Philosophy and Theology*, 98.

53. Terrence Tilley, *Inventing Catholic Tradition* (Maryknoll: Orbis Books, 2000) 45.

54. Tilley, "Toward a Practice-Based Theory of Tradition," in *Tradition and Tradition Theories: An International Discussion*, eds. Thorsten Larbig and Siegfried Wiedenhofer (Münster: Lit, 2006) 262.

55. Katherine Tanner, *Horizons* Symposium II, 311.

56. Tilley, *Inventing Catholic Tradition*, 122.

57. Terrence Tilley, "Author's Response," *Horizons* 28 (2001) 117.

58. Tilley, *Religious Diversity and the American Experience: A Theological Approach* (2007) xv–xvi

59. Tilley, *Religious Diversity and the American Experience: A Theological Approach* xv–xvi.

60. New American Bible (New York: Oxford University Press, 1990).

61. Catherine Cornille, ed., *Many Mansions? Multiple Religious Belonging and Christian Identity*, "Introduction: The Dynamics of Multiple Belonging" (Maryknoll, New York: Orbis Books, 2002) 1–6.

62. "The Basis, Purpose, and Manner of Inter-Faith Dialogue," *Scottish Journal of Theology* 10 (1977): 260.

63. *Summa theologiae*, I, 13, 5.

64. *Summa theologiae*, I, 13, 6.

65. Declaration *Dominus Iesus: On the Unicity and Salvific Universality of Jesus Christ and the Church*, no. 3; http://www.vatican.va/roman_curia/congregations/cfaith/documents/rc_con_cfaith_doc_20000806_dominus-iesus_en.html

Chapter 4: Transposing Richard McKeon's Philosophic Pluralism into a Theological Key

1. Richard McKeon, "Philosophic Semantics and Philosophic Inquiry" in Richard McKeon, *Freedom and History and Other Essays*, edited by Zahava K. McKeon (Chicago: University of Chicago Press, 1990), 242–256. This dense essay is summarized in Michael Buckley, *At the Origins of Modern Atheism* (New Haven: Yale University Press, 1987), 21–25. For a book-length development of McKeon's approach, see Walter Watson, *The Architectonics of Meaning: Foundations of the New Pluralism* (Chicago: University of Chicago, 1985).

2. Buckley, *Origins of Modern Atheism*, 21.

3. In addition to drawing upon the texts mentioned in note 1, I gather together insights gleaned from various conversations with Buckley over the years and add some additional reflections of my own, especially as McKeon's approach is applied to theological issues.

4. Aristotle, *Nicomachean Ethics*, 1098a28.

5. Buckley, *Origins of Modern Atheism*, 24. The quotation within the quotation is from Michael Buckley, *Motion and Motion's God: Thematic Variations in Aristotle, Cicero, Newton, and Hegel* (Princeton, N.J: Princeton University Press, 1971), 9.

6. Thomas Aquinas, *Summa theologiae* (Allen, Texas: Christian Classics, 1981) I, q. 13, a. 11, *sed contra*: "It is written that when Moses asked, 'If they should say to me "What is his name?" what shall I say to them?' The Lord answered him, 'Thus shalt thou say to them, "HE WHO IS" hath sent me to you.' "

7. Immanuel Kant, *Critique of Pure Reason* (New York: Macmillan, 1929), Preface to Second Edition, B xvi, 22.

8. Aristotle, *Ethics*, 1109b5.

9. Immanuel Kant, "Idea for a Universal History," in *On History*, ed. Lewis White Beck (London: Macmillan, 1963), 17.

10. Karl Barth, *The Epistle to the Romans* (Oxford: Oxford University Press, 1968), 10.

11. Karl Barth, *Church Dogmatics I.1: The Doctrine of the Word of God* (Edinburgh: T & T Clark, 1975), xiii.

12. Barth, *Church Dogmatics I.1*, xvi.

13. G. W. F. Hegel, *Encyclopaedia of Philosophical Sciences* (Indianapolis: Hackett, 1991), Part I, § 60.

14. "When we speak this way of 'being' and 'ground of being' we run the deadly risk that many contemporaries can hear the word 'being' only as an empty and subsequent abstraction from the multiple experience of the individual realities which encounter us directly. For this reason we want to try to call the term and source of our transcendence by another name.... We want to call the term and source of our transcendence 'the holy mystery,' although this term must be understood, deepened, and then gradually shown to be identical with the word 'God.' Karl Rahner, *Foundations of Christian Faith: An Introduction to the Idea of Christianity* (New York: Crossroad, 1995), 60–61.

15. Rahner, *Foundations*, 68, at the conclusion of chapter two's sub-section "The Knowledge of God," 51–71.

16. Rahner, *Foundations*, 69.

17. I am reliably informed by Michael P. Moreland that this line comes from W. S. Gilbert's "The Merry Zingara; or, The Tipsy Gipsy & The Pipsy Wipsy." My thanks to him for his seemingly boundless and instant recall. I am also grateful to John Montag for the grammatical assist to change "are" to "art."

18. Gustavo Gutiérrez, *A Theology of Liberation: History, Politics, and Salvation* (Maryknoll, New York: Orbis Books, 1988), 5–11.

19. For a helpful introduction to the notions of liberation and social grace, see Roger Haight, *The Experience and Language of Grace* (New York: Paulist Press, 1979), 143–186.

20. For the sake of clarity, I have altered three of the four names McKeon gave to designate the options within this coordinate. I believe these altered names are clearer because they draw upon the words that are actually used to describe each option within the coordinate of interpretation. Thus, McKeon's ontological interpretation, I am calling a transcendental interpretation, because this position claims that reality *transcends* appearances. His entitative interpretation, I am calling a substantive

interpretation, because this position holds that reality is a *substrate* of appearances. His existentialist interpretation, I am calling a perspectival interpretation, since in this view reality is seen in the *perspective* one has on what appears. I am retaining his designation of the essentialist interpretation.

21. For a classic study of this position, see Bernard Lonergan, *Insight: A Study of Human Understanding* (Toronto: University of Toronto, 1957).

22. In his study of modern arguments for God's existence, Buckley shows how different figures relied on either (#1) metaphysical arguments that transcend experience (Descartes), or (#2) evidence of an underlying order in nature that requires intelligent design (Newton), or (#4) religious experience that purports to gives immediate presence of the divine (Pascal). Buckley, *Modern Atheism*, 198–205. No mention is made of the theological casting of the essentialist interpretation (#3) in these pages.

23. Benedict's Augustinian sympathies, from his 1953 doctoral dissertation on Augustine to his 1996 self-description as "decidedly Augustinian," are well-documented (e.g., by Joseph Komonchak in "The Church in Crisis: Pope Benedict's Theological Vision" [*Commonweal* 132.11 (June 3, 2005) 11–14]) and lie behind his ambivalence over *Gaudium et spes*, a document heavily influenced by the decidedly Thomist thinker, Marie-Dominique Chenu. In *Spe salvi*, Augustine is by far the most cited theologian (seven times).

24. Karl Rahner, "Current Problems in Christology," *Theological Investigations*, vol. 1 (New York: Crossroad, 1982), 149–200, at 183: "Human being is rather a reality absolutely open upwards; a reality which reaches its highest (though indeed 'unexacted') perfection … when in it the Logos himself becomes existent in the world."

25. Karl Rahner, "On the Theology of the Incarnation," *Theological Investigations*, vol. 4 (New York: Crossroad, 1974), 105–20.

26. Jon Sobrino, "The Kingdom of God and the Theological Dimension of the Poor: The Jesuanic Principle," in *Who Do You Say That I Am? Confessing the Mystery of Christ*, eds. John Cavadini and Laura Holt (Notre Dame, Ind.: University of Notre Dame Press, 2004), 109–38, at 125. One of the best examples of a Christian evaluation of contemporary economics is Nicholas Boyle's *Who Are We Now? Christian Humanism and the Global Market from Hegel to Heaney* (South Bend, IN: University of Notre Dame Press, 1998).

Chapter 5: St. John of the Cross and Interreligious Dialogue

1. For example, a recent book argues that St. John of the Cross "serves as a bridge for dialogue with Eastern religions, offering critical guidance for assimilating practices from these religions that can enhance growth in Christian contemplative life." Both St. John of the Cross and the Buddha taught purification of conduct, mind, and heart *en route* to authentic humanity, and even though the Buddha spoke of *Nibbana*, while St. John envisioned participation in the life of the Trinity as the

ultimate end of purification, nonetheless the method of Buddhist Insight Meditation, "if practiced seriously with an attitude of faith and love, trusting in the merciful love of God...will bring about the healing and wholeness for which we long and for which God created us." Mary Jo Meadow, Kevin Culligan, and Daniel Chowning, *Christian Insight Meditation: Following in the Footsteps of John of the Cross* (Boston: Wisdom Publications, 2007) 177, 155. Buckley himself has referred to "the almost Zen-like verses in which [St. John of the Cross] summarized the movement of a human being into the contemplative possession of God." Michael Buckley, S.J., *Denying and Disclosing God: The Ambiguous Progress of Modern Atheism* (New Haven, CT: Yale University Press, 2004) 112. For Thomas Merton, the Buddhist doctrine of emptiness was akin to St. John of the Cross' "doctrine of 'night.'" Thomas Merton, *Zen and the Birds of Appetite* (New York: New Directions, 1968) 119.

2. This approach is represented by the little book of Miguel Asín Palacios, *St. John of the Cross and Islam*. The author uses philology, thematic analysis, and geography to argue for the possibility that St. John either read or assimilated through popular cultural influences the poetry and / or commentary of the Shadhili school of Islamic Mysticism. According to Asín Palacios, the most likely candidate to have influenced St. John is Ibn Abbad of Ronda (Spain) who died in 1389 or 1390 and whose employment of key Arabic terms such as *qabd* (translated as "contraction," or more importantly, as "dark night," *noche oscura* in Spanish) and *bast* ("expansion / dawn / light") is so similar to the peculiar emphases and vocabulary of St. John of the Cross, without any obvious Christian precedents, that it is reasonable to assume literary borrowing, either direct or indirect. Miguel Asín Palacios, *St. John of the Cross and Islam.*, Howard W. Yoder and Elmer H. Douglas, trans. (New York: Vantage, 1981) 24–27.

3. Paul Knitter, *Introducing Theologies of Religions* (Maryknoll, NY: Orbis Books, 2002) 126.

4. Paul Knitter, "Is the Pluralist Model a Western Imposition? A Response in Five Voices," *The Myth of Religious Superiority: A Multifaith Exploration*, Paul Knitter, ed. (Maryknoll: Orbis Books) 2005: 33, 34.

5. Knitter, "Is the Pluralist Model a Western Imposition?" 34.

6. Knitter, "Is the Pluralist Model a Western Imposition?" 35.

7. Raimon Panikkar, *The Intra-Religious Dialogue* (New York: Paulist Press, 1999) 12, 114.

8. Buckley, *Denying and Disclosing*, 131.

9. *Ascent* 1.3.1; All citations from John of the Cross are taken from *The Collected Works of Saint John of the Cross*. Kieran Kavanaugh and Otilio Rodriguez, trans. (Washington, D.C.: ICS Publications, 1991).

10. *Ascent* 2.2.1

11. Iain Matthew. *The Impact of God: Soundings from St. John of the Cross* (London: Hodder & Stoughton, 1995) 63.

12. *Ascent* 1.4.3.

13. *Ascent* 1.4.3.

14. Buckley, *Denying and Disclosing*: 115.

15. Buckley, *Denying and Disclosing*: 115; *Ascent* 2.4.3.

16. *Ascent* 2.4.3.

17. *Ascent* 2.4.4.

18. *Ascent* 2.4.4.

19. Buckley, *Denying and Disclosing*: 116; *Living Flame of Love* 3.48.

20. *Dark Night* 2.16.3.

21. Matthew, *The Impact of God*: 124.

22. *Ascent* 2.1.1.

23. Interestingly for St. John of the Cross the "deep things of God" include not only the Trinity and the Incarnation but also the unity and the infinity of God, which puts him somewhat at odds with a Thomist perspective about what can and cannot be known by reason alone. *Ascent* 2.9.1; *Ascent* 2.27.1.

24. *Ascent* 2.27.4.

25. Sometimes one hears or reads similarly skeptical interpretations of the submission to Church authority in the prologue to *The Ascent of Mount Carmel*, but it is possible that St. John's training led him to cultivate precisely the kind of humility—humility toward doctrine as Catherine Cornille puts it (see below)—that would lead him to defer to magisterial authority.

26. *Ascent* 1.5.8.

27. *Ascent* 1.13.3–7.

28. *Ascent* 2.7.2–3.

29. *Ascent* 2.7.5.

30. *Ascent* 2.7.5.

31. *Ascent* 2.7.9–11.

32. *Ascent* 2.7.11–12.

33. Edward Howells. *John of the Cross and Teresa of Avila: Mystical Knowing and Selfhood* (New York: Herder & Herder, 2002) 4, 123; *Canticle* 37. 3–4.

34. Buckley, *Denying and Disclosing*, 117, 118.

35. *Ascent* 2.22.5.

36. *Ascent* 2.22. 7–8.

37. Matthew, *The Impact of God*, 128.

38. *Dominus Iesus* (2001), section fourteen, sounds the same note: "Bearing in mind this article of faith [namely that salvation is accomplished once for all in the incarnation, death, and resurrection of Jesus, the Son of God], theology today, in its reflection on the existence of other religious experiences and on their meaning in God's salvific plan, is invited to explore if and in what way the historical figures and positive elements of these religions may fall within the divine plan of salvation." Iain Matthew points to the inexhaustible depths of *Christ* for St. John of the Cross. "For John, Christ is himself the receding depth which makes the divine 'always new and increasingly amazing.'" Matthew, *The Impact of God*, 127; *Canticle* 37.4.

39. *Dark Night* 1.12.3–6.

40. *Dark Night* 1.7.1.

41. "The Church, therefore, exhorts her sons, that through dialogue and collaboration with the followers of other religions, carried out with prudence and love and
in witness to the Christian faith and life, they recognize, preserve and promote the
good things, spiritual and moral, as well as the socio-cultural values found among
these men." *Nostra Aetate*, 2.

42. Catherine Cornille, *The Im-Possibility of Interreligious Dialogue* (New
York: Crossroad, 2008) 26–27.

43. Cornille, *Im-Possibility*: 27.

44. Cornille, *Im-Possibility*: 10.

45. Cornille, *Im-Possibility*: 33–44.

46. Cornille, *Im-Possibility*: 114–115.

47. Jacques Maritain, *Distinguish to Unite or The Degrees of Knowledge* (New
York: Scribner, 1959) 311.

48. Reginald Garrigiou-Lagrange, O.P. *The Three Ways of the Spiritual Life*
(Westminster: Newman Press, 1955) 29.

49. Joseph Maréchal, S.J. *Studies in the Psychology of the Mystics* (Albany,:
Magi Books, 1964) 232.

50. Joseph Guibert, S.J. *The Theology of the Spiritual Life* (New York: Sheed
and Ward, 1953) 21.

51. Gustave Poulain, S.J. *The Graces of Interior Prayer: A Treatise on Mystical
Theology* (St. Louis: Herder, 1957) 6.

52. Buckley, *Denying and Disclosing*: 131.

53. Buckley, *Denying and Disclosing*: 129–132.

54. Buckley, *Denying and Disclosing*: 118.

55. Buckley, *Denying and Disclosing*: 111.

56. Buckley, *Denying and Disclosing*: 129, 130.

57. St. John does say of mystics inebriated with love, that "with singular bold-
ness they do strange things, in whatever way necessary, in order to encounter him
whom they love." *Dark Night* 2.13.5.

58. Maréchal, *Studies in the Psychology of the Mystics*, 276.

59. Maréchal, *Studies in the Psychology of the Mystics*, 279.

60. *Dominus Iesus*, 21.

Chapter 6: Beyond Education for Justice: Christian Humanism in Catholic Higher Education

1. Michael J. Buckley, S.J., *The Catholic University as Promise and Project:
Reflections in a Jesuit Idiom* (Washington DC: Georgetown University Press, 1998),
108.

2. Buckley, *The Catholic University as Promise and Project*, 111.

3. Buckley, *The Catholic University as Promise and Project*, 115.

4. Buckley, *The Catholic University as Promise and Project*, 112.

5. Buckley, *The Catholic University as Promise and Project,* 116.

6. Buckley, *The Catholic University as Promise and Project,* 119.

7. Buckley, *The Catholic University as Promise and Project,* 107.

8. Peter-Hans Kolvenbach, "The Service of Faith and the Promotion of Justice in American Jesuit Higher Education <http://www.scu.edu/news/attachments/kolvenbach_speech.html>

9. Kolvenbach, "The Service of Faith and the Promotion of Justice."

10. Kolvenbach, "The Service of Faith and the Promotion of Justice."

11. Kristen E. Heyer, "Community Based Learning," in *Educating for Faith and Justice,* ed. Thomas P. Rausch (Collegeville: Liturgical Press, 2010) 103.

12. Heyer, "Community Based Learning," 105.

13. Heyer, "Community Based Learning," 105.

14. Stephen J. Pope, "Immersion Trips," in *Educating for Faith and Justice,* ed. Thomas P. Rausch, (Collegeville: Liturgical Press, 2010) 127–128.

15. Pope, "Immersion Trips," 132.

16. Pope, "Immersion Trips," 137.

17. Pope, "Immersion Trips," 138.

18. Pope, "Immersion Trips," 135.

19. Pope, "Immersion Trips," 140.

20. Buckley, *The Catholic University as Promise and Project,* 112.

21. Thomas Aquinas, *Summa Theologiae,* II-II 30.3.

22. See, for example, Archbishop Marcos McGrath, "The Puebla Final Document, Introduction and Commentary," in John Eagleson and Philip Sharper, eds., *Evangelization in Latin America's Present and Future: Final Document of the Third General Conference of the Latin American Episcopate* (Maryknoll: Orbis, 1979), 87–110, at 104.

23. United States Conference of Catholic Bishops, *Economic Justice for All: Catholic Social Teaching and the U.S. Economy,* (Washington, D.C.: United States Catholic Conference, 1986) no. 52.

24. David J. O'Brien, "The Option for the Poor in Undergraduate Education," in *Love of Learning, Desire for Justice: Undergraduate Education and the Option for the Poor,* ed. William Reiser, S.J. (Scranton: University of Scranton Press, 1995) 33.

25. O'Brien, "The Option for the Poor in Undergraduate Education," 33.

26. Sobrino, "The Samaritan Church and the Principle of Mercy," in *The Principle of Mercy: Taking the Crucified People Down from the Cross* (Maryknoll: Orbis, 1992) 16.

27. Sobrino, "The Samaritan Church and the Principle of Mercy," 16.

28. Sobrino, "The Samaritan Church and the Principle of Mercy," 16.

29. Sobrino, "The Samaritan Church and the Principle of Mercy," 21.

30. Sobrino, "The Samaritan Church and the Principle of Mercy," 25.

31. See note 22.

32. John Tracy Ellis, "American Catholics and Intellectual Life," *Thought* 30 / 118, 1955, 351–388, also see Thomas P. Rausch, *Educating for Faith and Justice: Catholic Higher Education Today* (Liturgical Press: Collegeville, 2010) 17–19.

33. Rausch, *Educating for Faith and Justice,* 17.

34. Rausch, *Educating for Faith and Justice,* 28.

35. Rausch, *Educating for Faith and Justice,* 34 and 35.

36. The lack of basic knowledge about religion that characterizes Catholic university students today is described by John Cavadini in "Ignorant Catholics: The Alarming Void in Religious Education," *Commonweal* 9 April 2004. Cavadini's remedy, a "renewed pedagogy of the basics," is not inconsistent with what is described in this essay, and may even complement the kind of spiritual transformation that results from service learning and immersion experiences.

37. Christine D. Pohl, *Making Room: Recovering Hospitality as a Christian Tradition* (Grand Rapids: William B. Eerdmans, 1999) 56–58.

38. Pohl, *Making Room,* 65.

39. Pohl, *Making Room,* 69–70.

40. Pohl, *Making Room,* 75.

Chapter 7: Theology as Architectonic Wisdom in the Catholic University: Promise and Problems

1. The widespread social (and student) ignorance about religion is well-documented by Stephen Prothero, *Religious Literacy: What Every American Needs to Know—And Doesn't* (New York, NY: HarperCollins, 2008).

2. Pew Forum on Religion and Public Life, "US Religious Landscape Survey (2008)," <http://religions.pewforum.org/reports> (9 August 2010). The study reports, however, that foreign-born Catholics help but do not completely offset the losses of native-born Catholics who leave.

3. Terry Eagleton, *Reason, Faith, and Revolution: Reflections on the God Debate* (New Haven and London: Yale University Press, 2009), 39.

4. Michael J. Buckley, S.J., *The Catholic University as Promise and Project: Reflections in a Jesuit Idiom* (Washington, D.C.: Georgetown University Press, 1998), 15.

5. Buckley, *The Catholic University as Promise and Project,* 15.

6. Buckley, *The Catholic University as Promise and Project,* 15–16.

7. For examples of gross misunderstanding of theology and religion, see Richard Dawkins, *The God Delusion* (Boston and New York: Houghton Mifflin, 2008) and Christopher Hitchens, *God Is Not Great: How Religion Poisons Everything* (New York: Hachette Book Group, 2009). Terry Eagleton exposes their ignorance and intellectual dishonesty in his masterful refutation, *Reason, Faith, and Revolution: Reflections on the God Debate.* Michael J. Buckley also criticizes the "new atheists" as does Nicholas Lash. See Michael J. Buckley, S.J., "The Madman and the Crowd," *America* 198, no. 15 (May 2008) and Nicholas Lash, "Where Does *The*

God Delusion Come From?" *Theology for Pilgrims* (Notre Dame, IN: University of Notre Dame Press, 2008), 1–18.

8. Buckley, *The Catholic University as Promise and Project*, 72.

9. Buckley, *The Catholic University as Promise and Project*, 174.

10. Buckley, *The Catholic University as Promise and Project*, 72–73.

11. Buckley, *The Catholic University as Promise and Project*, 172. In many ways, Buckley refashions John Henry Newman's warning about the danger of one discipline usurping the province or territory of another, opening both to distortion. See discourses two through four of *The Idea of a University* (Oxford: Clarendon Press, 1976), 33–93.

12. Buckley, *The Catholic University as Promise and Project*, 175–177. Buckley takes Bonaventure and Aquinas as plural instances of how theology unrestrictedly engages other liberal arts and disciplines. Bonaventure likes to show how all created reality can be traced to the pinnacle of creation, Jesus Christ. Aquinas, rather than reducing the disciplines back, shows how theology can clarify, support, and judge the conclusions of different sciences without annihilating their differences.

13. See Karl Rahner, "The Present Situation of Catholic Theology," *Theological Investigations* 21 (New York: Crossroad, 1988), 76–77.

14. For an excellent treatment of the history and fate of the theological encyclopedia, see Thomas A. Howard, *Protestant Theology and the Making of the Modern German University* (Oxford: Oxford University Press, 2006), 267–324.

15. Edward Farley, *The Fragility of Knowledge: Theological Education in the Church & the University* (Philadelphia: Fortress Press, 1988), 114. See Friedrich Schleiermacher, *Brief Outline on the Study of Theology*. Translated with Introduction and Notes by Terrence Tice (Richmond, VA: John Knox Press, 1970); Johann Sebastian Drey, *Brief Introduction to the Study of Theology*. Translated with an Introduction and Annotation by Michael J. Himes (Notre Dame and London: University of Notre Dame Press, 1994).

16. For the relationship of theology to other disciplines in the medieval university and later centuries, see De Ridder-Symoens, Hilde, *A History of the University in Europe*. 2 Vols. (Cambridge: Cambridge University Press, 1992).

17. This is evident for Drey. "The theologian who wants to understand Christianity historically and scientifically in all its ramifications is instructed in how to administer the polity and act in its spirit in practical theology." *Brief Introduction to the Study of Theology*, 149. See also, Edward Farley, *Practicing Gospel: Unconventional Thoughts on the Church's Ministry* (Louisville: Westminster John Knox Press, 2003), 30–35.

18. Edward Farley, *Practicing Gospel*, 17.

19. Edward Farley, *The Fragility of Knowledge*, 114.

20. Edward Farley, *The Fragility of Knowledge*, 108.

21. Edward Farley, *Theologia: The Fragmentation and Unity of Theological Education* (Philadelphia: Fortress Press, 1983).

22. Farley, *The Fragility of Knowledge*, 31.

23. Farley, *The Fragility of Knowledge*, 35.

24. Farley, *The Fragility of Knowledge*, 109.

25. Farley, *The Fragility of Knowledge*, 109.

26. Farley, *The Fragility of Knowledge*, 109.

27. Farley, *The Fragility of Knowledge*, 34.

28. One representative article that tends to reflect the inattention to genre is by Leo D. Lefebure, "Catholic Theological Education in a Religiously Pluralistic Age," *Teaching Theology and Religion* 9:2 (2006): 85–90. Edward Foley mentions the need for a "habitus" but does not touch directly on the issue of genre. "Theological Reflection, Theology and Technology: When Baby Boomer Theologians Teach Generations X & Y," *Theological Education*, 41, no. 1 (2005): 45–56.

29. Farley, *The Fragility of Knowledge*, 35.

30. Farley, *The Fragility of Knowledge*, 38–39.

31. Farley, *The Fragility of Knowledge*, 39.

32. Farley, *The Fragility of Knowledge*, 42.

33. Dennis O'Brien has a wonderful account of this paradigm in his chapter, "Science: The Truth of Universities." *The Idea of a Catholic University* (Chicago: University of Chicago Press, 2002), 23–32.

34. Felix Wilfred, "Theology in the Modern University: Whither Specialization?" *Theology in a World Of Specialization*, edited by Erik Borgman and Felix Wilfred (London: SCM Press, 2006), 25–26.

35. Criticism of the empirical paradigm in the sciences is not new. Wolfhart Pannenberg observed that "the differences in scientific procedure do not coincide with the classification of objects of study: not only are traditional human sciences increasingly using methods regarded as belonging to the natural sciences, but conversely there are also natural sciences which pursue 'historical' investigations."

36. *Theology and the Philosophy of Science*. Translated by Francis McDonagh (Philadelphia: Westminster Press, 1976), 135.

37. Nicholas Lash, *The Beginning and the End of 'Religion'* (Cambridge: Cambridge University Press, 1996), 50.

38. Another term Farley uses to chart the consequences of the empirical paradigm is what he calls the damaging process of 'objectification' that the postmoderns rightly criticize. 'Objectification' supposes, in its delusion, that sciences or the extensions of the paradigm actually provided us 'reality' in quantifiable bits and pieces. See Edward Farley, *Deep Symbols: Their Postmodern Effacement and Reclamation* (Valley Forge, PA: Trinity Press International, 1996), 63f.

39. Farley, *The Fragility of Knowledge*, 44.

40. Farley, *The Fragility of Knowledge*, 3.

41. Farley, *The Fragility of Knowledge*, 44.

42. Farley, *The Fragility of Knowledge*, 45.

43. Jodi Heckel, "Instructor of Catholicism at UI claims loss of job violates academic freedom," 7/9/2010. <http://www.news-gazette.com/news/university-illinois/2010-07-09/instructor-catholicism-ui-claims-loss-job-violates-academic-free> (9 August 2010)

44. Farley, *The Fragility of Knowledge*, 105.

45. Farley, *Practicing Gospel*, 36.

46. Farley, *The Fragility of Knowledge*, 135.

47. Farley, *The Fragility of Knowledge*, 136.

48. Farley, *The Fragility of Knowledge*, 134.

49. Farley, *The Fragility of Knowledge*, 137–138.

50. Farley, *The Fragility of Knowledge*, 138. One might draw a parallel between Farley's position here and what Rowan Williams maintains in considering the unity of Christian truth. Williams state that "the search for a *theological* unity in what we [Christians] say involves a high degree of sustained conversation with the history of Christian ethics and spirituality (in its full historical complexity and ambiguity) and with the history of how the vocation of human beings is imagined by Christians. And in reading the texts of faith in the context of the sacramental action of the community, we are reminded of what is, in fact, a significant aspect of all reading of texts: we are not the first or the only readers. We read *as* we perform identifiably similar actions to those performed by other readers, representing a single story which is believed to be the point of focus for all our analogies—what interprets and is interpreted by the life of the new community, and thus connects 'new' and 'old' worlds." *On Christian Theology* (Malden, MA: Blackwell, 2000), 24.

51. Farley, *The Fragility of Knowledge*, 139.

52. Gavin D'Costa, *Theology in the Public Square: Church, Academy and Nation* (Malden, MA: Blackwell, 2005), 112.

53. Gavin D'Costa, *Theology in the Public Square*, 1. Key texts in the postliberal tradition that inform D'Costa's view and which found his deeper philosophical presuppositions include Alasdair MacIntyre, *Whose Justice? Which Rationality?* (Notre Dame, IN: University of Notre Dame Press, 1988); *Three Rival Versions of Moral Enquiry: Encyclopedia, Genealogy, and Tradition* (Notre Dame, IN: University of Notre Dame Press, 1990); "Catholic Universities: Dangers, Hopes, Choices" in *Higher Learning and Catholic Traditions*, ed. Robert E. Sullivan (Notre Dame, IN; University of Notre Dame Press, 2001), 1–22; *God, Philosophy, Universities* (Lanham, MD: Sheed & Ward, 2009), 165–181; John Milbank, *Theology and Social Theory: Beyond Secular Reason* (Malden, MA: Blackwell, 2006; 1990), esp. 382–442; John Milbank, "Knowledge: The Theological Critique of Philosophy in Hamann and Jacobi," *Radical Orthodoxy*, ed. John Milbank, Catherine Pickstock, and Graham Ward (New York, NY: Routledge, 1999), 21–37.

54. D'Costa, *Theology in the Public Square*, 67. D'Costa relies heavily on the research of several scholars who trace the history of weakening and secularization of traditional Christian universities from their religious foundations. Philip Gleason, *Contending with Modernity: Catholic Higher Education in the Twentieth Century* (Oxford: Oxford University Press, 1995); James T. Burtchaell, *The Dying of the Light: The Disengagement of Colleges and Universities from their Christian Churches* (Grand Rapids, MI: W.B. Eerdmans, 1998); Frank Schubert, *A Sociological Study of Secularization Trends in the American Catholic University: Decatholicizing the Catholic Religious Curriculum* (Lewiston, NY: Edwin Mellen Press, 1990).

55. D'Costa, *Theology in the Public Square*, 4.

56. D'Costa, *Theology in the Public Square*, 144.

57. D'Costa, *Theology in the Public Square*, 75

58. D'Costa, *Theology in the Public Square*, 19.

59. D'Costa, *Theology in the Public Square*, 112.

60. D'Costa, *Theology in the Public Square*, 114. Italics his.

61. Farley spends much more time tracing the shift from *theologia* as a personal *habitus* to its location within the context of knowledge as divided into categories fitting the encyclopedia, which then becomes *wissenschaftlich* fields of specialization. Though D'Costa mentions the problem of theological specialization (*Theology in the Public Square*, 14), he does not attend to what Farley profoundly describes as the resultant four-fold pattern of theological education that still dominates today. *Theologia*, 49–124.

62. D'Costa, *Theology in the Public Square*, 14–15. Exceptions to this shift would be Prussian and central European universities which, as Thomas Howard states, "retained theological faculties as an integral, if reduced, part of the state's educational system." *Protestant Theology and the Making of the Modern German University* (Oxford: Oxford University Press, 2006), 5–6.

63. Michael J. Buckley, S.J., *At the Origins of Modern Atheism* (New Haven, CT: Yale University Press, 1987).

64. D'Costa, *Theology in the Public Square*, 15–17.

65. There is a legitimate place for the pursuit of a certain kind of religious studies. D'Costa does not jettison the term or the general idea. He would rather the discipline become more fruitful as a "theological religious studies." *Theology in the Public Square*, 145–176; see also Gavin D'Costa, "Theology and Religious Studies OR Theology vs. Religious Studies," in *Theology and Religious Studies in Higher Education: Global Perspectives*, eds. Darlene L. Bird and Simon G. Smith (London and New York: Continuum, 2009), 44–54

66. D'Costa, *Theology in the Public Square*, 17. An instance of alien methodology here would be the need for an observer to be utterly neutral and detached from his subject rather than somehow more involved with it. This is what D'Costa rightly criticizes, as Michael Buckley before him, as the religious *epoche*. See Michael J. Buckley, "The Rise of Modern Atheism and the Religious Epoche," CTSA *Proceedings* 47 (1992): 69–83.

67. D'Costa, *Theology in the Public Square*, 2.

68. This is the title of D'Costa's first chapter and highlights the theme of Christian theology's status as prisoner in a foreign land. *Theology in the Public Square*, 1–37. D'Costa seems to agree with John Howard Yoder about a fundamental opposition between "church" and "world" that underwrites and legitimates the impossibility of doing theology within the dominant paradigm of rational secularity, since theology too easily subordinates to non-Christian thinking or political forces. See John Howard Yoder, "The Otherness of the Church," *The Royal Priesthood: Essays Ecclesiastical and Ecumenical*, ed. Michael G. Cartwright (Grand Rapids, MI: Eerdmans, 1994), 54–64; 57f.

69. D'Costa, *Theology in the Public Square*, 16–37.

70. D'Costa, *Theology in the Public Square*, 92–111. For the document, see <www.vatican.va/holy_father/john_paul_ii/apost_constitutions/documents/hf_jp-ii_apc_15081990_ex-corde-ecclesiae_en.html> (9 August 2010).

71. D'Costa, *Theology in the Public Square*, 94–96. "It [theology] serves all other disciplines in their search for meaning, not only by helping them to investigate how their discoveries will affect individuals and society but also by bringing a perspective and an orientation not contained within their own methodologies. In turn, interaction with these other disciplines and their discoveries enriches theology, offering it a better understanding of the world today, and making theological research more relevant to current needs. Because of its specific importance among the academic disciplines, every Catholic University should have a faculty, or at least a chair, of theology." *Ex corde ecclesiae*, #19.

72. D'Costa, *Theology in the Public Square*, 99–100. D'Costa discusses particular institutions in the context of American Catholic university history and secularization. However, as he exegetes and comments upon *Ex corde ecclesiae*, he does not identify one institution as the "model."

73. D'Costa, *Theology in the Public Square*, 99.

74. D'Costa, *Theology in the Public Square*, 105.

75. Richard J. Janet, "*Ex Corde Fidei*: Toward a Taxonomy of Catholic Higher Education," *Current Issues in Catholic Higher Education*, 25, no. 2 (2006): 169–175; 172. Janet cites the University of St. Thomas in Minneapolis as another example of "canonical." Yet one does not clearly see this from its mission statement or from its historical overview which states that "the university is not owned or governed by the Archdiocese of St. Paul and Minneapolis." http://www.stthomas.edu/aboutust/history/default.html.

76. Janet, "*Ex Corde Fidei*: Toward a Taxonomy of Catholic Higher Education," 172.

77. Janet, "*Ex Corde Fidei*: Toward a Taxonomy of Catholic Higher Education," 172–173. Janet oddly omits Ave Maria University in Naples, FL, which explicitly refers to *Ex corde ecclesiae* as its foundational charter.

78. Janet, "Ex Corde Fidei: Toward a Taxonomy of Catholic Higher Education," 173.

79. D'Costa, *Theology in the Public Square*, 109.

80. D'Costa, *Theology in the Public Square*, 96; *Ex corde ecclesiae*, 27.

81. D'Costa, *Theology in the Public Square*, 110.

82. D'Costa, *Theology in the Public Square*, 112.

83. D'Costa, *Theology in the Public Square*, 116.

84. Denys Turner puts this well when he writes "I think at the very least, we all recognize that if theology were not done in this creedally and ecclesially interested spirit outside the university, there would be nothing for us to do as theology in our own academic way within the university." "Doing Theology in the University," in *Fields of Faith: Theology and Religious Studies for the Twenty-first Century*, ed. David Ford, Ben Quash, Janet Martin Soskice (Cambridge: Cambridge University Press, 2005), 25–38; 25.

85. D'Costa, *Theology in the Public Square*, 116f.

86. D'Costa, *Theology in the Public Square*, 114. Italics mine.

87. D'Costa, *Theology in the Public Square*, see chapters 5 and 6. Chapter six attempts to unify the disciplines of theology and representatives from the natural sciences. He describes the attempt as integrative: "The Marriage of the Disciplines," 177–214.

88. Under the section "General Norms," article 4, § 5, *Ex corde* states: "The education of students is to combine academic and professional development with formation in moral and religious principles and the social teachings of the Church; the programme of studies for each of the various professions is to include an appropriate ethical formation in that profession. Courses in Catholic doctrine are to be made available to all students" (51).

89. D'Costa, *Theology in the Public Square*, 88, 91. One might suppose that D'Costa's position evades the difficulty of public understanding of theological claims due to this approving description of how Hauerwas handles the issue. "Hauerwas is not arguing that Christians cannot engage with other forms of discourse. Rather, the warrants for Christian discourse are necessarily Christian, based on revelation, and thereby *sui-generis*. They nevertheless can make a claim on non-Christians both by their truthfulness and by their ability to call the non-Christian into question" (86). The problem is to hold simultaneously the view that claims are *sui-generis* while denigrating the possibility of some form of universal rationality that gives force and witness to *how* truth makes such claims influential and intelligible. I can only be accountable if I understand and see the reasons for your claim upon me. How does this happen if no sense of "shared discourse" is possible because no type of "universal rationality" is admitted? I find this view deeply problematic. It unnecessarily opposes grace and nature.

90. Buckley, *The Catholic University as Promise and Project*, 17; chs. 4–5.

91. D'Costa, *Theology in the Public Square*, 87. Second italics mine.

92. Buckley, *The Catholic University as Promise and Project*, 37. Second italics mine. Buckley has discussed the relationship between faith and truth before. See Michael J. Buckley, S.J., "Transcendence, Truth and Faith: The Ascending Experience of God in All Human Inquiry," *Theological Studies*, 39, no. 4 (1978): 633–655.

93. Thomas Aquinas, *Summa Theologia*, I.1. ad 2.

94. For a good overview of this debate as it concerns systematic theology, see William L. Portier, "Does Systematic Theology Have a Future?" in *Faith in Public Life*, edited by William J. Collinge, Vol. 53 (Maryknoll, NY: Orbis Books, 2008), 135–150.

Chapter 8: The Jesuits and the School of Salamanca: How the Dominicans Formed the Society of Jesus

1. Cf. Franz Ehrle S.J., *"Arnaldo de Vilanova ed i «Thomatiste»,"* *Gregorianum* 1 (1920) 475–501; cited in Melquíades Andrés Martín, *La Teología Española*

en el Siglo XVI. II volumes (Madrid: Biblioteca de Autores Cristianos, 1976–1977) 283.

2. Andrés Martín, *La Teología Española en el Siglo XVI*, 1976, 284–85.

3. Andrés Martín, *La Teología Española en el Siglo XVI*, 1976, 279.

4. The names "Prime" and "Vespers" derive from the liturgical hours of the day when lectures were given: morning and afternoon, respectively.

5. Cf. José García-Oro, *"Conventualismo y observancia,"* in *Historia de la Iglesia en España*, VII volumes, volume III-1. ed. Ricardo García-Villoslada S.J.. (Madrid: Biblioteca de Autores Cristianos, 1980) 211–349, especially 253–267.

6. José Barrientos García, *"La Escuela de Salamanca: desarrollo y carácteres,"* *La Ciudad de Dios* 1995: 208, 1040–1079, at 1046.

7. Andrés Martín, *La Teología Española en el Siglo XVI*, 1976, 25–29.

8. Barrientos, *"La escuela de Salamanca: 1044–47."* Martínez de Osma's denunciation took place two years before Isabela established the modern, state-controlled Inquisition, but the newly established organ only handed down its condemnation of him within the year after; see Andrés Martín 1977, I, 261.

9. Andrés Martín, *La Teología Española en el Siglo XVI*, 1976, 272–73.

10. Delgado Criado, 225.

11. The triple-chairs associated with Thomists, Scotists and nominalists (Durandus) date only to 1508, as a result of the pressure of Cardinal Cisneros and the growing influence of Alcalá and its structure; Andrés Martín, *La Teología Española en el Siglo XVI* , 1977, 32–39.

12. Barrientos, *"La escuela de Salamanca,"* 1058–59.

13. Cf. Henry Kamen. *Concise History of Spain* (Illustrated Natural History) (London: Thames and Hudson, 1974), 159–164; Stephen C. Ferruolo. *The Origins of the University: The Schools of Paris and their Critics, 1100–1215.* (Stanford, CA: Stanford University Press, 1985), 97.

14. Melchior Cano, *Opera* 3 vols., vol. 3 (Rome: Forzani et Soc., 1890), 1–2 (Book 12, prooemium).

15. On the theology and method of Cano's treatise, see Andrés Martín, *La Teología Española en el Siglo XVI*, 1977, 393–399; 411–424.

16. García-Villoslada, *Historia*, III-2, 286–87; on Agricola's 'place-logic,' and the spatialization of the word, see Walter J. Ong S.J., *Ramus, Method, and the Decay of Dialogue: From the Art of Discourse to the Art of Reason* (Cambridge MA: Harvard University Press, 1983), 92–130: "What helped make Melchior Cano, Francis Suárez, Robert Bellarmine, and even Francisco de Vitoria, not to mention Melanchthon, Bullinger, and Alsted, different from St Thomas Aquinas, stemmed, in great part directly, from Agricola, who supplied the initial impetus and the very exiguous theory, taken over verbatim by Cano and others, for the theologies of 'places' or 'loci'"; 93–94.

17. On this restructuring, see Delgado Criado, 217–222.

18. Juan de Guevara not only won the chair, but held it, in the teeth of all opposition, for 35 years until his death in 1600—although he retired from active teaching (according to statute) in 1584, when Báñes took Prime.

19. Melquiades Andrés, *"Pensamiento teológico y vivencia religiosa,"* in Garcia-Villoslada, *Historia*, 3-2, 299; cf. Elliott, 216.

20. Cf. Ong, 1983.

21. Indeed, quite ironically, Ramus drew on the same inspirations as did Cano in his revisions of scholastic theology.

22. Melquíades Andrés Martín, *"Pensamiento teológico y vivencia religiosa en la reforma española (1400–1600)."* In *Historia de la Iglesia en España*. 7 vols. Vol. III-2 (Madrid: Biblioteca de Autores Cristianos, 1980), 269–305, at 299.

23. Michel de Certeau S.J., *The Practice of Everyday Life*, 2 vols., trans. Steven Rendall, vol. 1. (Berkeley CA: University of California Press, 1984), 87.

24. *Constitutiones* SJ, IV, 7, [392]: *"Teniendo respecto a que en los Colegios nuestros no solamente los Scolares nuestros se ayuden en las letras, pero aun los de fuera en letras y buenas costumbres; donde cómodamente se podrán tener escuelas, se tengan a lo menos de letras de Humanidad y de allí arriba...."* (To take care that in our colleges not only our own scholastics may be helped in learning, but also those from outside in both learning and good habits of conduct, where schools [open to the public] can be conveniently had, they should be established at least in humane letters, and in more advanced subjects...); Ignacio de Loyola, *Obras*. 5th ed. (Madrid: Biblioteca de Autores Cristianos, 1991), 547.

25. *Cum litterarum*, 10 March 1571 *(Privilegia circa praelectiones in collegiis, etiam ubi aliorum sunt universitates, declarantur)*, in *Instituti Societatis Iesu, vol. I, Bullarium et compendium privilegiorum* (Florence, 1892), 44–46. *"...auctoritate apostolica per praesentes decernimus et declaramus, quod Praeceptores huiusmodi Societatis, tam litterarum humaniorum quam liberalium artium, theologiae, vel cuiusvis earum facultatum in suis Collegiis, etiam in locis ubi Universitates extiterint, suas lections etiam publicas legere (dummodo per duas horas de mane, et per unam horam de sero cum Lectoribus Universitatum non concurrant) libere et licite possint; quodque quibuscumque scholasticis liceat in huiusmodi Collegiis lectiones et alias scholasticas exercitationes frequentare, ac quicumque in eis philosophiae vel theologiae auditores fuerint, in quavis Universitate ad gradus admitti possint; et cursuum, quos in Collegiis praedictis confecerint, ratio habeatur, ita ut si in examine sufficientes inventi fuerint, non minus, sed pariformiter et absque ulla penitus differentia, quam si in Universitatibus praefatis studuissent, ad gradus quoscumque, tam baccalaureatus quam licentiaturae, magisterii et doctoratus admitti possint et debeant; eisque super praemissis specialem licentiam et facultatem concedimus; districtius inhibentes Universitatum quarumcumque Rectoribus et aliis quibuscumque, sub excommunicationis maioris, aliisque, arbitrio Nostro moderandis, infligendis et imponendis poenis, ne Collegiorum huiusmodi Rectores et scholares, in praemissis, quovis quaesito colore, molestare audeant vel praesumant."* The University was certainly within its authority in denying the Jesuits the right to teach during the regular university hours of Prime and Vespers. This issue was ultimately resolved, as we shall see.

26. Cf. Barrientos, *"Pleito de la Compañía de Jesús,"* 467.

27. de Certeau, *The Practice of Everyday Life*, 30–38.

28. de Certeau, *The Practice of Everyday Life*, 34.

29. de Certeau, *The Practice of Everyday Life*, 35–36.

30. de Certeau, *The Practice of Everyday Life*, 36.

31. de Certeau, *The Practice of Everyday Life*, 36–37.

32. de Certeau, *The Practice of Everyday Life*, 37–38.

33. Barrientos, *"Pleito de la Compañía de Jesús,"* 467.

34. Ferruolo, *The Origins of the University*, 314.

35. Hastings Rashdall, *The Universities of Europe in the Middle Ages*, III volumes, eds. F. M. Powicke and A. B. Emden (Oxford: Clarendon Press, 1936), volume I.4-6.

36. Barrientos, *"Pleito de la Compañía de Jesús,"* 471.

37. Barrientos, *"Pleito de la Compañía de Jesús,"* 473.

38. Cf. Michael Buckley, *The Catholic University as Promise and Project: Reflections in Jesuit Idiom* (Washington, D.C.: Georgetown University Press, 1998) 3–39.

Chapter 9: The Eternal Plan of Divine Providence and the God Who Dialogues: The Contribution of John H. Wright, S.J.

1. I would like to thank Michael Buckley, S.J., William Harmless, S.J., Michael Himes, Michael Legaspi, Eileen Burke-Sullivan, Brian Sholl, and John H. Wright, S.J. for their helpful feedback on previous drafts of this essay.

2. Augustine, *Retractiones* 2.1 (CCL 57:89–90). I have taken this from Augustine quoting his *Retractiones* in his *De praedestinatione sanctorum* 4.8 (BA 24:486–488). The English translation comes from St. Augustine, *Answer to the Pelagians, IV: To the Monks of Hadrumetum and Provence*, trans. Roland J. Teske, S.J., in *The Works of St. Augustine: A Translation for the 21ˢᵗ Century*, Part I, Vol. 26, ed. John E. Rotelle, O.S.A. (Hyde Park, New York: New City Press, 1999), 155.

3. The major shift in his thinking on grace occurred as he responded to questions of his friend Simplician concerning Romans 9. See *Ad Simplicianum* 1.2.9. For the development of Augustine's thought on grace see J. Patout Burns, *The Development of Augustine's Doctrine of Operative Grace* (Paris: Études Augustiniennes, 1980).

4. Augustine quoting his *Retractiones* 2.1 in his *De praedestinatione sanctorum* 4.8. The English translation comes from Augustine, *Answer to the Pelagians, IV*, trans. Roland J. Teske, S.J., 155.

5. Anne Carr, B.V.M., "'Not a Sparrow Falls:' On Providence and Responsibility in History," in *Proceedings of the Forty-Fourth Annual Convention of the Catholic Theological Society of America*, ed. George Kilcourse (Louisville, Kentucky: Bellarmine College, 1989), 37.

6. Wright's work has been recognized in that he wrote the dictionary articles for a prominent United States theological dictionary and encyclopedia. (See the entries on "God," "Predestination," and "Providence" in *The New Dictionary of Theology*, ed. Joseph A. Komonchak, Mary Collins and Dermot A. Lane (Wilmington,

Del.: Michael Glazier, 1987). See also the entry "Providence" in *The HarperCollins Encyclopedia of Catholicism,* ed. Richard P. McBrien (New York: HarperCollins Publishers, 1995).

In the scholarly literature, Wright's work has not been widely appreciated. I would suggest that this is largely a result of timing. His two articles in *Theological Studies* creatively drew upon Aquinas's philosophical theology and developed a quite technical and philosophically demanding theology. These articles, however, were published in the late 1960s and 1970s when the trend in systematic theology was away from Aquinas's thought and speculative philosophical theology toward the scriptural and historical renewal of dogmatic theology.

Those who have engaged Wright's thought have addressed it only tangentially in footnotes, and they have conflicting interpretations of his thought. From the perspective of process theology, Joseph Bracken criticizes Wright, in the context of his criticism of Thomas Aquinas, for stressing the immutability of God. Bracken maintains that if God is immutable then the eternal plan of providence is "fixed and immutable since it is one with God's willing of the divine being itself." Bracken concludes that the comprehensive character of the eternal plan of providence leads to a type of theological determinism that leaves nothing to chance and that does not allow for human freedom. (See Joseph A. Bracken, S.J., *The One in the Many: A Contemporary Reconstruction of the God-World Relationship* [Grand Rapids, Michigan: William B. Eerdmans Publishing Company, 2001], 20 n. 12.) From the perspective of classical theology, Thomas Weinandy, drawing upon Thomas Aquinas, criticizes John Wright for not sufficiently stressing the immutability of God. More particularly, Weinandy argues that several theologians of Thomistic background, including Wright, respond to the attacks on Aquinas's understanding of God's relation to the world by emphasizing God's intentional relation to the world through God's knowing and loving the world, but they do not sufficiently highlight the immutability of God as the foundation for God's relation to the world. See Thomas G. Weinandy, O.F.M. Cap., *Does God Suffer?* (Notre Dame, IN: Notre Dame Press, 2000), 137 n. 69; Thomas G. Weinandy, O.F.M. Cap., *Does God Change? The Word's Becoming in the Incarnation* (Still River, Mass.: St. Bede's Publications, 1985), 95–96 n. 110.

7. John Wright was kind enough to provide a copy of his manuscript prior to its publication. He worked on the manuscript for over thirty years and was in the last stages of editing it when he died in April 2009. The manuscript has been published in two-volumes treating the theology of providence of the Old and New Testaments respectively: *Divine Providence in the Bible: Meeting the Living and True God—Volume I: Old Testament* (Mahwah, NJ: Paulist Press, 2009) and *Divine Providence in the Bible: Meeting the Living and True God—Volume II: New Testament* (Mahwah, NJ: Paulist Press, 2010).

8. John H. Wright, S.J., "The Eternal Plan of Divine Providence," *Theological Studies* 27, no. 1 (1966), 27–57.

9. The use of the terms "antecedent," "before," and "prior to" in reference to God's knowledge or will should not be understood in temporal terms because God is eternal; rather, they need to be understood in terms of a natural order of priority.

An example of a natural order of priority is found in Trinitarian theology. The one God is eternal and unchanging, yet the Father is prior to the Son because the Father generates the Son. Another example of a natural order of priority can be found in the one human being who is both soul and matter. The two aspects of soul and matter exist simultaneously in the order of time; one, however, can speak of a natural order of priority of the soul in relation to matter.

10. Wright, "Eternal Plan," 30.

11. Molina maintained that God infallibly knows what free creatures would do in every possible set of circumstances (i.e., free conditioned futures) before any actual divine decree, while Bañes maintained that God knows these free conditioned futures through a divine decree. For Bañes God knows what creatures would do in any possible set of circumstances not because God sees what they would do, but because God knows what God will do. God determines prior to any action of creatures how God will infallibly influence creatures in the created order, and through God's determination God knows what creatures would do in any set of circumstances. The contradiction in Bañes's thought concerns his idea that God moves the free creature infallibly to one choice, while maintaining that the creature still has free choice among alternatives. Molina, on the other hand, has God knowing what is unknowable: namely, a possible free choice that as such has not yet been determined to one choice through the creature's power of choice. Molina has God knowing as actual something that is only possible. See Dominico Bañes, *Scholastic commentaria in primam partem Summae theologicae S. Thomae Aquinatis* (Madrid: Editorial F.E.D.A., 1934) especially q. 14. See Luis de Molina, S.J., *Liberi arbitrii cum gratiae donis, divina praescientia, providentia, praedestinatione concordia,* ed. Johann Rabeneck, (Oña and Madrid: Societatis Iesu Selecti Scriptores, Collegium Maximum, 1953). For an English translation of part IV of the Concordia with an extensive introduction, see Luis de Molina, *On Divine Foreknowledge (Part IV of the Concordia),* trans. Alfred. J. Freddoso (Ithaca, NY: Cornell University Press, 1988). There has been a resurgence of Molinism in the past thirty years that began with the work of Alvin Plantinga, who developed his thought without any awareness of Molina. See Alvin Plantinga, *The Nature of Necessity* (Oxford: Clarendon Press, 1974); Alvin Plantinga, *God, Freedom, and Evil* (Grand Rapids, Mich., Eerdmans, 1977); Thomas P. Flint, *Divine Providence: The Molinist Account* (Ithaca, N.Y.: Cornell University Press, 1998).

12. Wright, "Eternal Plan," 56–57.

13. John H. Wright, S.J., "Divine Knowledge and Human Freedom: The God Who Dialogues," *Theological Studies* 38, no. 3 (1977), 450–477.

14. John H. Wright, S.J., "Human Freedom and Divine Action: Libertarianism in St Thomas Aquinas," in *Human and Divine Agency: Anglican, Catholic, and Lutheran Perspectives,* ed. F. Michael McLain and W. Mark Richardson (Lanham, MD.: University Press of America, 1999), 42.

15. Wright, "Divine Knowledge and Human Freedom," 450.

16. Wright, "Divine Knowledge and Human Freedom, 450—451 n. 4. Wright is quoting from Alfred N. Whitehead, *Process and Reality* (New York: Harper, 1960), 522.

17. Wright, "Divine Knowledge and Human Freedom," 450.

18. Wright, "Divine Knowledge and Human Freedom," 450. See also *Divine Providence in the Bible—Volume I: Old Testament,* especially 18–19, 34–37.

19. Many of these examples are taken from Wright's abbreviated treatment of the scriptural data in his article "The Eternal Plan of Providence," 33–39.

20. See Wright, "Eternal Plan," 33.

21. Wright, "Eternal Plan," 33–34.

22. Wright, "Eternal Plan," 34.

23. Wright, *Divine Providence in the Bible—Volume I: Old Testament,* 19.

24. Wright, *Divine Providence in the Bible—Volume I: Old Testament,* 19.

25. See Wright, "Eternal Plan," 34, where he quotes from George Ernest Wright, *The Old Testament Against its Environment* (London: SCM Press, 1950), 53.

26. Wright, "Eternal Plan," 34.

27. Wright, "Eternal Plan," 34.

28. Wright, "Eternal Plan," 36.

29. Wright, "Eternal Plan," 37.

30. Wright, "Eternal Plan," 37.

31. See Justin Martyr, *The First Apology*, I,42; Irenaeus, *Against the Heresies*, 4,29,1–2; Clement of Alexandria, *Stromata* 7,17; Origen, *On First Principles* 3,1,12–13. For Augustine's early view see his *Commentary on Propositions from the Epistle to the Romans*. For his later view see the major shift in his thinking in *To Simplician—On Various Questions* and the maturation of his thinking during the Pelagian controversy. For Augustine's development in the thirteen works he produced during the Pelagian controversy see the modern critical edition of Augustine's Latin texts *Corpus Scriptorum Ecclesiasticorum Latinorum* (CSEL) vols. 60, 42, 85, and for those texts that are not yet in the *CSEL* see the older *Patrologia Latina* (PL), vols. 44, 45. For an English translation of the texts of the Pelagian controversy see St. Augustine, *Answer to the Pelagians I–IV,* trans. Roland J. Teske, S.J., in *The Works of St. Augustine: A Translation for the 21ˢᵗ Century*, Part I, Vols. 23–26, ed. John E. Rotelle, O.S.A. (Hyde Park, New York: New City Press, 1997–1999). For the development of Augustine's thought on grace see P. Burns, *The Development of Augustine's Doctrine of Operative Grace* (Paris: Études Augustiniennes, 1980). The assumption that God's sovereignty requires that God's election or decrees cannot be frustrated in individual instances has led to insoluble theological problems. Once you make this assumption concerning God's sovereignty, you have only two theoretical options. First, you can ground God's sovereignty in the divine intellect by appealing to divine foreknowledge, which was the route taken (in the early Church) by Justin, Irenaeus, Clement, Origen, and the early Augustine, but then you will have God knowing what is unknowable. Second, if you do not ground God's sovereignty in God's intellect (i.e., God's foreknowledge) then you must ground it in God's will. If you ground it in the divine will, then you will have God determining the choices

of free creatures, which leads (as it did for the later Augustine) to God's predestining some to salvation antecedent to their free choices. For a further analysis of this problem, see my "The Church as Potential Key to Unlocking the Problem of Providence, Predestination, and Human Free Choice" in G. Mannion, P. De Mey, and P. De Witte, eds., *Believing in Community: Ecumenical Reflections on the Church* (Leuven: Peeters Press, 2011).

32. Wright, "Eternal Plan," 38–39. See also Joseph A. Fitzmyer, *Romans: A New Translation with Introduction and Commentary,* 1st ed. (New York: Doubleday, 1993), 522.

33. Wright, "Eternal Plan," 37.

34. Wright, *Divine Providence in the Bible—Volume I: Old Testament,* 37.

35. Wright, "Eternal Plan," 37.

36. Wright, "Eternal Plan," 37–38.

37. Wright, "Eternal Plan," 38, Cf. 1 Jn 1:3.

38. Wright, "Eternal Plan," 38.

39. Wright, "Eternal Plan," 39.

40. Wright, "Divine Knowledge and Human Freedom," 450.

41. Wright, "Eternal Plan," 459.

42. In speaking of God's knowing and willing and "of the divine intellect and will as principles of these activities" (Wright, "Eternal Plan," 454), we are not simply transferring a facultative psychology to God, but we are trying to get some understanding of God's activity. As Wright maintains, "Although we must finally say that God is God's intellect and will, just as He is God's knowing and willing, still the simplicity of the divine reality involves a richness and diversity known by God Himself and not merely fashioned by our faltering distinctions. God Himself perceives a difference between God's knowing and willing. Even for Him, the grasping of an intelligible content (knowing) differs from the intention to communicate that content with another (willing)." (Wright, "Eternal Plan," 454).

The distinction of the divine intellect and will that are integral to Wright's argument can also be defended on Trinitarian grounds. In a Thomistic context, the immanent activities of the divine intellect and will have as their term the person of the Son and the person of the Holy Spirit. The Father knows God's self in speaking God's self in the Word which He generates and loves God's self through the Holy Spirit which He spirates through the Son. Indeed, these two modes of procession (intellectual and voluntary) are, according to Giles Emery, "for Saint Thomas, the only way in which understanding guided by faith can coherently represent the real distinction of persons who are truly God." See Giles Emery, O.P., "Trinity and Creation" in *The Theology of Thomas Aquinas,* ed. Rik Van Nieuwenhove and Joseph Wawrykow (Notre Dame, IN: University of Notre Dame Press, 2005), 62. See also Aquinas S.T. I.27; S.C.G IV.11; De Potentia q. 9 a.9 ad. 7.

43. The divine goodness is God's being as communicable and desirable. In a Thomist understanding goodness is a transcendental that is common to every being in so far as it is. The transcendentals are not extraneous additions to being but are included in being as intrinsic to being, expressing a mode of being not expressed

by the term "being" (e.g., the true, the one). Goodness expresses that being can be communicated and is desirable. When attributed to God it expresses that God's being is communicable and it is desirable. God's being is communicable in that God can share God's being with others such that they can exist as limited participations in God who is the Infinite act of existence. God's being is desirable because it is perfect. Since all perfections exist super-eminently in God, creatures in their natural desire for their own perfection naturally desire God. The good of creatures is the end proper to their natures. Creatures desire the good or end proper to their natures because they do not possess it. The end or object of God's will is God's goodness, but unlike creatures God is identical to God's end. God does not seek what God lacks but loves and delights in what God is.

44. Wright, "Divine Knowledge and Human Freedom," 453.

45. Wright, "Divine Knowledge and Human Freedom," 455.

46. W. Norris Clarke expresses the central point here: "The necessary, immutable, and objectively founded *intelligibility* of the possibles we accept as rigorously and adequately established by the traditional Thomistic analysis. We also recognize it as an extremely important and absolutely necessary truth in order to safeguard the wisdom of God in creating, God's providence in governing the universe, the permanence of ethical laws based on permanent essences, etc., lest we flounder helpless in a compassless relativism and empiricism. The whole great tradition of Christian exemplarism fits in here, but interpreted precisely as an exemplarism of divine *ideas* only, which acquire formally distinct intelligibility only in the divine mind and exclusively as the result of its infinitely fecund, artistically inventive activity, which does not find them somehow ready-made in God's essence (what could that possibly mean ontologically?), but literally "invents," "excogitates" them, using the infinitely simple plenitude of *Esse* that is God's essence as supreme *analogical* model or norm, so that all God's "inventions" will be only so many diversely limited modes (or "variations on the theme") of the one great central perfection of God's own act of existence." W. Norris Clarke, S.J., "What Is Really Real?" in *Progress in Philosophy,* ed. James Aloysius McWilliams (Milwaukee: Bruce Pub. Co, 1955), 85 n. 45. Clarke adds that "St. Thomas deliberately uses the terms '*rationes quasi excogitates*' (*De Potentiae,* q. 1 a. 5 ad. 11m) and '*advenit, ut ita dicam*' (*De Veritate,* q. 3 a. 2 ad. 6m). *Adinvenio* in his vocabulary is the precise term he uses to signify not 'discover'—*invenio*—but 'invent' or 'make up' logical relations: cf. *Lexicon of St. Thomas, Defarrari.*" (Clarke, "What Is Really Real?" 85 n. 45).

47. Wright, "Divine Knowledge and Human Freedom," 455.

48. The actual execution of this choice and the concomitant communication of existence are through the divine power. As we will see, this ordered relation of the divine will to the divine intellect that determines the divine power to a definite effect is the structure of God's causative knowledge.

49. Wright, "God," in *The New Dictionary of Theology,* 432.

50. Wright, "God," 432. See also *Divine Providence in the Bible—Volume I: Old Testament,* 8.

51. Wright, "Eternal Plan," 42.

52. As will be shown, the antecedent plan is the possible means for achieving God's purpose and the consequent plan is those means for achieving God's purpose that become actual in the world and salvation history.

53. Wright, "Eternal Plan," 42.

54. Wright, "Eternal Plan," 42–43.

55. Wright, "Eternal Plan," 41 n. 40.

56. Wright, "Eternal Plan," 41 n. 40.

57. Wright, "Eternal Plan," 43.

58. Wright, "Eternal Plan," 43.

59. Wright, "Human Freedom and Divine Action: Libertarianism in St Thomas Aquinas," 42.

60. Wright, "Eternal Plan," 44.

61. Wright, "Eternal Plan," 44.

62. Wright maintains that personal union with God requires freedom of choice which involves the possibility of failure: "if God by God's 'absolute power' as the theologians say were to create men simply in possession of the end He would be placing them in a situation for which they as persons were in no way responsible. There would be a union of persons, but it would not be really a personal union, for it would not respect the distinctness and uniqueness of the created person." John H. Wright, S.J., "A Theological Analysis of Freedom in Terms of Grace," in *Proceedings of the Society of Catholic College Teachers of Sacred Doctrine, Eleventh Annual Convention* (Weston, MA: Published by the Society at Regis College, 1965), 84. In my own writings, I agree with Wright's conclusion that the intelligibility of created persons called to personal union with God involves the possibility of their rejecting God's call, but I arrive at this conclusion through a different argument. I maintain that the created spirit must exist initially outside the beatific vision in the order of grace so that she can become a person to whom God can give God's self in the beatific vision; for if the creature did not live initially outside the beatific vision in the order of grace, there would not be an "I" or a person to whom God could give God's self in union. And in this state of existence outside the beatific vision, the free creature is capable of sin, moral evil, moral imperfection, and error. See my "The Mystery of God and the Suffering of Human Beings," *Heythrop Journal* (2009), 846–863.

63. Wright, "Eternal Plan," 45.

64. Wright, "Eternal Plan," 45.

65. Wright, "Eternal Plan," 45.

66. Wright, "Eternal Plan," 46.

67. Wright, "Eternal Plan," 45.

68. Wright, "Eternal Plan," 45.

69. Wright, "Eternal Plan," 46.

70. All analogies involve elements of similarity and dissimilarity. The dissimilarity is incomprehensibly greater in these analogies because they are drawn from creatures in order to make true judgments about God who is mystery. As the Fourth Lateran Council maintained—"For between creator and creature there can

be noted no similarity so great that a greater dissimilarity cannot be seen between them." Norman P. Tanner, *Decrees of the Ecumenical Councils Vol. I* (London: Sheed & Ward; Washington, DC: Georgetown University Press, 1990), Fourth Lateran Council, Constitution 2, 232. These examples are trying to get a sense of the infallibility of God's knowledge. Our knowledge that the human race will be in existence in two hundred years and that a certain number (certain in the sense of falling within a predictable range) of people will get married next year has a passive element to it: namely, the cumulative experience of the human community. God's infallible knowledge that there will be a society of the blessed united to God is not passively received from something outside of God; rather, God's knowledge is active and God knows infallibly in knowing God's self that there will be a society of the blessed united to God.

71. Wright, "Eternal Plan," 48.

72. Wright, "Human Freedom and Divine Action: Libertarianism in St Thomas Aquinas," 42.

73. To preserve God's perfection, we must maintain that God's knowledge is in no way caused by another (like our knowledge is), but is causative. We know that the wind is blowing through the effect on us of the pressure, sound, and temperature of the air in motion. God knows that the wind is blowing because God causes it to blow. See Wright, "Divine Knowledge and Human Freedom," 452.

74. Wright, "Divine Knowledge and Human Freedom," 462.

75. Wright, "Divine Knowledge and Human Freedom," 462–463.

76. Wright, "Divine Knowledge and Human Freedom," 456.

77. Wright, "Divine Knowledge and Human Freedom," 464.

78. Wright, "Divine Knowledge and Human Freedom," 464.

79. Wright, "Divine Knowledge and Human Freedom," 464.

80. This is necessarily so, such that if God is going to create, creation will necessarily be ordered toward God as its end.

81. *S.T.* I.19.2 as quoted in Wright, "Divine Knowledge and Human Freedom," 464.

82. Wright, "Divine Knowledge and Human Freedom," 464–465.

83. Wright, "Divine Knowledge and Human Freedom," 465.

84. Wright, "Divine Knowledge and Human Freedom," 465.

85. Étienne Gilson, *Being and Some Philosophers* (Toronto: Pontifical Institute of Mediaeval Studies, 1949), 184.

86. Wright, "Divine Knowledge and Human Freedom," 467.

87. Wright, "Divine Knowledge and Human Freedom," 467.

88. Wright, "Divine Knowledge and Human Freedom," 467.

89. This is John Wright's example. See Wright, "Eternal Plan," 53.

90. Wright, "Eternal Plan," 53.

91. See Thomas Aquinas, *Summa contra Gentiles* III.2.[8].

92. See Norris Clarke, "Freedom as Value," in *Freedom and Value*, ed. Robert O. Johann (New York: Fordham University Press, 1976), 14.

93. Clarke, "Freedom as Value," 14–15.

94. Wright, "Divine Knowledge and Human Freedom," 470.

95. Wright, "Divine Knowledge and Human Freedom," 470.

96. Clarke, *Freedom as Value*, This is a paraphrase of Clarke from page 14.

97. Wright, "Divine Knowledge and Human Freedom," 471.

98. Wright, "Divine Knowledge and Human Freedom," 471. God's applying a creature to act simply means that God moves a creature to act according to its nature.

99. Here is where a creature's free choice and God's free choice are intrinsically analogous; for, in free choice, God and the free creature are simply determining how their perfection will be shared. The difference is that the perfection that the creature orders to communication is a continual gift of God.

100. Wright, "Divine Knowledge and Human Freedom," 472.

101. Wright, "Divine Knowledge and Human Freedom," 472.

102. Wright, "Divine Knowledge and Human Freedom," 453.

103. Wright, "Divine Knowledge and Human Freedom," 454.

104. Wright, "Divine Knowledge and Human Freedom," 454. This is precisely the contradiction in Luis de Molina's thought and all the variations of Molinism in contemporary philosophy of religion.

105. Wright, "Eternal Plan," 50.

106. Wright, "Human Freedom and Divine Action: Libertarianism in St Thomas Aquinas," 43.

107. Wright, "Eternal Plan," 50.

108. Wright, "Eternal Plan," 475.

109. Wright, "Eternal Plan," 475.

110. Augustine quoting his *Retractiones* 2.1 in his *De praedestinatione sanctorum* 4.8. The English translation comes from Augustine, *Answer to the Pelagians*, IV, trans. Roland J. Teske, S.J., 155.

Chapter 10: Trinity, Community, and Social Transformation

1. See especially Karl Barth, *Church Dogmatics* Volume 1/1, originally published 1932. Karl Rahner, "Remarks on the Dogmatic Treatise *De Trinitate*," *Theological Investigations IV* (Baltimore: Helicon, 1966).

2. James P. Mackey, *The Christian Experience of God as Trinity* (London: SCM, 1983), 3.

3. Stanley J. Grenz, *The Social God and the Relational Self* (Louisville: Westminster John Knox, 2001), 4.

4. Nicholas Lash, *Holiness, Speech and Silence* (Burlington, Vermont: Ashgate, 1994), vii.

5. Rowan Williams, *Tokens of Trust: An Introduction to Christian Belief* (Louisville: Westminster John Knox, 2007), 117.

6. Mark Searle, "Private Religion, Individualistic Society, and Common Worship," in *Liturgy and Spirituality in Context: Perspectives on Prayer and Culture*, ed. Eleanor Bernstein (Collegeville, Minn: Liturgical Press, 1990), 29.

7. Searle, "Private Religion," 37.

8. Hans Urs von Balthasar, *The Von Balthasar Reader*, ed. Medard Kehl and Werner Löser, trans. Robert Daly and Fred Lawrence (New York: Crossroad, 1982), 331.

9. Williams, *Tokens of Trust*, 137.

10. Williams, *Tokens of Trust*, 137.

11. "We often yearn for a roomy, isolated home (a thing we easily adapt to) when, in fact, it will probably compromise our happiness by distancing us from neighbors. (Social interaction and friendships have been shown to give lasting pleasure.)" John Gertner, "The Futile Pursuit of Happiness," *New York Times Magazine*, September 7, 2003, 86.

12. "Wendell Berry," in *Current Biography Yearbook*, vol. 63 (2002), 35.

13. Wendell Berry, *Sex, Economy, Freedom and Community* (New York: Pantheon, 1993), 147.

14. Berry, *Sex, Economy,* 119–120.

15. Berry, *Sex, Economy,* 120.

16. Berry, *Sex, Economy,* 155.

17. Berry, *Sex, Economy,* 120.

18. Berry, *Sex, Economy,* 120.

19. Berry, *Sex, Economy,* 133.

20. Berry, *Sex, Economy,* 161.

21. Berry, *Sex, Economy,* 161.

22. Berry, *Sex, Economy,* 121.

23. Berry, *Sex, Economy,* 132.

24. KC Flynn, "The Joining of Heaven and Earth: A Look at Wendell Berry and the Church," *The Everyday Journal* 1.3 (August 2008). <http://everydayliturgy.com/magazine/august-2008/articles/the-joining-of-heaven-and-earth-a-look-at-wendell-berry-and-the-church> (15 October 2009).

25. Flynn, "The Joining of Heaven and Earth."

Chapter 11: Incarnate Meaning and Mimetic Desire: Notes toward the Development of a Theology of the Saints

1. Michael J. Buckley, *Denying and Disclosing God: The Ambiguous Progress of Modern Atheism* (New Haven: Yale University Press, 2004), xv.

2. Buckley, *Denying and Disclosing God*, xv.

3. Buckley, *Denying and Disclosing God*, xv.

4. Buckley, *Denying and Disclosing God*, 129.

5. Buckley, *Denying and Disclosing God*, 135.

6. Buckley, *Denying and Disclosing God*, 130.

7. Buckley, *Denying and Disclosing God*, 130.

8. Patricia A. Sullivan, "A Reinterpretation of Invocation and Intercession of the Saints," *Theological Studies* 66 (2005), 395.

9. Lawrence S. Cunningham, *A Brief History of Saints* (Malden, MA: Blackwell, 2005), 136.

10. Cunningham, *A Brief History of Saints*, 136.

11. Cunningham, *A Brief History of Saints*, 136.

12. Lawrence S. Cunningham, "Saints," *The New Dictionary of Theology*, ed. Joseph A. Komonchak, et al. (Collegeville: The Liturgical Press, 1987), 927.

13. Cunningham, "Saints," 928.

14. Balthasar, *Love Alone Is Credible*, D.C. Schindler, ed. (San Francisco: Ignatius Press, 2004), 12.

15. This theme pervades Balthasar's writings. See, for example, "Theology and Sanctity," *Explorations in Theology I: The Word Made Flesh*, 181–209. Here, I limit my focus to Balthasar's concise presentation in his book *Two Sisters in the Spirit: Thérèse of Lisieux and Elizabeth of the Trinity* (San Francisco: Ignatius Press, 1992), 26.

16. Balthasar, *Two Sisters in the Spirit*, 26.

17. Balthasar, *Two Sisters in the Spirit*, 26.

18. Balthasar, *Two Sisters in the Spirit*, 26.

19. Balthasar, *Two Sisters in the Spirit*, 27.

20. Balthasar, *Two Sisters in the Spirit*, 25.

21. Balthasar, *Two Sisters in the Spirit*, 26, 25.

22. See John D. Dadosky, "'Naming the Demon': The 'Structure' of Evil in Lonergan and Girard," *Irish Theological Quarterly* 75.4 (2010), 355–372 and "Woman Without Envy: Toward Reconceiving the Immaculate Conception," *Theological Studies* 72.1 (2011), 16–40; Robert M. Doran, "Lonergan and Girard on Sacralization and Desacralization," *Revista Portuguesa de Filosofia* 63 (2007), 1171–1201 and "The Nonviolent Cross: Lonergan and Girard on Redemption," *Theological Studies* 71.1 (2010), 46–61; Charles Hefling, "About What Might a 'Girard-Lonergan Conversation' Be?," 95–123; and, Neil Ormerod, "Questioning Desire: Lonergan, Girard and Buddhism," *Louvain Studies* (forthcoming) and "Desire and the Origins of Culture: Lonergan and Girard in Conversation," *Heythrop Journal* (forthcoming).

23. Lonergan, *Method in Theology* (New York: Herder and Herder, 1972), 57.

24. John Henry Newman, *An Essay in Aid of a Grammar of Assent* (Notre Dame: University of Notre Dame, 1979), 89.

25. Lonergan, *Method in Theology*, 73.

26. Lonergan, "The Analogy of Meaning," *Philosophical and Theological Papers 1958–1964*, Collected Works of Bernard Lonergan, vol. 6, Robert Croken, et al., eds. (Toronto: University of Toronto Press, 1996), 188.

27. Lonergan, *Method in Theology*, 73.

28. Lonergan, "Time and Meaning," *Philosophical and Theological Papers 1958–1964*, Collected Works of Bernard Lonergan, vol. 6, Robert Croken, et al.,

eds. (Toronto: University of Toronto Press, 1996): 94–121. See Georges Morel, *Le Sens de l'existence selon s. Jean de la Croix* (Paris: Aubier, 1960–61).

29. Lonergan, "Time and Meaning," 102.

30. Since we made a connection to Balthasar above, we would be remiss if we did not mention the importance of John of the Cross for Balthasar's theological reflection, especially his controversial theology of Christ's consciousness on the Cross. Balthasar writes, "This timelessness is confirmed, in some precision, by those Christian mystics who were privileged to experience something of the dark night of the Cross." He refers in the footnote to this selection to John of the Cross. *Theo-Drama IV: The Action*, Graham Harrison, trans. (San Francisco: Ignatius Press, 1994), 337. Find Balthasar's sustained analysis of the works of John of the Cross in *The Glory of the Lord*, volume III: *Studies in Theological Style: Lay Styles*, Andrew Louth, John Saward, Martin Simon, and Rowan Williams, trans. (Edinburgh: T&T Clark, and San Francisco: Ignatius Press, 1986). In fact, Michael Buckley used Balthasar's monograph in his course on John of the Cross.

31. Buckley, *Denying and Disclosing God*, 108.

32. Buckley, *Denying and Disclosing God*, 119.

33. Buckley, *Denying and Disclosing God*, 110.

34. Buckley, *Denying and Disclosing God*, 117.

35. Buckley, *Denying and Disclosing God*, 117.

36. Buckley, *Denying and Disclosing God*, xv.

37. See Lonergan, *Method in Theology*, 73.

38. See Rosenberg, "The Drama of Scripture: Reading Patristic Biblical Hermeneutics through Bernard Lonergan's Reflections on Art," *Logos: A Journal of Catholic Thought and Culture* 11:2 (Spring 2008): 126–148 and "Lonergan on the Transcendent Orientation of Art," *Renascence: Essays on Values in Literature* (Spring 2009): 141–151. I draw selectively from these essays in a slightly adapted presentation.

39. Lonergan's theory of art is worked out most carefully in "Art," *Topics in Education: The Cincinnati Lectures of 1959 on the Philosophy of Education*, Collected Works of Bernard Lonergan, vol. 10, Robert M. Doran and Frederick E. Crowe, eds. (Toronto: University of Toronto Press): 208–232.

40. Lonergan, "Art," 224–225. I expand on this theme more thoroughly in Rosenberg, "Lonergan on the Transcendent Orientation of Art."

41. Lonergan, "Art," 216.

42. Lonergan, "Art," 217.

43. Lonergan, *Method in Theology*, 63.

44. Lonergan, "Art," 229.

45. Lonergan, "Art," 229.

46. Lonergan, *Method in Theology*, 63.

47. Lonergan, "Art," 222.

48. Lonergan, "Art," 222.

49. Frances Young, *Biblical Exegesis and the Formation of Christian Culture* (Peabody, MA: Hendrickson, 2002), 158.

50. Cunningham, *A Brief History of Saints*, 139–140. Cunningham is drawing from Frances Young's *The Art of Performance: Towards a Theology of Holy Scripture* (London: Darton, Longman, and Todd, 1990).

51. Cunningham, *A Brief History of Saints*, 140.

52. Cunningham, *A Brief History of Saints*, 140.

53. René Girard, *Mimesis and Theory: Essays on Literature and Criticism, 1953–2005*, Robert Doran, ed. (Stanford, CA: Stanford, 2008), 246.

54. *Things Hidden Since the Foundation of the World* (London: Continuum, 2003), 431.

55. René Girard, *Violence and the Sacred*, Patrick Gregory, trans. (Baltimore, The Johns Hopkins University Press, 1977), 146.

56. Girard, "The Goodness of Mimetic Desire," *The Girard Reader*, James G. Williams, ed. (New York: Crossroad, 1996), 63

57. Girard, "The Goodness of Mimetic Desire," 64.

58. Girard, "The Goodness of Mimetic Desire," 64.

59. Girard, *I See Satan Fall Like Lightning*, James G. Williams, trans. (Maryknoll, NY: Orbis, 2001), 15.

60. *I See Satan Fall Like Lightening*, 16.

61. For a sustained discussion of "interdividual psychology," see Girard, *Things Hidden*, 283–431.

62. Hefling, "About What Might a 'Girard-Lonergan Conversation' Be?," 104.

63. Hefling, "About What Might a 'Girard-Lonergan Conversation' Be?," 104.

64. Hefling, "About What Might a 'Girard-Lonergan Conversation' Be?," 104.

65. René Girard, *Deceit, Desire, and the Novel: Self and Other in Literary Structure*, Yvonne Freccero, trans. (Baltimore: The Johns Hopkins University Press, 1965), 9.

66. Girard, *Deceit, Desire, and the Novel*, 9.

67. Girard, *Deceit, Desire, and the Novel*, 9.

68. Girard, *Deceit, Desire, and the Novel*, 10.

69. Buckley, *Denying and Disclosing God*, 129.

70. Buckley, *Denying and Disclosing God*, 129.

71. Buckley, *Denying and Disclosing God*, 129.

72. Buckley, *Denying and Disclosing God*, 129.

73. Buckley, *Denying and Disclosing God*, 129. As constitutive as the categorical disclosures were to Edith Stein and the Maritains, Buckley also identifies a transcendental form of "religious" experience operative: the unrelenting search for and commitment to discovering the truth. In terms of the Lonergan-Girard conversation, Robert Doran, in *The Nonviolent Cross*, has argued that both thinkers are "responsible for two of the most vital and far-reaching intellectual and cultural discoveries of the 20th century.... Lonergan has articulated the structure of what he calls the transcendental intentions or notions of intelligibility, truth and being, and the good.

Girard has elucidated the mimetic, indeed acquisitively mimetic and potentially violent, character of a great deal of human desire" (47).

74. *The Autobiography*, trans. Parmananda R. Divarkar, *Ignatius of Loyola: Spiritual Exercises and Selected Works*, George E. Ganss, ed. (New York: Paulist, 1991), 70.

75. Cunningham, *A Brief History of Saints*, 66.

76. See Lonergan, *Method in Theology*, 281–288.

77. Buckley, *Denying and Disclosing God*, 130.

78. See Randall S. Rosenberg, "Christ's Human Knowledge: A Conversation with Lonergan and Balthasar," *Theological Studies* 71.4 (December 2010), 817–845. See also Lonergan, *Method in Theology*, 335–353.

Chapter 12: Vatican II and a New Church Mission to the World

1. Michael J. Buckley, S.J., *The Catholic University as Promise and Project: Reflections in a Jesuit Idiom* (Washington, D.C.: Georgetown University Press, 1998), 105.

2. Richard Gaillardetz, *The Church in the Making: Lumen Gentium, Christus Dominus, Orientalium Ecclesiarium* (New York: Paulist Press, 2006), 2.

3. Brian Gleeson, C.P., "Commemorating Lumen gentium: A Short History of a Ground-breaking Charter," in *The Australian eJournal of Theology*, Issue 3 (August 2004) < http://dlibrary.acu.edu.au/research/theology/ejournal/aejt_3/Gleeson. htm> (6 January 2011).

4. *Mystici corporus Christi*, 1943, no. 1. <http://www.vatican.va/holy_father/ pius_xii/encyclicals/documents/hf_p-xii_enc_29061943_mystici-corporis-christi_ en.html> (6 January 2011). Where necessary, I have altered Vatican documents to incorporate gender inclusive language.

5. *Mysticis corporus Christi*, 1943, "mystical body of Christ" is used 56 times, the "spotless bride" is used in paragraph 106, while "bride" is used in no. 86 and no. 96. "Holy Mother Church" is used in no. 3, 92, 105 and 109.

6. *Mysticis corporus Christi*, 1943, no. 53.

7. *Mysticis corporus Christi*, no. 63.

8. José Comblin, *People of God*, ed. and trans. by Phillip Berryman, (Maryknoll: Orbis Books, 2004) 8.

9. Comblin, *People of God*, 8–9.

10. Gustavo Gutiérrez in his landmark article "Toward a Theology of Liberation" implies as much when he states: "The absolute salvation provided by God in the hereafter, which diminishes the present life, has led to a very peculiar outlook: human institutions will be considered important if they are oriented to the hereafter. All other institutions have no value because they will pass away." In *Liberation Theology: The Documentary Heritage*, ed. Alfred Hennelly, (Marknoll: Orbis, 1990) 67.

11. Gleeson, "Commemorating *Lumen gentium*: A Short History of a Ground-breaking Charter,"

12. Gleeson, "Commemorating *Lumen gentium*: A Short History of a Ground-breaking Charter." This paragraph summarizes Gleeson's section titled "Abstract."

13. *Lumen gentium* states this clearly in no. 30. "For their pastors know how much the laity contribute to the welfare of the entire Church. They also know that they were not ordained by Christ to take upon themselves alone the entire salvific mission of the Church toward the world. On the contrary they understand that it is their noble duty to shepherd the faithful and to recognize their ministries and charisms, so that all according to their proper roles may cooperate in this common undertaking with one mind." <http://www.vatican.va/archive/hist_councils/ii_vatican_council/documents/vat-ii_const_19641121_lumen-gentium_en.html> (7 January 2011).

14. For an excellent study on the relationship between the papacy and episcopacy actually commissioned by Cardinal Joseph Ratzinger when he was head of the Congregation for the Doctrine of the Faith, see Michael J. Buckley, S.J., *Papal Primacy and the Episcopate: Towards a Relational Understanding* (New York: Crossroad, 1998).

15. This message from the prophets is a major theme of the Hebrew Scriptures and is evident in Jeremiah, Amos, Isaiah, and the Psalms, among many others. Recall that in a patriarchal society one's social status depends on one's relationship to the oldest male of the clan. Widows and orphans were cut off from that relationship and thus were the most vulnerable in that culture.

16. José Comblin, *People of God*, 8.

17. *Lumen gentium*, para. 9.

18. *Lumen gentium*, para. 8, italics mine.

19. John Henry Newman, *On Consulting the Faithful in Matters of Doctrine*, ed. John Coulson (Kansas City, MO: Sheed and Ward, 1961). Newman originally published the article in the July 1859 issue of *The Rambler*. I am indebted to Rev. Michael Himes for material in this section.

20. John Henry Newman, *On Consulting the Faithful in Matters of Doctrine*, 41, emphasis mine; see also Rev. Michael J. Himes, "Lay Ministers and Ordained Ministers" in *Lay Ministry in the Catholic Church: Visioning Church Ministry Through the Wisdom of the Past*, ed. Richard Miller (Liguori, MO: Liguori Press, 2004) 79–87.

21. *Mystici corporis Christi*, no. 17 (emphasis and italics mine).

22. *Mystici corporis Christi*, no. 20.

23. *Mystici corporis Christi*, no. 20.

24. *Mystici corporis Christi*, no. 93. "If the faithful strive to live in a spirit of lively faith, they will not only pay due honor and reverence to *the more exalted members of this Mystical Body, especially those who according to Christ's mandate will have to render an account of our souls,*[180] but they will take to their hearts those members who are the object of our Savior's special love: the weak, We mean, the wounded and the sick who are in need of material or spiritual assistance; chil-

dren whose innocence is so easily exposed to danger in these days, and whose young hearts can be molded as wax; and finally the poor, in helping whom we recognize as it were, through His supreme mercy, the very person of Jesus Christ." (emphasis and italics mine).

25. *Mystici corporis Christi*. no. 108.

26. *Lumen gentium*, no. 30.

27. *Lumen gentium*, no. 31.

28. *Apostolicam actuositatem*, no. 2 < http://www.vatican.va/archive/hist_councils/ii_vatican_council/documents/vat-ii_decree_19651118_apostolicam-actuositatem_en.html> (7 January 2011).

29. *Lumen gentium*, no. 31.

30. *Lumen gentium*, no. 11.

31. Comblin, *People of God*, 16.

32. *Lumen gentium* even supports this understanding. "If therefore in the Church everyone does not proceed by the same path, nevertheless all are called to sanctity and have received an equal privilege of faith through the justice of God." no. 32.

33. *Lumen gentium*, no. 42.

34. Comblin, *People of God*, 6.

35. *Lumen gentium*, no. 39.

36. *Lumen gentium.*, no. 40.

37. *Lumen gentium*, no. 42.

38. *Immortale dei*, no. 10.

39. *Gaudium et spes*, no. 43. < http://www.vatican.va/archive/hist_councils/ii_vatican_council/documents/vat-ii_cons_19651207_gaudium-et-spes_en.html> (7 January 2011).

40. *Gaudium et spes*, no. 1.

41. *Gaudium et spes*, no. 5.

42. *Gaudium et spes*, no. 3.

43. *Gaudium et spes*, no. 14

44. *Gaudium et spes*, no. 12.

45. *Gaudium et spes*, no. 24.

46. For an excellent discussion of this see chapter 6 of Robert Bellah, et al., *Habits of the Heart: Individualism and Commitment in American Life*, 3rd edition (Berkley: University of California Press, 2007).

47. *Gaudium et spes*, no. 29.

48. *Gaudium et spes*, no. 63.

49. *Gaudium et spes*, no. 66.

50. *Gaudium et spes*, no. 69.